The
Parenting
Encyclopedia

OTHER BOOKS BY CARYL WALLER KRUEGER

Six Weeks to Better Parenting, Pelican Publishing, 1985

1001 Things to Do with Your Kids, Abingdon Press, 1988

Working Parent—Happy Child, Abingdon Press, 1990

The Ten Commandments for Grandparents, Abingdon Press, 1991

101 Ideas for the Best-Ever Christmas, Dimensions for Living, 1992

Single with Children, Abingdon Press, 1993

365 Ways to Love Your Child, Abingdon Press, 1994

The Family Party Book, Abingdon Press, 1995

222 Terrific Tips for Two, Abingdon Press, 1995

1001 More Things to Do with Your Kids, Abingdon Press, 1997

Family Traditions, Abingdon Press, 1998

The
Parenting
Encyclopedia

Caryl Waller Krueger

Abingdon Press
Nashville

THE PARENTING ENCYCLOPEDIA

Copyright © 2000 by Caryl Waller Krueger

Line Art by Jack Kershner

Library of Congress Cataloging-in-Publication Data

Krueger, Caryl Waller, 1929-
  The parenting encyclopedia / Caryl Waller Krueger.
    p. cm.
  ISBN 0-687-08927-1 [alk. paper]
  1. Parenting—United States—Encyclopedias. 2. Child rearing—United States—Encyclopedias.
  3. Child psychology—United States—Encyclopedias. I. Title.

  HQ755.8 .K68 2000
  649'1'03—dc21

                                                                00-038577

The author has made every effort to make the information and suggestions in this book practical and workable, but neither she nor the publisher assumes any responsibility for successes, failures, or other results of putting these ideas into practice.

00 01 02 03 04 05 06 07 08 09—10 9 8 7 6 5 4 3 2 1

MANUFACTURED IN THE UNITED STATES OF AMERICA

To the next generation of parents—
the children and grandchildren
of those who contributed ideas for this book:

Aaron, Amy, Austin, Brian, Cameron, Casey, Charles, Christopher, Claire, Collin, Eddie, Emily, Hudson, Jeremy, Kristin, Lindsay, Maxwell, the three Michaels, Molly, Nicholas, Paula, Stephen, Tim, and Will

Before you begin . . .

In the pages that follow, you will find hundreds of facts that will make your family life more productive and more happy.

This book by no means presents an exhaustive discussion of each topic. Other books, including my own twelve books, give far more details. The purpose of this book is to give you some immediate answers and helpful ideas on the most common questions that I address in lectures, newspaper columns, and radio and television interviews. It is based on years of research with families around the world and provides practical solutions that have been successful for others.

Subjects relating to health are only dealt with in a basic informative way. When the question concerns the health of a child, you should quickly consult the nurse/practitioner/doctor who can best give you comprehensive advice and comfort.

Your children are a precious responsibility. Your prime gift to them is your unconditional love. Good character training, solid academics, and after-school activities, plus time to build memories, are essential parts of that love. You have so few years to guide them into responsible adulthood that I know you want to and will make the most of this time.

Those of us in the child development field appreciate your dedication and applaud you for the time you are spending to build a better family.

Cordially,
Caryl Waller Krueger

P.S. Should you ever have a question you'd like to ask me, write me an e-mail at: Caryl@betterparenting.com. And you can learn more about effective parenting on my website: www.betterparenting.com. The website for Abingdon Press is www.abingdon.org.

A-1.

The very best in parenting is what you want to give your children. At the same time you want to enjoy doing it. Exercise your parenting skills and be an A-1 parent by utilizing many of the listings in this book. "A" represents your positive attitude and "1" reminds you to give your family a high priority.

ABANDONMENT. *See also Absence of Parent, Communication, Love, Neglect.*

Many youngsters feel abandoned by their parents—even when they live under the same roof. Starting with infants (through holding, feeding, singing, kissing, and so forth) and continuing with good family communication skills and activities, you can replace feelings of abandonment with feelings of affection.

However, there can be circumstances (illness, travel, divorce) that may prevent a parent from day-to-day contact with a child. The absent parent needs to vigorously maintain a connection in ways such as telephone calls, letters, greeting cards, small gifts, cassette tape messages, and e-mail. Reassure a child that he will always be precious to you, no matter what.

If the child is permanently abandoned by a parent (for example, the father), it is important for the remaining parent (the mother) to find positive male role models for the child. Otherwise, this abandonment can lead to feelings of low self-worth, which can lead to self-defeating behavior.

Sometimes youngsters feel so angry and upset they would like to abandon their families. Do your best to keep estrangement from continuing. Try ethical compromise and keep open those important lines of communication.

ABILITY. *See also Lessons, Success, Talent.*

Every child has a unique ability. Some just cover it up better than others! While some children will display a variety of aptitudes, others will show just a few or even none. Be patient because the development of special skills can take time.

At least twice a year, encourage a youngster to try a new activity. Provide opportunities for experiencing various sports, music, arts, crafts, clubs, and academics because such endeavors can widen a youngster's horizons. Pay attention to the ones that your child enjoys and encourage him to repeat these. Be supportive but also be ready for him to shift gears and try something entirely new.

ABORTION. *See also Adoption, Pregnancy, Sex.*

While this subject is one that each woman must consider for herself, we are gradually seeing a rise in the number of pregnancies carried to term and followed by adoption. Abortion, when used as a form of birth control, is certainly not as wise or health-giving as more usual birth control methods. Psychologists active in counseling women who have had abortions find lingering feelings of guilt and sorrow. If you are unable to keep and care for a baby, think and talk about all the options with your spouse/partner. The popular term "pro-choice" can also mean that a woman has a choice NOT to engage in activity that could result in pregnancy.

At the right time, discuss with teens the problems resulting from an unwanted pregnancy and how it can dramatically change their lives. Cover all the alternatives, including abstinence.

ABSENCE OF PARENT. *See also Communication, Separation Anxiety.*

Because the parent is the preponderant emotional and educational connection for most children, the absence of a parent (due to business, travel, illness, social events) can be difficult for a youngster unprepared for the separation.

Never "sneak" away from children. If they will be asleep when you leave, explain your absence in advance. If you will be leaving a baby who is still awake, take time for interaction between you, the caregiver, and child. A visible affection connection with the child will help make your departure happier for both of you. With older children, oversee the start of a game or other activity that will keep them occupied after you depart.

Always tell a child the approximate time of your return, and that you will look in on her when you get home. When you can't be with your child as much as you'd like, tie a gold ribbon (or one in her favorite color) on her wrist or somewhere in her room. Tell her that it is a reminder that you will be thinking of her and loving her while you are separated.

When the separation is for an extended period of time, take advantage of these other ways to connect:

1. Make a daily phone call, specifically asking to talk with the child first (so that she feels special) before talking with the other parent or caregiver.
2. Record a cassette tape of bedtime stories, ending with an expression of your love.
3. Leave a set of envelopes containing short messages, one to be opened each day.
4. Write out a promise of something special you will do together on your return.
5. Designate a special time each day, such as 8 P.M., when you will think of each other. Or, view the evening star (Venus) each night just after sunset, knowing the other one is doing the same thing.

ABSENTMINDEDNESS. *See Forgetfulness.*

ABUSE. *See also Anger, Discipline, Molestation, Punishment.*

The definition of abuse can be very fluid, depending on one's point of view. However, effective parenting never includes mental or physical abuse in any degree. Expressing outrageous anger, hitting, and giving extreme punishments that degrade a child do not promote a parent's goal of rearing a happy, responsible, mentally and physically healthy, intelligent child.

Abuse begets abuse. Abusive parents raise children who themselves may become abusive. If you have abusive feelings toward a child, examine the true motive for your actions and choose more reasonable ways to achieve obedience. At first this may take extra time and great patience, but it will bring about the desired results more quickly in the long run. If you can't manage your feelings, get immediate professional help as this is an issue that could destroy your family.

When you speak to an errant child, choose words that soothe and heal the problem, words you would be proud to see on a billboard in front of your house. For example, "I love you too much to let you do that." This does not mean that you excuse wrong actions. Rather, you assume your role as parent/teacher and show the better way for him to accomplish his desire.

Do not permit your child to be abused. Tell him that no one has the right to molest him. Calmly go through hypothetical situations to show how he should react to bullies, strangers, and anyone who tries to touch him in a private place (any place a swim suit covers). Reassure him that you will work to keep him safe.

Teach children that sexual abuse is not their fault and that they can trust you to stand up for them. Insist that you be told if there is any improper action. Explain that he must not give in to suggestions to keep certain forms of "touching" a secret. Talk about the difference between good and bad kinds of touching and good and bad kinds of secrets.

You should come back to the subject of abuse many times through your child's growing up years. Do not ignore it.

ACADEMICS. *See also Homework, School, Tests.*

A good education is one of the most powerful gifts from parent to child. Your encouragement of academic success has little to do with your own educational background.

Begin by supporting reading in the home by reading to very young children. (This improves attention span and increases vocabulary.) Then, provide the time and place for quiet activities even before there is school homework. (This gives opportunities for creative thinking.)

Starting when your child enters preschool or kindergarten, take an active interest in the school by being a volunteer. There are opportunities for both stay-at-home parents and parents who work outside the home. Respond immediately to notes from the teacher. In most cases, oppose social promotion (promoting a child regardless of achievement). Make a plan for combating learning difficulties rather than permitting them to drag on and become entrenched. Each day talk together about what is being learned and ask nonjudgmental questions. Laud improvement and express appreciation over every success. After all, academics is the child's "work" and should be highly important to both child and parent.

ACHIEVEMENT. *See also Appreciation, Determination, Praise, Self-Worth, Success.*

Every youngster needs to feel a sense of accomplishment at the end of the day and it is important that a parent find something that is worthy of mention. This is sometimes difficult with certain children! Verbal applause can be given a youngster for something as large as a good grade on a paper or as small as remembering to brush her teeth. Provide places to display achievements: the hall walls for artwork, the coffee table for hand-crafted pieces, shelves in the family room or a child's bedroom for trophies, and bulletin board space for good school papers and sports awards.

Don't overplay small achievements in your zeal to give youngsters self-esteem. Keep your praise in proportion. (This means that you don't reward picking up toys with a trip to the ice-cream shop.) And remember that esteem isn't given, it is gained through experiences.

Do give a child opportunities each day to achieve something positive. Remember to thank her when she helps to clear the table or comforts a crying sister. Your aim is to compliment more than you complain.

ACNE.
Skin problems can be very frustrating and embarrassing to youngsters. Research shows that almost all teens get skin problems, starting in puberty. They are usually caused by the overproduction of oil in the follicles. It used to be thought that certain foods caused acne, but that hasn't been proved. Most treatments do little more than keep the skin clean, which of itself is good. Acne usually disappears by the end of the teenage years but that can be of little comfort to a self-conscious youngster. While a parent should not trivialize acne by saying "Don't complain, it doesn't matter," he needs to regularly reinforce the youngster in other ways. A sincere compliment now and then on a teen's appearance is always welcome.

ACTIVITIES. *See also After-School Activities, Arts and Crafts Projects, Evening Activities, Extracurricular Activities, Games, Lessons, Outdoor Play, Sports, Team Sports, Weekends.*
Each day deserves at least one small highlight. It can be of short duration, but you need to provide some memorable event. It could be as simple as lighting candles on the dinner table in honor of a badge earned by your Boy Scout, taking a family walk around the block after dinner, or doing a puzzle together.

Make it a given that in addition to chores, errands, and religious observances your weekend always has one other togetherness activity. Early in the week, talk together about what you will do: a trip to the zoo, a picnic in the woods—something that involves the entire family.

Let children be children. Don't involve a child in organized activities at too early an age just because you think she'll look cute in the soccer uniform or because you always wanted to play a saxophone.

👎 Avoid overbooking youngsters with a string of organized activities. Leave some afternoon time for creative, unstructured play at home, at a friend's home, or at the caregiver's home. It is sufficient for youngsters to have a maximum of two or three organized activities each week (perhaps one sport for teamwork, one music lesson to develop a talent, one club for social interaction).

👍 Make a list of all the after-school activities that you approve of, then let the choice be made by the child. Youngsters should understand that they are committed to an activity for a minimum of six months before dropping out. However, let them explore a wide variety. Keep the list, add to it, and let the child select some for this year and save others for subsequent years. Encourage group activities that teach leadership, responsibility, new skills, being part of a team, and democracy in action. Sports activities can teach sportsmanship, diligence, team spirit, athletic skills, precision, and poise. But most important, after-school activities should be fun.

ADD/ADHD. *See also Hyperactivity.*

Not every overactive child has attention deficit disorder or attention deficit hyperactivity disorder. Some kids just have a less-developed attention span and are more prone to mischief. Pediatricians say it is normal for three-to-five-year-olds to race from one activity to another when they are overexcited, hungry, or tired. However if this lack of focus continues, these youngsters may be at risk for long-term social and academic problems.

Attention deficit hyperactivity disorder is marked by failure to pay attention, listen, and follow directions. The child is forgetful and fidgety, blurts out answers or questions, and has difficulty taking turns. Although the drug Ritalin was heavily prescribed in the past, new nonchemical methods of control seem to be gaining in effectiveness.

The drug-based approach to ADD/ADHD may have a connection with later use of illegal drugs. Its continued use could be habit-forming. Long-term effects of this approach have not been studied in humans as yet but long-term use in laboratory test animals has shown heart and brain damage and psychotic problems. So, institutes that promote medical but non-drug approaches are gaining in popularity and showing some success.

While there exists no scientific basis for classifying ADHD as a mental illness, there is substantial evidence that stimulants such as Ritalin can produce symptoms such as mania, insomnia, nervousness, irritability, and

14

other syndromes. However, failing to reach the source of the problem can bring on depression that could result in suicide, already at high levels among teens. Some pediatric neurologists say that there is no such illness as ADHD and that normal childhood activity has been wrongly labeled as a mental illness.

Before jumping into the long-term use of a drug, work with your child to develop a sustained interest in books, coloring, play with toys, and conversation with you. Monitor the worrisome behavior for about three months and if there is no improvement, seek professional help.

ADOPTION. *See also Abortion, Bonding, Cultural Differences, Heritage, Pregnancy, Sex.*

The number of couples hoping for a family and not succeeding on their own far exceeds the number of babies available for adoption in this country. Turning to fertility clinics is costly and painful, and doesn't have a high success rate, yet some couples persist, thinking that a baby they produce will be the absolute best because it will have their genes. At the same time many babies are aborted while others around the world go unwanted and unloved.

Many people would like to adopt a child or add a child to their existing family but they are reluctant to adopt due to the media attention focused on a few failed adoptions or occasions when birth parents reappeared and problems surfaced due to inadequate private adoptions. However, government agencies, usually in the county, are licensed adoption agencies that legally terminate the rights of birth parents. Such public adoptions are very low in cost and avoid many of the pitfalls associated with private agency adoptions.

Today more and more research is showing that a good child-raising environment usually plays a greater role than genes, so a foreign adoption can make good sense and is a loving response to a world problem. There are reputable agencies connecting would-be parents with healthy children, and although the costs and waiting times differ, the average cost is similar to a private adoption in the United States. Some foreign-born babies are delivered to the United States by professional couriers, but in other cases the new parent may be required to travel to the foreign country. Parents who adopt have found that they usually bond quickly with these eager children and that their love knows no cultural or national boundaries.

Teach birth children that adopted children are just as much a part of a loving family as they are, and that the adopted child's parents are truly their "real" parents.

AFFECTION. *See Love.*

AFTER-SCHOOL ACTIVITIES. *See also Activities, Clubs and Youth Groups, Latchkey Children.*

Winding down after the school day is highly important for a child's well-being. After a sharing time complete with snacks, encourage change-of-pace activities (not sitting in front of the television) and then chores and homework. Active play outdoors is best, but it is also possible indoors during bad weather with games of tag, Ping-Pong, a chinning bar or exercise equipment, or a mat for stunts.

If a parent is not home to hear the triumphs and tragedies, a phone call can help. This reassures the parent that all is well and it reassures the child of the parent's care. An at-home parent can provide neighborhood headquarters for enjoyable and safe play by remembering to include youngsters whose parents are not at home.

To keep connected, working parents can create a message jar on the kitchen counter that contains the day's timely messages such as "Fruit sticks in the freezer," "Gotta alota homework? Play first!" or "Please start the potatoes at 5:30." (By putting messages in a jar, they can't be easily overlooked or lost amid other papers on the counter.) Some parents leave a cassette tape message for children who are home alone.

AGGRESSION. *See also Anger, Assertiveness, Bullies, Discipline.*

Out-of-control behavior stems from a child's inability to know how to respond when something is disappointing, bewildering, or frightening. He wrongly and fiercely demands what he deems his inherent right. While a certain amount of pushing/shoving can be playful (and can often be handled by children without adult intervention), some children respond to every disagreement with excessive physical force.

An aggressive child should usually be removed from the scene of action and controlled until he is calm (and the adult is, too). This is especially true with very young children who cannot yet verbalize their frustrations.

Never respond in kind by hitting a child who is hitting, pinching the pincher, or punching the puncher. Rather, use your mature wisdom to get to the motive behind the wrong action. Find the reasons behind the action and you lessen further occasions for aggression. Do not reward aggression with extra attention. Get to the point in a solemn way, using a serious low voice to show that you feel strongly about the problem.

Be consistent in not permitting aggressive behavior. Take action every single time and immediately. By separating the errant child from the play, you will show that there is no benefit derived from aggression or violence. Talk together about a better way to achieve a desired result. Finding the usual triggers for aggressive behavior will help to eliminate it.

AIDS (Acquired Immune Deficiency Syndrome). *See also Homosexuality, Sex.*

The spread of AIDS and other sexually transmitted diseases (STDs) is a major concern of every parent. Be informed by getting current facts from the CDC National Prevention Information Network (Center for Disease Control), P.O. Box 6003, Rockville, MD 20849-6003; (800) 458-5231.

While sexual abstinence is the best option, those who lack this self-control can greatly reduce the spread of any sexually transmitted disease by the use of condoms. The problem is that young people think it is other people who get AIDS or they feel that if they use condoms the act is planned, not spontaneous. If the latter, they feel it is out of their control and this lessens their guilt.

Open discussions at home and at school should address the options of abstinence, testing partners, and using condoms. A healthy and increasingly popular alternative is abstinence, postponing sex until entering a monogamous marriage. This option is obviously very attractive but it requires parents to reinforce the idea of chastity *before* the age when youngsters tend to become sexually active.

Be clear that a discussion of AIDS cannot be interpreted as a tacit permission to be sexually active but rather the point is to be extremely careful. (Most STDs are treatable or curable, with the exception of AIDS, which at present is not.) Since this continues to be a life-and-death issue, parents must speak up with resolve.

ALCOHOL. *See Substance Abuse.*

ALLOWANCE. *See Money.*

ANGER. *See also Aggression, Biting, Discipline, Hatred, Kicking, Running Away.*

An angry child is feeling hurt in various ways and needs to be comforted before you can pursue the cause of the anger. Comfort can come from a parent's calm words, cuddling the angry child, or removing her from the unhappy scene. Teach good alternatives to hitting or screaming: hitting a pillow on a bed, tearing up old newspapers, going for a walk or jog, or taking a soothing bath. Anger is often caused when: a child doesn't get her own way; she is asked to do something she dislikes; she is punished for doing-wrong; she is frustrated in her attempts to achieve something; and when someone says something hurtful to her.

Use simple words of reason to show how to act in these situations. Role playing will help both before a problem arises or afterward. Take the role of the child and act in an inappropriate way and then ask the adult (the child) what she might say to you. This takes time, of course, but it can be very helpful.

Don't add to the problem by minimizing the child's anger and saying "That's not important," "How silly, just do it," "It's for your own good," or "Don't talk that way." Rather talk about the problem and how it can be solved in a better way.

Never discipline a child when you are angry. In those cases when you are so infuriated that you feel you are losing control, try to separate yourself from the scene by sitting quietly and calming down, or by telephoning someone who will help you to be more reasonable. Then put your anger in words such as, "I'm very disappointed in what you have done and I'm too angry to consider your punishment now, but we will talk about it in ten minutes."

Do work closely with a child who is frequently angry to help uncover the cause. Be sure to point out successes and happy events so that these become more important than disappointing or frustrating occasions. When a youngster can read, make a list of things for her to do when angry—those things that will cheer her or take her mind off the problem.

ANOREXIA. *See also Bulimia, Mealtime.*

This eating disorder that afflicts teens and young adults is starting to affect younger children. Although it is most common in girls, it is occasionally seen in boys. Start early to help youngsters achieve a good self-image. Reinforce the truth that a person's inner self is far more important

18

than outward appearances. See that regular meals and/or food supplements are consumed.

If there is a weight problem, it is easier to control when a child is five pounds overweight than when she has fifteen pounds of excess. Learn together how to cook tasty and nutritious low-calorie meals that can benefit the entire family. Should a youngster starve herself to the point of being underweight, it is time for you to seek professional help.

ANXIETY. *See Stress.*

APATHY. *See also Activities, Boredom, Determination, Laziness.*

Like a contagion, apathy can creep from parent to child. We need to have enthusiasm for what is important and to slough off what makes little difference in our lives. The problem is that youngsters often choose to be apathetic about what should be vital to their well-being such as: tackling academic problems; health, including good personal habits and outdoor activities; friendships and socialization achieved through neighborhood and group play; spirituality, gained through meditation, religion, prayer, charitable activities; and a joyful approach to life including a variety of activities and experiences.

Research shows that the interest a parent takes in a child is vital in combating apathy. An ignored child easily becomes an apathetic child. Explore as a family interesting ways to spend free time. When you discover a glimmer of interest or excitement in an activity, build on it. Also, give youngsters *interesting* responsibilities and chores (opportunities to feel needed). And don't fail to tell a child how much you love and need him as an integral part of family life.

A wise person said: "A couch potato parent begets a mashed potato child." Don't permit your own apathy to mash down your youngster's zest for living.

APOLOGIZING. *See also Forgiveness.*

It's important to say "I'm sorry." Start with young children to teach these valuable words. When a wrong has been committed by child or parent, and when the wrong is acknowledged, an apology sets the stage for forgiveness. Apologizing doesn't require the pressure of the promise "I'll never do that again," but it does require regret—sorrow for having hurt someone, for having broken a family rule or community law, for having disappointed another person. Even if the wrongdoer doesn't think he's

19

done wrong, he can say "I'm sorry for hurting your feelings" or "I'm sorry to have made you unhappy."

When the apology is given, the incident should be forgotten. Don't keep bringing it up, however, you can mention the lesson that was learned without being critical. And when all is forgiven, there is nothing like a good hug!

APPEARANCE. *See also Cleanliness, Clothing, Fads, Haircuts, Makeup.*

What a child wears is not the essence of who he really is. Start when a child is young to help him choose comfortable, pleasant-appearing clothes. Work together with other parents to encourage children to dress as children, not as circus clowns or streetwalkers. Don't let youngsters be walking ads for products and manufacturers that you disapprove of.

Talk about fads and how and why some are acceptable to your family and some are not. Assure youngsters that when they are on their own they may spend the money they earn on what they please, but while living under your roof they will not dress like bums or spend money on trashy or over-priced fads.

When a child enters kindergarten, set standards for appearance, including cleanliness, hair care and style. Later discuss standards on makeup use, body piercing, and club or gang clothing. With kid-input, look over a youngster's wardrobe and select one or two outfits that both of you like and that you would want him to wear when he is with you. Be sure to compliment a good appearance with lines like "You look marvelous!" Above all, remember it is what's inside that counts.

APPRECIATION. *See also Achievement, Encouragement, Gratitude, Love, Praise, Toasts.*

How good it feels to be appreciated! If you verbally appreciate children, you may find that they may express appreciation for what you do. Remember to recognize small things: for doing homework, finishing chores, clearing her place at the table, playing with the dog.

Use lines such as "I'm so glad you're my kid." "There's nobody like you." "What would we do without you!" "You will always be special to me." "How good that you let baby Bruce join in your play."

A nice idea for showing you care is to serve the youngster's meal on a special plate—the kind that is imprinted "You are special" or any one-of-a-kind dish. Plan a once-a-month award night

20

honoring family achievements. Appreciate chores well done. Share good school work and also the satisfaction of a good project at a parent's work. Make up paper certificates for each family member, noting something they've accomplished: Best Pet Caretaker, Gourmet Cook, Tidiest Room, Greatest Grade, Chauffeur Extraordinaire, and so forth.

APRIL FOOL'S DAY. *See also Fun.*

While good fun should be a part of every day, make it special on this silly holiday. Color the orange juice green. Hide an alarm clock in with the toys. Put a fake plastic bug in the school lunch box. Place a paper cup of water on top of the bathroom door. Short-sheet a bed. Serve dinner on paper grocery bags used as place mats set under the dining room table. Anything goes as long as it isn't mean or dangerous.

ARGUING, ARGUMENTS. *See also Family Meeting, Fighting, Getting Even, Ombudsman, Sharing, Yelling.*

Constant arguments can stifle family love. Teach kids to ask themselves these questions before starting or continuing a quarrel. For very young children, ask in simple terms:

• Is this argument worth stopping play?
• Does this make a real difference?
• Does a parent need to be involved in this?

For older children, add these to the above:

• Is this the time to work on solving the dispute?
• Are there facts to be gathered before settling it?
• Even if I'm right, is it worth the time to argue?
• Can we just agree to disagree?
• Could we end this with a handshake or a hug?

List these questions on the bulletin board. When you're asked to referee a quarrel, ask if the participants have considered each question. Intervene as little as possible. Soon youngsters will find that it isn't worth their time to be constant arguers.

 Don't permit arguments over toys. If one arises, simply remove the toy from play. Eventually the kids will develop the skills of taking turns and sharing.

 When youngsters share a room, they still need their own space so that arguments don't prevail. For a temporary solution, use a yellow ribbon (like police use to cordon off a crime scene) to divide play space. A parent can also use ribbon to mark off the area around the computer or workbench—areas that youngsters should not enter uninvited.

Give praise at bedtime for a day without an argument. However, don't ignore legitimate disputes that require adult help to solve. Set aside a quiet time to search together for a solution that is mutually satisfying.

ARROGANCE. *See also Bragging, Bullies, Humility.*

No one likes an arrogant child. Tell him so! There is a big difference between arrogance and quiet pride over an achievement. Arrogance is usually the result of low self-esteem and indicates a cry for approval. While a youngster should recognize his self-worth, this shouldn't be the main topic of family or peer conversation. A parent who is quick to compliment good work will help a child to do the right thing with or without praise from others—and the child will not have to always boost himself.

Encourage a youngster to keep a little book in which he can write his achievements. Remember to ask him occasionally if he'd like to read these to you.

ARTS AND CRAFTS PROJECTS. *See also Museums, Recipes for Craft Projects.*

You won't know if you have a pint-sized Rembrandt if you don't expose children to at-home art opportunities. Many parents hold back because they feel art is so messy. It is, but you can control the mess in several ways:

• For toddlers, use big, unbreakable crayons.
• Provide aprons or old T-shirts to cover clothes.
• Put the painting easel in the kitchen where floor spills are easily wiped up (and teach young artists to do this).
• In nice weather, plan finger-painting outdoors where hands and patios can be hosed off.
• Let kids use water-based paints to paint murals on the outside of sliding glass doors (they wash off easily).
• Chalk play is fun on sidewalks and safe driveways and can easily be hosed off.
• Place newspaper on a picnic or patio table to make a work space for modeling clay projects.

- Set up a special table for projects such as model building or weaving that are not completed at one sitting.
- Use a plastic laundry basket or large covered bin as a receptacle for paper, crayons, paint, and other craft supplies.

Provide far more interesting supplies than boring coloring books. Don't overlook computer art projects, clay modeling, soap carving, model building, collage, bead work, felt pictures, flower arranging, and times for art appreciation and art museum visits.

A few ideas will help a project run smoothly: have only one messy project going at a time, invest time in first explaining the project, see that the equipment works well, don't hover but check often, and appreciate what a child does and show it off to the rest of the family. To start you thinking of interesting art projects, here are three that are easy-to-do.

Fantasy Candles give old crayons a new life. Let youngsters gather stubby crayons as a parent melts paraffin and old white candles in a heavy pan. Add crayons for the desired color. Use quart and pint milk cartons and place a taper candle or a fixed string in the middle. Then let children fill them with crushed ice. Add the melted wax and do not touch until the wax is firm. (The wax will eventually melt the ice.) When the wax is completely cool, pour off the water, then peel off the carton and see the unique shape of the candle (due to the spaces left by the ice). When lighted, you will see an unusual lighting effect.

Personalized place mats can be made with crayons, colored paper, and wax paper. For each family member, let youngsters make a drawing or design using eight-inch by ten-inch colored paper and crayons. Then place two nine-inch by twelve-inch pieces of wax paper over and under each drawing. The parent then gently irons the wax paper to fuse the two pieces of wax paper together. Pinking shears can make a nice edge.

Window Wonders are made with old crayons, a grater, and wax paper. Working on a piece of wax paper, let a child grate the crayons, using one color, and then another. Remember that overlapping colors will produce new colors, such as red and blue will make purple. Push the shavings into an area about three inches square and at least one-quarter inch deep. Then place a small hardware nut near one edge of the shavings. (This will be used later for hanging.) Cover the arrangement with another piece of wax paper and top with a newspaper. With parental help, run a warm iron over the newspaper until the

23

crayon shavings are all melted. Do not touch until the shavings are again totally cool and hard. Then remove the paper to reveal the creation. Thread a ribbon through the nut and hang in a window for all to admire.

Provide places (other than the refrigerator door) to display art: in poster frames down a hallway, under glass on coffee tables, hanging on a clothesline or on the stairway bannister. Keep at least one piece of art each year for inclusion in the family's yearly scrapbook of achievements and events. Occasionally take a piece of art to the office and tape it on the wall to share with coworkers, or share a masterpiece with grandparents. The artist will be impressed!

Borrow from the library age-appropriate books on art and artists, read them together and then let kids create a piece of art in one of the styles described. Small school budgets often eliminate art classes so encourage your school to ask businesses to underwrite art instruction for children.

ASSERTIVENESS. *See also Aggression.*

There is a difference between aggression and assertiveness. The first involves verbal and physical force, while assertiveness means standing up for an idea or principle. We want kids to be assertive in areas of honesty, human rights, fairness, appreciation of others, and good values. They can do more than be assertive for themselves, they can also defend these rights for others. Family dinner-table discussion as to how and when to be properly assertive can be helpful to both parent and child. Give specific examples such as how to respond to incidents of teasing or discrimination, or the correct response when a schoolmate tries to take over a project all for himself. Talk about the importance of logical debate techniques and dealing in facts not unsubstantiated rumors.

ATTACHMENT. *See also Bonding.*

Although similar to bonding, attachment is the mutual connection between the parent and child that usually comes later than bonding but during the first year or two. It happens when a parent or certain objects (such as a toy animal or doll) become very important to a child. Attachment can also occur between the child and other regular caregivers.

Attachment defect is the term used when the youngster fails to make any connection. It arises when a youngster is ignored when very young or not treated as a special individual as could happen in a large care facility. It can even happen to a baby who is very sick. He can be physically well

24

cared for by parents and professionals, yet is mainly the object of tests and medication with little time for normal babyhood activities. Consequently the child fails to bond to people or things, seems not to care, and flits from person to person or activity to activity without any commitment or visible affection. Some also become irrationally attached to certain objects, such as food.

Attachment disorders are most severe in youngsters who, although physically cared for, lacked loving caregivers who did not use opportunities to connect. While these children appear not to care about others, as if they were very independent, actually they are extremely dependent but are not able to show it.

This can be overcome with dedicated loving care and firm discipline. One-on-one activities with lots of eye contact, being talked to (even before the child can respond), and being held, touched, stroked, and massaged can help a great deal.

ATTENTION, NEED FOR. *See also Showing Off, Tantrums.*

We all like to be noticed but our kids need to learn how to both give and get attention—and it isn't by throwing a tantrum in the middle of the grocery store! Usually a youngster's bad attitude is really a cry for attention. Often he gets attention—but it is the wrong kind of attention: the parent lectures or punishes and stops there. And thus the cycle is repeated: the call for attention followed by the short-lived negative response.

When there are several children in a family, a parent must be sure to regularly acknowledge each child individually, rather than giving the most attention to the neediest or the noisiest. Each one needs to be appreciated as unique or special. One-on-one time with each child is essential and can be accomplished through a walk and talk, playing a game or sport, doing a work project, reading books together, talking at bathtime, or having a quiet conversation at bedtime.

Teach children to *ask* for, not demand, attention when they need it. Respect requests such as "I need you to help me." "Can you give me an answer?" "I want to play this game and nobody will play with me." As children mature, there is still need for attention and you will find that in giving it, you also get it in return.

ATTENTION/RETENTION/RECALL. *See also Attention Span.*

These are three essential points you want to make so that your words are listened to, have meaning, and are remembered. (Start using the actual terms *attention, retention,* and *recall* with early grade-school children.) First, show them how they learn more when they give the subject their undivided attention. For example, give directions as to how to change a lightbulb. When you have finished (telling where bulbs are kept, how to unscrew the dead ones, the safety features of having the switch off, and what to do with the dead bulb), have the child repeat the instructions back to you, showing how much she has retained. Then at some later time, ask the youngster to do the project, showing how well she can recall the information.

Teachers need these skills reinforced at home since attention, retention, and recall are integral in mastering the basics of a subject and then building on those basics. There is failure if no attention was given at the start, thus there is nothing to retain in thought, or recall when needed.

Increase a young child's attention span through activities such as reading books together and naming the pictures, lining up blocks in a certain unique formation, talking quietly on one subject only, or creating an entire village of cars, boats, planes, and buildings. Later, see if he has retained any of these skills in his play alone.

ATTENTION SPAN. *See also Attention/Retention/Recall, Homework.*

Lengthen a child's attention span through activities that take concentration. Have the child sit with you while you read an entire children's book and focus on pictures or letters. Color together, finishing one picture completely before starting another. Rather than dumping out a bunch of toys, provide fewer toys at one time so that a child can play more in depth with them.

Don't keep a child so busy he can't "play out" to conclusion the project he's working on. Only suggest a new line of play when the first is totally exhausted. Ask questions like "What else can we do with these blocks?"

Remove distractions, such as other toys, when playing or reading together. Rotate toys so when certain toys become boring they can be put on a shelf and different ones can be brought out. The newness of these will also increase the attention span. This is preferable to having all toys available all the time which can cause lack of focus on any one. Have "Train Week," "Doll House Day," or an evening of building blocks.

ATTITUDE. *See also Behavior Problems, Character Building.*

A child's reaction and response to words and happenings is often displayed in verbal and body language — and these can be negative or positive.

Bad attitudes include defiance, aggression, stubbornness, sarcasm, disdain, self-pity, and apathy. Body language may be as significant as words. Constant negative attitudes offer little hope of happiness and success in life.

Good attitudes include determination, teachableness, affection, forgiveness, friendliness, respect, obedience, cheerfulness, and optimism, which bring joy to the youngster and others.

A parent teaches good attitudes by helping youngsters focus on positive goals and ways to properly achieve them. Children take their lead and mimic their parents' attitudes. For example, when a child says "I can't do this!" a parent needs to encourage the child to at least start, and then offer help along the way. Parents who say things like "Nothing good ever happens" are setting negative examples. For example: When dad is up for promotion, mom makes negative remarks about the boss and other candidates, saying, "Well, you probably won't get the job because of that stupid office policy." How much better to adopt a positive attitude and say, "You certainly have worked hard and been a loyal employee, so you are deserving of recognition." Another example, upon hearing a loud sound upstairs a parent says "Sounds like someone fell down and killed himself!" (On examination, it may be a door slamming.) Again the attitude in this case is negative.

Thus parents need to watch their own responses and keep hopeful attitudes toward a youngster's ability to succeed in school, in sports, or in life in general. A child's bad attitude may be the result of fear of failure, fear of disappointing a parent, or fear of doing something punishable. A calm and caring environment with firm but gentle training will usually result in a family with positive attitudes.

AUTHORITY. *See also Discipline.*

For most children the parent is the authority figure at home, and teachers, coaches, youth leaders, ministers, and law enforcement officers are the authorities away from home. Parents should set an example of respecting the authority of these other people and being patient and appreciative of their efforts.

27

When the parent is away from home, authority is often transferred to a caregiver. Children need to know that the person who is in charge has authority. Insist on respectful behavior and use corrective methods for disobedience to other authority figures.

Because a child sees you as an authority on most everything, don't make the mistake of appearing to be infallible. Share those times when you make a mistake or when you accede to the authority of others.

Never undermine the authority of law enforcement officers. The vast majority are honest and helpful and can aid a child in trouble. Consider a visit to a police department or a court to see how the law protects.

One parent should not undermine the authority of another. When children are very young, talk over your parenting style and agree on certain parental issues so that you have a united front. If one parent is the authority and disciplinarian during the day, the other should do it for evenings and weekends. One parent shouldn't always be the meanie and the other the softie.

Do let children know that (most of the time) you as the authority have a wealth of experience, and that you know what is right. But explain that you want them to gradually assume responsibility in many areas such as what to wear, classes to take, and selection of friends. As children gather information in school and other activities, let them become miniauthorities on certain topics: ancient literature, astronomy, soccer, bee-keeping, and so forth. And encourage teens to become authority figures in appropriate areas to siblings.

AUTOMOBILE TRAVEL. *See Travel.*

BABYHOOD CONCEPTS. *See also Playpen, Toddler Concepts.*

A child's first year is an important learning time. These are the concepts that parents should emphasize:

• patience—everything needn't be done in a rush.
• a sense of value—certain things are more important than others.
• obedience to simple words such as "no," and that we mean what we say.
• unselfishness—fussing won't always make baby the center of attention.
• care of possessions—a toy thrown is not returned.
• a sense of accomplishment—praise and applause for doing something good.
• being loved—no matter what.

In general, babies go through several stages of activity: reflex actions (those first smiles), coordinated actions (holding a finger), manipulating objects (shaking a toy), understanding cause and effect (playing peek-a-boo or throwing a toy), and so forth. Fully explore and enjoy each learning experience during this first year because you are setting the foundation for actions and attitudes in the years to come.

Be alert to a baby's early years, which are crucial to learning. Interact by talking, singing, playing, hugging. Research shows that a baby's brain grows to 90 percent of its adult size in the first three years.

BABYPROOFING. *See also Environment, Safety.*

Start to babyproof your home before a baby is born as you may be too busy to do much of it later. Here's a checklist for right now and the next few months:

• Be sure that crib and playpen rails are safely designed. (You may find some older models that can permit a child's head to be caught.) Be sure that the mattress and pad fit securely without gaps.

- Remove and discard plastic wrappings on all equipment.
- Anchor to the wall any tall dressers, bookcases or television stands that a young child could pull over on himself. Cushion sharp corners of furniture.
- Obtain a bath seat and a padded faucet cover to protect a child in the tub.
- Store harmful cleaning solutions and medicines out of reach.
- Use electric outlet cover plugs, cupboard and toilet latches, cord shorteners, and kitchen appliance latches where needed.
- Install safety gates at stairways and fencing on balconies.
- Check that screens and storm windows are properly installed.
- See that car seats are safely located and latched into place.
- Obtain a fire extinguisher for each floor of the house and learn how to use it.
- Have an emergency chain ladder if the house has a second floor.
- Write a list of emergency numbers, including the poison control center, and post it where everyone can see it.
- Have a simple intercom system if you cannot easily hear a child.
- Install night lights in halls, bathrooms, and bedrooms for safe walking at night.
- Remove from clothes, toys and bedding any tags that a child might chew on.
- Check an older home for dangerous lead paint and asbestos.
- Create one or more safe changing areas and determine never to turn away when changing or dressing a baby.
- If you wish to have the baby in your bedroom, choose the new bedside cribs that fit directly on the side of your bed. These are far safer than having the baby in your bed where a parent could roll onto him.

BABY-SITTERS. *See Caregivers, Child Care Facilities, Grandparents.*

BACKYARD ACTIVITIES. *See Activities, Outdoor Play, Play.*

BALLOONS.

Although balloons can be part of many happy activities, they can also be a danger. Keep balloons away from babies and toddlers who might put them to their mouths, break them, and then suck them into their throats.

 Enjoyable balloon games include "Balloon Barber" in which each participant has a filled balloon and a bladeless razor.

Smear each balloon with shaving cream and then let participants "shave" all the lather off the balloon without popping it. Balloon volleyball and dropping water-filled balloons into a target from a ladder or tree can also make good fun.

BATHTIME. *See also Bedtime Routine, Cleanliness.*

This prelude to good sleep is an important time for young children since it provides play tied to cleanliness. A warm, soothing bath is ideal about thirty minutes before bed. Conversation, storytelling, and fun with bath toys combine with the simple lessons on how to clean various body parts.

Never leave young bathers alone, even for a minute. Never let them turn on water while in the tub. Have a padded cover over the faucet to protect them from bumps. To prevent burns from scalding water, the parent should prepare the bath ahead and be the only one to add any additional water.

By the time youngsters are in grade school, they prefer to bathe or shower solo. A radio or cassette player—placed a safe distance away from the water—can add to the enjoyment. Don't intrude on privacy, but be aware when youngsters are in the bathroom, should there be a fall. Teens seem to prefer morning showers and both boys and girls like the use of a variety of body-care products.

Train youngsters to leave the bathtub, shower, shower curtain or door, and entire bathroom in good condition for the next user.

BEDTIME ROUTINE. *See also Fears, Naps, Nightmares, Sleep, Touching.*

Going to bed should be one of the most cherished times for child and parent. Set age-appropriate bedtimes and change them each year before the start of school. For their own well-being and ability to learn in school, see that youngsters get adequate rest.

Don't rush kids off to bed; let it be a gradual winding down from the day. Try to put youngsters to bed every night, but if you will be away at their bedtime, still wish a child "good sleep," "happy dreams," "sweet waking up."

Bedtime comes easier if a parent gives a child some warning, such as "Fifteen minutes 'til bedtime." For young children, set a timer to ring in fifteen minutes. You can teach an older child to look at a clock and see (for example) when the big hand is on the twelve and the small hand on the eight.

Activities leading up to bedtime should be more quiet and calming (save the tussling for earlier in the evening) and can include a snack, a warm bath, a trip to the bathroom, a drink of water, a story, a chat about the best thing that happened that day, a song, a prayer, and then soft music. Having friendly stuffed animals and dolls in bed makes the parting less lonely. If needed, provide a night-light and a bedside bell to call parents in case of emergency.

Most kids love to be really tucked in with the covers firmly around them. Then comes a prayer, a hug, a kiss, and reassuring words such as "All is well," "I love you," "See you in the morning," "I'll be checking on you," "It was a good day." If you haven't reaffirmed your love earlier, do it now.

Never get in the habit of lying down with a child to help her sleep. If it is absolutely necessary to reassure a sick or fearful child, sit quietly in a bedside chair in the dark. Don't permit children to become bedtime pests—getting out of bed with weak excuses and complaints. Take care of every physical and emotional need/fear and then gently say farewell. Instruct children that there are just three reasons to get out of bed: they are sick, the house is on fire, or they want to be punished.

Sometimes children are truly afraid to be left alone. Letting siblings sleep in the same room, or letting there be an animal in the room (a guinea pig in a cage or a dog by the bed) gives comfort. A night-light, a flashlight on the night table, an under-the-bed check by the parent, and the soft sounds of music can be reassuring.

As soon as children can read on their own, give a fifteen-minute reading bonus. This quiet activity promotes sleep.

BED-WETTING. *See also Toilet Training.*

Parents may be surprised to know that it is not unusual for children over age five to still urinate at night. Many young children are not yet physically ready to make it through the night. The problem can also be caused by stress, excitement, failure to completely empty the bladder before going to bed, or excessive drinking in the evening hour.

When bed-wetting occurs, an older child is often embarrassed and ashamed. Help him to handle the problem quickly and responsibly by having him change his clothes, remove soiled sheets and put on clean sheets. Many youngsters prefer to do this themselves without their involving parents. Be supportive and patient since this phase usually doesn't last for more than a year. If it does, seek professional help.

For many children, wearing a pull-up diaper at night is the answer. This can be a blessing but also can become a crutch if the pull-up habit is extended for too long a period.

BEHAVIOR DRUGS. *See also ADD/ADHD.*

The modern practice of medicating youngsters for every behavioral problem is beginning to backfire. Often a drug prescribed to cure one ailment causes another more serious one. Certainly a medicine may be a quick fix, but it is not a permanent cure. These medications are often used as substitutes for self-control, parental and child professional counseling, and teaching good social values and etiquette. They can inhibit the natural growth from childhood to maturity.

While we spend millions of dollars warning children about the dangers of taking drugs, at the same time we are encouraging parents to use drugs for minor childhood behavior problems, implying that a drug is the answer to every problem. Some more common drugs are Ritalin (often prescribed for ADHD), the antidepressant Luvox, and Prozac, which is often surreptitiously used for youngsters but not approved as yet.

When a child is physically well but mentally troubled, parents should consider all the possibilities before treatment with mood-altering drugs. Much of the violence in schools today can be directly traced to the use of these drugs. Before giving their consent, parents should ask many questions of professionals and other knowledgeable parents concerning long-term use, addiction, side-effects, and alternate treatments.

BEHAVIOR PROBLEMS. *See also Aggression, Anger, Biting, Discipline, Rules.*

Parents have about eighteen years to teach children how to behave as responsible adults. So let kids be kids—don't downgrade childhood and don't force kids into adult ways before they can handle adult occasions. Teach little by little and remember that childish actions are normal during most of these years and that some youngsters just mature more slowly than others.

A positive behavior once learned is frequently forgotten or ignored so a parent must be patient but firm in teaching and re-teaching. Writing down rules for proper behavior is a big help for youngsters who can read.

Often inappropriate behavior arises when a child just doesn't know the right things to do. A parent can easily correct this with role playing: taking turns acting out how to react to anger, fighting, lying, cheating, and so forth.

Sometimes the unacceptable behavior comes because parents are not consistent in requiring youngsters to adhere to family values and rules. This is a bit harder to correct since parents have been actually permitting the bad behavior. But an announcement of a new routine of following the rules, and then following through and being firm about discipline, will usually correct the behavior.

Children who exhibit behavioral problems such as violence or excessive dishonesty are often trying to communicate another message that is difficult for them to put into words. If a parent is tuned into his youngster, he may be able to ferret out the cause of a severe behavior problem. This requires patience and understanding. If behavioral problems continue, a responsible parent will not ignore these cries for help but seek guidance. Some schools have counselors to advise or they can guide you to other professional help.

BICYCLING. *See also Safety.*

Bicycles are one of the best forms of fun and exercise for every age, providing certain steps are taken for safety. Wagons, scooters, soap box racers, roller skates, and in-line skates also provide outdoor fun and exercise. The use of wheels builds strength and endurance and provides older children with a form of transportation.

A first bike is a big moment for child and parents, and the removal of training wheels is another important step. Cycling can be on the patio, on a blocked off driveway, on neighborhood sidewalks, and in parks (especially useful in urban areas).

Take youngsters on several neighborhood bicycling safaris and make sure they understand the dynamics of avoiding pedestrians and how to safely cross streets. Teach them to abide by these safety tips:

• Always wear a properly fitted safety helmet, strapped in place. If a child fails to wear the helmet, prohibit bike riding for a period of time, such as a week. Elbow and knee pads are also helpful for new riders.
• Ride defensively. Teach youngsters to use their eyes to be aware of other riders and pedestrians, looking out for potholes and other hazards on the cycling surface.
• Ride at a speed that is safe in keeping with age and ability. If youngsters want to race, find an area that can be marked off safely.

- Be alert to water and slippery wet leaves. Wet conditions slow braking time.
- Respect traffic. All states require cyclists to ride with the traffic flow. Wrong-way riders are much more apt to have accidents and get traffic tickets. Obey stop signs, actually putting one foot down; don't just slow to a glide. Look back, signal, and check for on-coming traffic before turning.
- Dress safely. Wear clothes that won't impede the pedals. At night, be sure the bike has lights and reflectors and the cyclist is wearing light-colored or reflective clothing.
- Never pack another rider or play tricks in traffic. Save the wheelies for a safe area.

If your neighborhood has ample sidewalks and driveways, it's helpful and fun to create a safe area for kids to practice skills. Sometimes you can cordon off several driveways for safe play by parking cars at the curb to block the driveway. Use chalk markings to indicate sidewalks, "parking lots" and traffic lanes, and cardboard to make a variety of traffic signs and signs for school, market, bank, and so forth.

Family cycling can be very satisfying. There are fine safety seats to hold very young children. Consider having a weekend day when all transportation is by bicycle. Ice or roller skating at a rink is another great sport for the family to enjoy as part of a memorable weekend.

BIRTH ORDER.

The characteristics of children can be affected by the order in which they are born. Thus parents need to be alert to the way they treat each child and be as evenhanded as possible.

The oldest child is used to dominating conversations, having had the parent's undivided attention at first. She usually has a very good vocabulary and enjoys adult company. There is often pressure on the firstborn child to excel and cries of "You're not fair!" are not uncommon when asked to do something she thinks is beneath her. She usually enjoys being a leader in play and is good at nurturing since she considers herself wiser than her younger siblings. However, the birth of a sibling has its downside since "the little princess" may feel dethroned. Advance conversation before the second child is born, a set of very fair rules, and a few special privileges will promote better behavior that is worthy of having younger ones mimic.

The middle child is the younger child for a while and enjoys the "baby perks" while they last. But a middle child can often feel ignored, feel a lack of attention, and thus be more prone to tantrums. He tries hard to be different from the older sibling who excels. In creating his own identity he often chooses inappropriate ways to do so. He will benefit most from one-on-one time with an understanding parent.

The youngest child is usually the most mellow, reflecting the parent's more relaxed attitude since they've been through babyhood before. Often this child is a clown or comic and she really enjoys all the attention received as baby of the family. She can be subtly competitive, striving to keep up with the elder siblings. Some young children rely on their siblings to speak for them, hence they don't practice speaking skills and talk later and less. They also count on older siblings to stick up for them and even fight for them. With the youngest, it's important not to make comparisons with the early achievement of the elder children.

No matter what the birth order, parents should strive to let youngsters grow up without labels and allow each to develop as a unique individual.

BIRTHDAYS. *See also Gifts, Parties.*

Plan parties for ages three up to eighteen, or beyond if you choose. Kids younger than age three don't comprehend the occasion and the party will be primarily for parents and friends. Permit one guest child for each year of age; thus a three-year-old invites three friends and a sixteen-year-old entertains up to sixteen. Home or park parties can be delightful and much less expensive than celebrations at kid-oriented restaurants and amusement parks.

About a month ahead, go with a child to the store and make a wish list so that others have some idea of what the honoree would like. Avoid giving in to television advertised toys, ones that require little creativity, and ones that break easily. Also, pick out the party supplies together, being sure to get plenty of inexpensive prizes so everyone is a game winner.

To help a child know how to act at a party, rehearse how to accept a gift, what to say when opening gifts, how to graciously win or lose at a game, how to bid guests good-bye.

When a youngster is about five, consider planting a birthday tree either in your yard or with permission at a nearby school or park. Pick one about the height of the child and watch how both grow each year. For young children, make a crown out of cardboard and aluminum foil with a clip to adjust it at the back. Make it a family tradition that the celebrant does one good deed on her birthday—something for someone else.

For party themes, games, favors, and foods see *The Family Party Book* (Caryl Krueger, Abingdon Press, Nashville, Tenn.).

BITING. *See also Behavior.*

The child who bites another child is usually one who is frustrated because she does not have the words to express her feelings or needs.

Never bite back! Instead, express your overwhelming disapproval of the action and put the child in time-out. Check that the bitten child is not harmed, that the skin hasn't been broken. Do remember to very thoroughly wash any marks on the bitten child.

Return to the biter and sit with her until she is very calm. Then talk about what caused her to bite. Discuss better ways of achieving her aim. If this bad habit persists, explain to her that she cannot play with others until she learns how to control herself. Do not invite other children to play at your house or permit her to go to other homes for three to five days, and then see that she doesn't repeat the biting. This behavior usually ends by kindergarten or the age when a child can speak clearly and can handle frustrations in less angry and acceptable ways.

"BLANKIES." *See also Pacifiers, Thumb Sucking.*

Before youngsters can verbalize many of their needs, they find comfort in an object. It could be a blanket—commonly called a blankie—or a favorite stuffed animal, or a thumb or pacifier. Such items are called *transitional objects* or *connecting objects* since they ease the time from wakefulness to sleep or they mitigate the fear or confusion of some new experience. They are as normal as an adult's desire to wear a certain comfortable shirt or have a special food on unsettling occasions.

The connecting object is really a stand-in for the comfort of a parent or caregiver. The object often performs a useful service since without it a child is more apt to dissolve into tears or withdraw from an activity. The object is usually abandoned by school age, so the parents' only worry should be the possibility of the thumb causing crooked teeth.

Children can also find comfort in a small stuffed toy pinned inside a pocket where it can be felt but remain unseen by others. Or, it can be carried by a parent until the time of separation when it is then given to the child. A mother's cologne or dad's aftershave sprayed on it can be a further connection to home.

 Don't force a child to give up the connecting object. Peer pressure might bring this about, but let it be the child's choice.

Cut a blanket (such as a receiving blanket) into four equal pieces and if the material will ravel, hem it. Give the child two pieces. Children who need a security blanket will favor one piece since it has the smell (and dirt) that is familiar to him. However, he will usually accept the second one to be used at naptime. Then the first one can be washed, and when it is clean, introduce it with the third piece. The second one can then be washed. By rotating them a child will be comfortable with more than one and this averts noisy distress when one is misplaced. And, a parent can be sure that there is always a sanitary one for the child to have.

BONDING. *See also Separation Anxiety, Touching.*

Bonding is a deep sense of loving commitment and is initially brought about by the nurturing care of the needs of an infant. Then bonding is extended to feeling trust that begins to take root by the important act of touching a baby on a day-to-day basis. This sense of touch is the first means of communication between parent and child, and the earliest expression of love.

This important link between parent and child is not a one-time connection. Formerly it was thought that bonding had to take place shortly after birth, usually in the busy and sterile atmosphere of the hospital. The myth of early bonding gave many parents a lot of guilt when it didn't happen very quickly. Now we see that bonding and rebonding is a life-long happening. Research shows that the development of a lasting and loving tie can come despite age, adoption, or illness.

BOOKS. *See also Library, Reading.*

Among the most precious gifts to children are books, quality literature. Start reading to infants and continue until children can read alone. Then let the child read to you! Also continue reading longer books, called chapter books, together. Encouraging your child to read increases vocabulary and attention span. Create a bookshelf in his room and keep on it the books he is currently reading and the ones he doesn't wish to part with. Pass on books that have been outgrown. Libraries have lists of books recommended for various age groups. Don't forget classics such as *Heidi*,

The Jungle Book, and *Little Women*. You can save money by visiting the library and by buying good books at yard sales.

Consult with the school librarian and give a new book to the library "In honor of Craig Keller's eighth birthday." Place a name plate in the front of the book. The book can be presented in the classroom and class members can be the first to read it.

BOREDOM.

Boredom is defined as weariness by tedious repetition. Youngsters often appear bored with school and activities. The way to cure it is to carefully consider how a youngster actually spends her time.

Sit down together and make a chart of a typical day, hour by hour, filling in times for the essentials: sleep, meals, school, extracurricular activities, homework, and chores. You will find that many additional hours remain that are frittered away and become the basis for tedium; boredom sets in when a youngster doesn't know what to do with this free time. Next let the youngster take the lead by choosing from a number of possible activities to try: a club, sport, reading, crafts, experiments, cooking, shooting baskets, service to others, and so forth.

Of course there can be some television time, but it will be more worthwhile if you suggest a second activity, one that she can do at the same time, such as sewing or model building. Even the essential activities can be enhanced (meals, homework, chores) by creative thinking about how to make these more enjoyable by working as a team, by racing against the clock, or by setting minigoals. The aim is to create a variety of interesting options, things that are fun, creative, and adventuresome.

BORROWING.

Teach children that it is good manners to ask before taking another's possessions. (Borrowing without asking could be called stealing, even if you plan to return the item.) The borrowed item must be returned in the same condition. If it is not, the borrower should buy it or recompense the owner for repair or replacement. It helps to keep a list on the bulletin board of things borrowed within the family and by friends and neighbors. That way you'll know where they are when you need them.

BOTTLES, BOTTLE-FEEDING. *See also Breast-feeding, Colic.*

It's important for bottle-fed babies to be snuggled just as closely as nursing babies. And bottle-feeding gives fathers the opportunity to take part in the closeness of infant feeding times. Parents should be alert to a baby who doesn't enjoy feeding or has upset stomach, rash, colic, or other indications of allergies to cow's milk.

Young children may indicate when they're ready to give up bottles in favor of drinking from a cup. There is nothing wrong with a combination that could include a cup at mealtimes and a bottle before nap or bedtime. Children gradually learn other ways of self-comfort and the bottle won't be necessary.

Bottle props are not recommended as there is a psychological advantage in holding the newborn. Bottles should be warmed to body temperature and if the microwave is used to warm the milk, great care should be taken to vigorously shake the bottle and test the temperature since there can be hot spots.

Never put a baby to bed with a bottle. If a baby needs comfort, feed him first, then give him a pacifier or other object if he doesn't settle down.

A bottle-fed baby can thrive as well as a breast-fed baby providing the parent chooses a quality formula and prepares it in a sanitary way. Be alert to how much formula the baby is actually drinking as opposed to how much is in each bottle since some babies don't drain every bottle. While you can encourage an infant to drink an entire bottle, never force her to finish.

BRAGGING. *See also Arrogance, Bullies, Humility.*

Building up oneself is not attractive in adults or children. Show children acceptable ways to talk about their achievements without offending or putting down others. Help children to rephrase comments on their achievements in a modest way that includes others in the conversation and induces questions on the subject that they can then answer.

A child who brags is usually seeking validation or praise to boost a low self-esteem. Parents who regularly give youngsters the opportunity to excel and who regularly appreciate the good things youngsters achieve will not raise braggarts.

BREAKFAST. *See also Morning Routine.*

This is a most important meal since it reconnects family bonds of love and caring. Breakfast follows the long nighttime period of separation after which children need sustenance and reassurance. Don't skimp on food or time.

Set the breakfast time so that the entire family can participate; some may be getting ready to go out the door, others just getting up, but usually all can come to the table. This valuable meal prepares youngsters to function better in school because teachers say that hungry, sleepy children are not in the mood to learn.

Though this will often be a brief meal, include "I love you" hand squeezes around the table, a summary of each person's plans, and reminders of things to take. Send each family member off with wishes for a great day and the fact that you're looking forward to being together later in the day.

Go beyond cold cereal and juice. Consider a fruit smoothie and peanut butter on toast, a peach or other fruit filled with yogurt, French toast made the night before and reheated, or oatmeal/raisin cookies with cocoa.

Don't use this time to correct or nag. Building confidence is far more important at the beginning of the day. Remember that the mood of the day is often set during the first hour of the day, so make breakfast time a pleasurable experience.

BREAST-FEEDING. *See also Bottle-feeding.*

This is the most common and preferred method of feeding babies today. Even if a mother plans formula feeding, breast-feeding in the first few days provides benefits in protecting children from certain diseases. Most newborns are content on a two-to-three-hour schedule, a few can go four hours. It isn't wise to let a child go for much more than four hours as he will awaken very hungry and nurse vigorously, but usually just enough to satisfy the immediate hunger. The aim is calm, consistent nursing.

For mothers who work outside the home, using a breast pump will let the baby continue to have the benefits of mother's milk. A nursing mother needs to relax, eat a healthy diet, and find a comfortable position for the entire nursing time, even though 80 to 90 percent of the milk is drained within the first four minutes of nursing. Some pediatricians feel that an occasional bottle combined with breast-feeding is acceptable while others feel that it could upset a child's stomach.

Most babies are weaned by the end of their first year, but there is nothing wrong with nursing longer, providing the mother is able and the child is progressing.

While there are many benefits to breast-feeding including cost, purity, and availability, a bottle-fed baby can be cared for by the father or other caregivers, which in some ways can be much easier for the mother. No doubt the debate over breast-feeding and bottle-feeding will continue, but parents should decide what is best for them and know that a baby can thrive with either method.

BRUSHING TEETH. *See Dental Care.*

BUDGETS. *See Money.*

BULIMIA. *See also Anorexia, Mealtime.*
The excessive desire to remain thin has caused many eating disorders including bulimia, which typically causes the sufferer to alternate between binge eating and starving or purging. Bulimics attempt to keep the problem a secret and are often repulsed by their own purging activities.

The causes are multiple, one factor being a chemical malfunction in the brain that alters appetite regulation. Thus, a bulimic youngster needs loving parental attention and immediate professional care—sooner rather than later. Research also shows that a healthy approach to eating and a positive approach to body size can be reinforced through example and conversation starting with very young children.

BULLETIN BOARDS. *See Home Headquarters, Home Management, Organizational Skills.*

BULLIES. *See also Aggression.*
Neither youngsters nor adults should get their way through intimidation or terror. In the long run it is wiser to rule by kindness and reason than by fear and threats. Well-adjusted children are taught how to be assertive without being obnoxious. They are applauded by showing respect for the diversity of others and are encouraged to develop a high sense of ethics.

The attitudes and actions of the family greatly affect a child's tendency to be a bully. These harassers often have parents who fail to talk to them with love and encouragement but instead specialize in criticism and verbal put-downs. These parents use phrases such as "Shut up and just do it." "I don't want to hear a word from you." "Don't even think of asking that!" If not redirected, bullies can turn out to be teen troublemakers and dropouts, leading to antisocial adults with criminal behavior.

Bullies are usually cowards. They look for slights and other occasions that they believe give them the right to be aggressive against others. Often they pick on youngsters who are different from themselves; their victims are those who are smaller, overweight, of a different race, or not able to defend themselves.

A child has several responses when being bullied: to make light of the taunt, to totally ignore it, to smile about it, to report it to a teacher or parent. It's important for youngsters to learn to stick up for themselves but to do it in a safe way.

Encourage children to talk about, rather than hide, the problem of being bullied. Be suspicious when a child can't explain wounds or pretends sickness to stay home from school. Also, children who rush home from school and into the bathroom may be avoiding school bathrooms where much bullying takes place. Many schools have been slow to take steps to stop bullying, even though it is thought that one-third of all youngsters are bullied with some regularity. Metal detectors and closed-circuit television can be part of the solution but education of both teachers and students is the best answer. Unfortunately, few teachers have had specific training in how to handle bullies.

Some enlightened schools have started programs of asking students, with a guaranty of anonymity, to name bullies. They have found the same youngsters are consistently named. The bullies are then put on notice they are being watched, and required to sign a contract that they will not engage in certain bully-related behaviors. Specific punishments for breaking the contract are explained in advance. Antibullying rules are clearly posted. At the same time training is given to all students about how to respond to bullies and how to aid those being bullied. Such plans have produced good results.

Parents must press schools to protect their children from this kind of violence and they must not pass it off as childish pranks. Bullying has a detrimental effect on the socialization of a child and on his ability to concentrate on learning. The administration and teachers need to know that it is their duty to watch out for the well-being of students.

Discuss bully behavior with your child and the probable reasons behind the action: the person is unsure of himself, he doesn't know how to discuss problems, he doesn't have friends, he perceives himself as disliked, or his parents threaten or intimidate him and he needs to show the world that he is important.

Remember that verbal bullying can be very damaging and has no part in school or family life.

43

BUSINESS AND GOVERNMENT. *See also Jobs, Politics.*

What makes the world tick can be fascinating for youngsters. Talk about your work and let children actually see what you do. Ask them for suggestions about your work and try some of them. Participate in "take a child to work" days, in a trip to the bank, a behind-scenes visit at the grocery store, a courthouse, or a polling place on voting day. Talk about the businesses in your own town that are essential to family life, for example the grocer, the cleaners, the restaurant.

Don't let youngsters be naive about business or about community or national government. Support honest people and good issues. Don't blindly support officials who accept graft or engage in other dishonest practices. Explain how government affects big businesses and how business is supported by the stock and bond markets.

Encourage summer jobs as a good way for kids to earn extra money for the school year. This allows them to enjoy the school year activities without the pressures of an after-school job. Summer work lets youngsters see businesses in action and will give them some ideas for future careers.

Engage preteens and teens in following one particular election issue or one particular stock. Plan a visit to a stock brokerage house or to see a state, county, or local governing body in action.

44

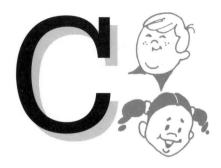

CALENDAR. *See also Home Headquarters, Organization.*

Keeping track of family activities provides both handy organization and healthy anticipation. Using a large monthly calendar, placed in a conspicuous location, fill in activities of parents and children: major tests, sports events, lessons, club meetings, recitals, business meetings, weekend family events, parties, trips, and so forth. In this way you can see where additional recreational activities might be needed and where activities may conflict.

To be most useful, make the calendar very inclusive and encourage all family members to list their activities and use the calendar. At the first of each week, look ahead to the upcoming events and see that there is something during the week of interest to each family member.

CAMP. *See also Homesickness.*

Camping provides great opportunities for fun and for learning new skills. Start camping experiences in your own backyard, then with a neighbor or family member, then at a day camp. By the time youngsters are about eight, they may be ready to go away to overnight camp, first for a short period of time, then for a longer time.

Start with a simple traditional camp that features water sports, crafts, horsemanship, and hiking mingled with campfire-style camaraderie. If possible, visit the camp and also learn about the management of the camp and the ratio of counselors to campers. Another year your child may want a more specialized program (marine biology, mountaineering, space exploration, sailing) but don't be surprised if your youngster prefers to return to the same camp each year, enjoying the company of the same fellow campers, and eventually becoming a junior counselor and finally a counselor.

 Let the first-time camper take along a small photo of the family. Write short, cheerful messages and seal them in small envelopes that the camper can open if she gets lonely. Provide a small notebook to record experiences worth sharing at her homecoming celebration dinner.

CANDY. *See Nutrition, Sweets.*

CAR POOLS. *See also Driving.*

Chauffeuring youngsters can be pleasant if they understand that safety (buckling up, not shouting, carefully exiting the car) is of highest importance. If the riders get unruly, the driver can cure that by pulling over and just stopping the car in a safe place until calm is restored.

The parent should set a good example by greeting each rider as they get on board and saying farewell at the end of the trip, also checking that they take their possessions with them. Youngsters usually talk among themselves, but the driver can initiate conversation, if needed, by asking silly questions or suggesting a song. Best of all, a parent can learn a few things just by listening to the conversation.

When alone with one's own child, the chauffeur can also use the time to share feelings about growing up, school subjects, boy-girl relationships, upcoming vacations, and so forth. In turn, a youngster will often share his feelings more readily since there is not the scrutiny of eye contact that there is in face-to-face conversation. Make the most of this precious time together!

CAR SEATS. *See also Safety.*

While it was formerly thought that a baby was most safe in its parent's arms when traveling in a car, a car seat is now mandatory for young children. Yet, research shows that countless children still ride in laps or without seat belts. Be sure you select a seat that meets current government standards; a seat purchased at a yard sale may not meet those standards.

The placement of the seat and the installation of it are of prime importance. Much as a parent would like to be able to see the baby, the safest placement is in the middle of the backseat, with the child facing the rear. This is because any impact will be against the baby's strongest body part, the back. Age and weight determine the car seat placement for older children who will face forward. Don't take shortcuts in installation of the seat; carefully follow the directions.

Since car seats make children immobile, attaching toys and providing other activities will make travel in a car seat more enjoyable.

CAR TRIPS AND GAMES. *See also Travel.*

Much family time is spent—and wasted—in the car. Quickly teach the basics of safe car travel and then set out to enjoy it! Before leaving home, talk about the purpose of the trip, and choose a time when youngsters are fed and rested.

Give youngsters assignments: navigator, refreshment chairman, safety engineer, games coordinator, song leader. Have a car activity bag with age-appropriate toys that are only played with in the car: books, art materials, dolls and trucks, playing cards, audiotapes, and so forth.

Play car games such as finding the letters of the alphabet on signs along the roadside. Before the trip, tear pictures out of magazines and then deal them out to youngsters who then find those things along the way. Older kids can race one another to total the numbers on license plates or decipher the word messages.

CAREER CHOICES. *See also College, Jobs.*

It is not unusual for young people to have little or no idea about their choice for a career. A parent can help most by exposing them to a variety of worthwhile career possibilities, giving some unbiased pros and cons. Letting youngsters get to know adults whose job choices are varied will also educate them. Summer jobs and internships will expose the student to on-the-job experiences.

High schools and colleges present career seminars that offer information on qualifications, scope of work, remuneration, and fields where workers are most needed. Usually by the junior year of college, a student has found a field of interest. Be sure that he chooses his own (not your wished for) career since the number of years that one works is now greater than it was a generation ago, and thus it is important to really like one's choice. However, it is also interesting that a generation ago a worker held an average of two jobs during his working years. Today, job switching is more prevalent, and it is not unusual for someone to work for five or more different companies and in two or more fields.

CAREGIVERS. *See also Child Care Facilities, Grandparents, Preschool.*

Those you empower to care for your children should be as loving and responsible as you are.

Investigate all caregivers by asking for references and inquiring if they have ever had a complaint waged against them. Seriously look into the family and educational background of each caregiver. At a visit to the facility before registering, listen to and watch the actions of employees. See how they speak to the children. Are they affectionate? Playful? Apathetic? Overly strict? Observe the activities of the children, and hope that the television isn't on. Consider the number of caregivers in relation to the number of children cared for.

Important qualifications for the facility itself will be found in the listing "Child Care Facilities," but kindness, creativity, cleanliness, patience, and honesty are imperatives for those who work there. After your child has been accepted at the facility, do not hesitate to drop in unannounced and assess the mood of those in charge of your children, as well as the children being cared for.

If children are cared for by neighbors, baby-sitting co-ops, or grandparents, the same high standards should apply.

CARING. *See also Empathy, Golden Rule, Selfishness, Service.*

Making others happy through words and deeds is a skill that can be taught to very young children, and is a skill that lasts a lifetime. A caring child often lets another choose the snack, the game to play, the video to watch. A caring child is aware when others are falling behind and help is needed. A caring child will do more than is asked. Caring for others is not done with the idea of self-gain but rather out of kindness and love—qualities taught at home by parents.

CHARACTER BUILDING. *See Communication, Happiness, Honesty, Intelligence, Leadership, Love, Patience, Responsibility, Self-Government, Self-Worth.*

CHARITABLE GIVING. *See Caring, Christmas Family, Christmas Outreach, Giving Versus Getting, Service.*

CHARTS FOR CHORES. *See also Chores.*

Until helping around the house becomes automatic, consider making charts or using other gimmicks or incentives to help youngsters accomplish tasks without reminding them. Incentive and reward are far better than nagging or punishment.

The old standard is a monthly chart where a youngster gets a stick-on star for doing his chores. You can substitute small colored squares of paper as building blocks to let youngsters make a tall tower of squares on the bulletin board, a block for each successful day. At holidays, you can put a large paper Christmas tree on the bulletin board and let a child put paper "chore circles" (like ornaments) on his tree. During the spring you can award pink paper ears for good work and play "pin the ears on the bunny" each evening.

To encourage teamwork, pair two children together and give the chart award when both have done their tasks. Older children respond to other types of awards—more phone time, special cosmetics, extra computer or car time for completing helpful jobs around the house. Your goal is to eventually have no gimmicks at all, as everyone does his share of the work voluntarily and cheerfully.

For more ideas on how to get kids to do their chores, see *Working Parent, Happy Child* (Caryl Krueger, Abingdon Press, distributed by Belleridge Press, Escondido, Calif.).

CHEATING. *See Honesty.*

CHILD CARE FACILITIES. *See also Caregivers, Preschool.*

The choice of day care or child care can be one of the most difficult and emotional decisions a parent must make. The difference between the two terms is slight, but day care is usually defined as supervised play with a group of children while child care is with fewer children and is often considered more structured and nurturing. Research shows that children who have had quality child care exhibit greater self-confidence and learning skills, and also relate better to adults. A nonquality day care situation can be stifling to creativity and curiosity.

Proper care during the early, formative years is vitally important and the lack of quality facilities is one of the weakest links in our child care system. For this reason, many parents plan ahead to stay at home with their children until kindergarten age. But this is not always financially possible. Use these guidelines when you plan to inspect a facility—a visit that should take at least one hour:

• a limited number of children—the fewer the better
• a valid up-to-date license for the number of children cared for
• calm and loving staff, at least one for every four children
• clean cribs and diaper-changing areas
• sanitary kitchen and eating areas with posted menus featuring healthy foods
• clean playpens and floors

- a variety of safe, creative toys in good condition
- opportunities for outside play, music time, book-reading time
- little or no television or video time
- a safe atmosphere with electric plug cover caps, stairway gates, fire extinguisher, and more than one exit
- colorful child-oriented decor at child eye level
- a posted schedule of activities for the week

Be sure there is a full-time staff person with CPR and first-aid training, and a posted fire/emergency plan. Ask if there has ever been a formal complaint filed against the facility or an employee. Be sure to ask if you are welcome to drop in unannounced. Find out what happens when a child or caregiver becomes ill. Ask for the names of families you can call as references.

Do not assume that attendance at a child care facility will teach your toddler all the essential age-related skills. You must be alert to what your child is or is not learning and be prepared to fill in the gaps.

CHOICES. *See also Control, Independence, Leadership, Order, Responsibility, Self-Government.*

Youngsters feel empowered when they are permitted to make some choices for themselves, and they will then not resent the choices that are still yours as a parent. Give more and more options with each passing year.

Start letting preschoolers choose what to wear, what snack to have, what to play, which book to read. Grade school youngsters can choose what extracurricular lessons to take and what after-school groups to join, what clothes to wear (from a preapproved selection you make together), how to spend extra money, what television to see (from a list you've approved ahead of time). Teens can make the previous choices and also what classes to take (with help from a school counselor), which summer job is best, and how to spend vacation time.

Often you can give two specific alternatives such as "Do you want to see a half-hour of TV first, or empty the dishwasher first?" Do you want to clean up your room now or after you call Marcy?" The phrase "Do you want" is very important for it shows youngsters that you respect them enough to trust their decisions.

CHORES. *See also Charts for Chores, Laundry.*

The purpose of giving children tasks to do is to share the load of work at home and to prepare them for life on their own. These are equally important. Failing to give chores on a regular basis is not a kindness but is handicapping your child. Chores are not sexist: boys can fold laundry and bake cookies, and girls can change lightbulbs and mow the lawn.

Carefully go over the proper procedure for each chore—you may have to do this several times, but eventually kid help will save you time. Each day, young children should have about fifteen minutes of work, grade-schoolers and teens at least thirty minutes. And, the family should work together for an hour each weekend, plus a once or twice-a-year work day. Total that up and see how much extra time it will give you: two children helping out will provide you with about seven extra free hours each week!

Use praise for all work done and lots of praise for work well done. Have a celebration dinner for especially good work. Switch chores every two weeks or so; repetition does make for more perfect work. List the chores to be done on the family bulletin board so that there is no doubt as to who does what.

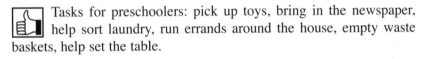 Tasks for preschoolers: pick up toys, bring in the newspaper, help sort laundry, run errands around the house, empty waste baskets, help set the table.

Tasks for young school children (in addition to above): empty dishwasher, sweep floor, wipe countertops, deliver laundry, bring in mail, put up the flag, feed and clean up after pets, make flower arrangements, entertain a baby, make sandwiches.

Tasks for preteens (in addition to above): wash the car, make weekend breakfasts or lunches, rake leaves, fold laundry, clean bathtub and lavatories, run sprinklers, make home repairs with supervision, bake, water house plants, dust and vacuum, paint a fence, plan a party, stamp and post mail, polish silver, sew, load dishwasher, change lightbulbs, shovel snow, run errands by bicycle, wash piano keys and mirrors, build a fire, read stories to younger children.

Tasks for teens (in addition to above): make dinner, wash windows, clean up after a party, defrost and clean freezer, clean cupboards, polish shoes, sew and mend, iron, babysit, serve guests at parties, address Christmas card envelopes, keep the family scrapbook, scrub floors, cut grass, do errands in the car.

When you have a job at home that is not assigned, write an "ad" describing it, the time involved, and the pay. No doubt you'll get a willing worker. This method works well for spring cleaning and other once-a-year tasks.

CHRISTMAS. *See also subsequent listings, Santa Claus.*

Don't confine the Christmas spirit to just one or two days each year. Love is the spirit of Christmas so show children that there is much more to this best-loved holiday than receiving gifts. As soon as you have properly celebrated Thanksgiving, make plans for a monthlong Christmas celebration.

Create a special Christmas calendar and pencil in times for these events: Christmas crafts/gift making, school and church productions, shopping excursions, gift wrapping and sending, card mailing, parties at your house and others', tree trimming and decorating, making cookies and other festive foods, holiday phone calls, driving around to see decorations, and so forth. Space these out over the weeks so that a few are done each week before Christmas.

Go to the library and borrow age-appropriate Christmas books including Dickens's *Christmas Carol.* For stories, recipes, and new ideas, borrow *101 Ideas for the Best-Ever Christmas* (Caryl Krueger, Abingdon Press, distributed by Belleridge Press, Escondido, Calif.).

Consider creating an extra Christmas each year on July 25 and call it "Five Months to Christmas." Bring out a few decorations, play with the train, make Christmas cookies, exchange silly gifts, play carols on the stereo, prepare a small turkey with all the trimmings.

CHRISTMAS ACTIVITIES, DECORATIONS, AND TRADITIONS.

Enjoy these activities in the month of December:

• Exchange names to become another family member's "Christmas Angel." Do secret good deeds for that person without being caught. Reveal the angel identities on Christmas Eve.

• Buy an inexpensive Advent Calendar and open one door each day at breakfast.

• Using shelf paper or other large, durable paper, let children make holiday place mats for the family.

• Light the Christmas candle at dinner each night: a candle made from stubs saved all year, melted together with a new wick or new candle in the middle. Surround it with fresh greens.

• As a family, go to purchase the Christmas tree. Buy one with character (not perfectly shaped) and see how beautiful it looks when decorated.

• Go outside and look up at the stars as the shepherds did. See if you can find a very bright star.

• Let family members have a decoration in their room or on their door.
• Hang mistletoe, and remember to give kisses.
• Display Christmas cards by hanging a sheet from the ceiling to the floor on a hall wall. Pin on the cards for a colorful display.
• Hang Christmas stockings that will be filled with small gifts and treats.
• Give family members new pajamas to wear Christmas Eve so they will look good in the Christmas morning pictures.
• Quietly read the story of Jesus' birth.
• Sing a Christmas carol in the dark before going to bed.
• Place one last gift, a book, under each person's pillow on Christmas Day night.
• Write thank-you notes together, lying under the Christmas tree; let preschool children draw pictures as thank-you notes.
• Write funny messages to put in with the decorations when it's time to pack them up.
• Attend after-Christmas sales, and buy one gift and one ornament for the next year.

CHRISTMAS FAMILY.

"Adopting" a family for Christmas can be one of the most satisfying activities. Depending on your finances, decide how involved you wish to be. Will you provide dinner? Gifts? Decorations? Toys? Everything? Contact your church, civic group, YMCA or YWCA or social services agency early in December. Then work together as a family to gather good new and used items for each member of your adopted family. Sometimes you will bring your contribution to a distribution center, but if you are permitted to deliver it to the family, prepare your youngsters for the visit.

CHRISTMAS FOODS.

Each family has its traditional specialties, but try to add a new recipe each year. Let youngsters help in cooking and baking and also teach them how to carve a roast or turkey. Here are a few culinary ideas to start you thinking.

• Let a big family meal be potluck, with your family providing the entree and others bringing the trimmings. Don't hesitate to serve dishes such as chili, roast duck, spaghetti, a hearty soup, or pheasant/venison for the outdoor lovers.
• For an elegant appetizer, mix eight ounces of crabmeat (can be imitation or canned) with an eight ounce package of cream cheese, one-quarter

53

cup of mayonnaise, and the heads of eight green onions. Heat until warm and serve with crackers.

- For a special touch on Christmas morning, add just one large pecan to the coffee cake (homemade or purchased). The person who finds it gets to open the first gift.
- Make an easy Christmas cake with white cake mix. Add red food coloring to one layer, green to the other. When baked, split these in half and layer them with white frosting, alternating the red and the green.
- For a delicious after-Christmas meal, place extra stuffing in the bottom of a rectangular baking dish, layer sliced turkey over it, and generously top with gravy. Bake at 350 degrees for about forty-five minutes or until hot. This can also be frozen.

CHRISTMAS GIFTS. *See also Wish lists.*

Start early to collect wish lists from family members, with the understanding that they may get some of the things on the list and some surprises. Share ideas with grandparents and other relatives.

Since a handmade gift comes straight from the heart, let youngsters make most of their gifts: candles, bottles of flavored vinegars, woven place mats, small carving boards for cheese, Christmas ornaments, beaded napkin rings, and so forth. A wonderful gift for grandparents is a photo calendar easily made at a quick-print shop from twelve of your own photos or slides.

If there are lots of gifts under the tree, open those from friends and relatives a day or two before Christmas so that they are not rushed through on Christmas morning. In this way, kids can better remember the givers.

Don't let weeks of work be over in a few minutes Christmas morn. Let kids rip open the stocking gifts, then all can have a buffet breakfast in the living room. Finally, let each family member "present" her gifts, starting with the youngest up to the parents. This puts the emphasis on giving, rather than getting. Don't hesitate to take a break to play with a gift or put one together.

After several days of play, let each youngster choose one or two gifts to be saved for play in the future, bringing them out on a date such as February first, when other gifts may have become tiresome.

CHRISTMAS OUTREACH. *See also Christmas Family, Service.*

Decide in advance on a "giving" project and include as many family members as possible in carrying it out. Here are some ideas:

- Adopt a needy family.
- Help give a party at a senior or youth facility.

- Help an older neighbor with shopping or home decoration.
- Include a U.S. service person or a student from another country in your celebration.
- Carol for neighbors and shut-ins.
- Volunteer to serve meals at a shelter.
- Make a gingerbread house with a child whose parents both work.
- Make extra cookies to give to busy families.
- Provide supper for a person with a disability.
- Baby-sit for busy parents so they can shop.
- Take part in a toy or food drive.
- Telephone faraway friends and relatives.
- Make ornaments or other gifts to give to teachers, librarians, coaches, and helpful service workers or shopkeepers.

CHRISTMAS PARTIES. *See also Parties.*

Plan ahead for your Christmas party and decide on a theme: caroling in the neighborhood, making door wreaths or ornaments, trimming your tree, baking and eating cookies, or having a surprise supper. The surprise supper is when each family member secretly invites one guest for a simple supper of casserole, salad, sundaes, and cookies. You'll be amazed at the interesting combinations of guests!

Welcome guests to your front door by filling brown paper lunch bags with some sand and a votive candle, placing these luminarias along your entry walkway.

Games can include "Pin the Red Nose on Rudolf" (make a large, simple sketch of a reindeer and cut circles out of red construction paper). For a relay race, divide into two teams, and provide each team with a big Santa cap and a pair of big boots. Each runner must put on the hat and boots, run to a line and back, take them off and give them to the next team member. For older guests, have each write down their favorite childhood Christmas memory. Let one person read the memory as others try to guess the writer.

CHRISTMAS STORY.

A memorable tradition is telling the Christmas story from the Bible over the course of several Sundays before Christmas. At the same time, add the appropriate figures to the family nativity scene.

On the first Sunday read the prophecy of Jesus' coming from Micah 5:2, Isaiah 40:1-5, and Isaiah 9:2, 6, 7. Place the stable and animals on a table or shelf to await the Messiah.

On the second Sunday read the story of Mary and Joseph from Matthew 1:18-23 and Luke 2:1, 3-7. Place the figures of Mary and Joseph in the stable.

On the third Sunday read the story of the shepherds from Luke 2:8-18, 20. Add the shepherds and sheep to the scene.

On the fourth Sunday, read about the Kings (even though their arrival was later) from Matthew 2:1-12. Place kings and camels next to the stable.

On Christmas Eve, read about Jesus from Luke 2:40; Matthew 4:23-24; Matthew 5:2, 16; Matthew 10:8; John 13:34; John 21:25; and Revelation 19:6, 16. Then place the figure of baby Jesus in the crèche.

CHURCH / TEMPLE / SYNAGOGUE ATTENDANCE. *See also Faith, Religion.*

If you wish your child to have a religious background, start when young to make attendance at services a given part of family life. While a child may have religious classes separate from adults, there are many times when the family is together for a service and it is important to help youngsters understand the protocol. For young children who may find the hour or more a long time, a small notebook for drawing may help. Teach children to sing "la-la-la" when they can't read the words of hymns. Create sign language to remind of no talking or eyes shut for prayer. Let youngsters find the hymns. Tell them to listen to what is said so they can share one good idea on the way home.

Take an interest in activities before and after the service and other special church events so that your family gets to know others and really feels a part of the church family.

CIGARETTES, CIGARS. *See also Substance Abuse.*

Children sometimes see tobacco use as glamorous. As soon as they understand the words, explain exactly how cigarettes and cigars can spoil their lives and cause death. Both smokers and those breathing secondhand smoke are in danger. Tell them that if they never start, they can't become hooked for life into a habit that consumes their money and destroys their health. Appeal to a youngster's intelligence and logic to avoid this habit.

CLEANLINESS. *See also Bathtime.*

Start with very young children to teach habits of cleanliness. A nightly or every-other-night bath, or shower as children get older, is basic. Beyond that, a child needs to remember the all-important rule of washing hands after using the toilet, after playing with pets, and before eating. Actually give youngsters how-to lessons on cleaning their private parts, fingernails, navel, ears, toes, and hair.

Wearing clean underwear and socks each day is another good habit. Older children should be instructed in the use of powders, creams, oils, and lotions for skin care and the regular use of a deodorant.

Personal cleanliness carries over into the habits of cleanliness when a child prepares snacks or part of a meal and also into the cleanliness of one's own space, like a bedroom or playroom. Every child should be taught simple cleaning procedures such as dusting/vacuuming/scrubbing, tasks that can be rotated on a youngster's chore list.

CLIQUES. *See also Bullies, Gangs.*

Good friendships should not be confused with cliques. Cliques promote insiders and outsiders and this exclusiveness leads to unmerited feelings of superiority and to hurtful snubs of others. By encouraging youngsters to have a wide variety of friends and to include others (those less popular or ethnically different) in activities, there can be a healthy feeling of belonging. Of course a small group of good friends can be supportive for teens, but parents should discourage the feeling that no one else could ever add something beneficial to the group.

When children are giving a party, encourage them to invite their good friends but also new kids who don't have many friends at the present. They will be surprised at the resulting interesting combinations of people.

CLOTHING. *See also Appearance, Fads.*

Starting when children are young, set parameters about what is acceptable clothing. You may want to look over clothing together and put outfits in three categories: ones that a child can choose from for school, ones for play, and some that should be worn at a parent's request. Ribbons tied on the closet clothing rod to separate the three categories, or separate stacks in drawers will then enable a child to choose without parent help.

When youngsters enter the preteen years, give them a clothing allowance so that they can decide between having more less-expensive clothes or having fewer but more expensive outfits. This teaches money management and values.

Refuse to allow gang clothing and discourage fad outfits that may soon be out of fashion and thus a waste of money. Don't permit a youngster to wear clothing advertising a product or place of which you disapprove.

CLUBS AND YOUTH GROUPS. *See also After-School Activities.*

Making friends and learning how to interact with others is part of maturing and learning how to function in the real world. Be sure your youngster has at least one group activity each week, but be careful not to let her become overbooked so that there is no time for creative free play. These youth groups also expose kids to activities that parents may not be skilled in, and they put youngsters in touch with other responsible adults who can become mentors through the years.

The success or failure of many clubs or groups is often directly dependent on the abilities and enthusiasm of the leaders. Certainly get to know them and be sure they are proper influences on your child.

Parents also have a part in the process, seeing that youngsters get to the event each week, chaperoning trips and parties, and taking leadership when needed. Working parents are not excused from participation and should inquire about how they can be supportive.

Consider Scouting, Camp Fire, Indian Guides, Y groups, church clubs, and special interest groups such as a rocketry club, youth theater, line or square dancing, 4-H and so forth. Let a youngster choose one activity with the understanding that the commitment will be for at least one semester or for the school year.

Children need to be aware of the cost of belonging to a group and it is beneficial to both parent and child if he shares the cost of equipment, uniforms or other supplies. Even if he doesn't help pay for the activity, be sure you explain the costs so he will feel some obligation to participate fully.

COACHES.

An athletic coach will have a large influence in your child's after-school life. Get to know the people who run the programs in which your children participate. Be sure to ask the coach what you can do to support the team. A coach whose prime focus is winning every contest should be avoided. Learning the mechanics of a sport, practicing good sportsmanship, enjoying teamwork and team spirit should be the emphasis.

Should you question the coach's actions, talk first with other parents to see if they also recognize the problem. (The problem could be favoritism, foul language, undue pressure, and so forth.) If you feel comfortable talking about it with the coach, do so. Or, go to those who supervise the program and share your complaint. Sometimes the only solution is to remove a child from an impossible situation. However, also remember that teams teach youngsters to take some bumps—sometimes physical ones, sometimes verbal ones in the form of helpful criticism. Coaches teach youngsters to be tough, brave, and competitive, and you can monitor the activity so that it is done in a positive and kind way.

COLIC. *See also Crying.*

Colic is a catch-all term to cover many of the causes for a baby's unhappy crying. Happily, in most cases, it ends by about the fourth month. Gastrointestinal disorder brought on by formula intolerance was originally thought to be a reason for this frantic type of crying, usually in the evening. Newer research indicates that colic may come from overstimulation. Certain babies have nervous systems that can't abide too much activity, thus necessary feeding, bathing, diaper-changing may be almost all a baby can take during the day. So when a parent adds too much cooing, rocking, singing, bouncing, plus the loud household sounds (television, dishwasher, shouting siblings), the baby just gets overstimulated and screams to block it out.

Don't ignore the problem. Be sure that the child is not sick, is eating well, and keeping food down. Endure about ten minutes of crying, then try to quietly calm the baby with a minimum of activity. Sometimes rubbing the baby's back or putting a warm washcloth on the back of the neck will do the trick.

Keep a record so that you can find a pattern for the crying. See if it follows or precedes nursing, eliminating, burping, passing gas, or is tied to acid reflux. If the baby is frequently miserable, call your pediatrician.

COLLECTIONS. *See also Arts and Crafts Projects.*

Collections educate, provide topics for discussion, can make a pleasant display, provide gift ideas for relatives, and may even become a valuable hobby. And at the same time, they're fun. Let a child consider rocks, stamps, bugs, shells, coins, postcards, marble eggs, dolls from around the world, matchbox cars, bells, pressed flowers, recipes, carved animals, and so forth.

Start with a collection subject that is not expensive and is readily available. Don't insist on continuing a collection when a child has lost interest; perhaps a sibling or friend may want to take it over. If not, a simple collection could be discarded; one worth money could be donated to a Boys or Girls Club, Y, or seniors facility.

COLLEGE. *See also Education.*

Today a college education is more valuable than ever before. Research shows that people with an advanced education not only have higher earnings, they are also more satisfied and happy with their lives. So parents need to plan ahead for this schooling. Money can be saved by attending a junior college prior to going away to a college or university. Money can be saved by attending a state school, by applying for grants, loans, and scholarships, or through a teen contributing earnings from summer jobs.

Sometimes a year off from college can be a useful maturing time, but if at all possible encourage a student to complete two or four years of college before a break. Statistics show that those not going directly from high school to college, or who drop out for a break, are less apt to obtain a degree.

Start in a student's freshman or sophomore year of high school to work with him and school counselors to plan course selections that fit the academic requirements of most colleges. Then, two years in advance, check the specific entrance requirements of several schools your youngster may wish to attend.

Don't believe that a college degree is an absolute necessity for every student. For a young adult not interested in four or more years of advanced schooling consider special learning opportunities such as police academies, beautician schools, art and design schools, computer and technical training and internships, and adult night school. Many of these can lead to good careers with fewer years of academic study.

COMMUNICATION. *See also Language, Listening, Openness, Profanity, Show and Tell, Speech, Words, Writing.*

The ability to communicate is a skill that starts in infancy. It is built on love and trust that provide a foundation for explaining ideas, asking questions, sharing feelings, and comfortably speaking the truth. It is essential that a family find occasions for good communication during times that are open-ended and not rushed.

Phrases such as "Shut up," "That's silly," "It's a dumb idea," and "Not now!" turn off communication. Don't overreact to things kids say—sometimes they are just sending up a trial balloon to see your reaction or to get your attention. Don't be so critical that a child becomes fearful about sharing ideas.

Be available when youngsters want to talk, and if you absolutely don't have the time at that moment, set a specific time to talk later, and see that you do. Going for a walk or talking in the dark can make communication easier. Be open to ideas that may seem outlandish—consider them seriously before making a decision.

Use the many opportunities for conversation: at dinner, in the car, waiting for appointments, before bed. Help youngsters to polish oral school reports by home rehearsal. Before a social event, encourage easy conversation with friends and relatives by giving kids a few conversational hints on topics they can share.

Of great importance is the discussion of subjects that affect a youngster's future: dating, driving, and drugs. Talk about these well in advance of need so that you know your youngster's attitudes toward these topics. Have an open discussion, utilizing facts and personal experiences. Create a home atmosphere where your youngster feels she can talk with you about anything.

Encourage written forms of communication—short notes that express interest and love, whether they be hand written, computer written, or e-mailed.

Casual, nonjudgmental talk with family members will avert many problems. See that there are daily opportunities for one-on-one conversations without interruptions. Agree that there are times that you will disagree. Weekly family meetings keep everyone well-informed and provide opportunities to settle problems and consider good ideas. Take turns moderating these meetings. Make the talk free from criticism or profanity.

Once a month have "Friendly Talk Day." This means there will be no arguing, mean words, or insolence, for the entire day. Compliment good efforts and the idea may catch on!

At mealtimes, talk about the events of the day, upcoming activities, things seen on television, local and world news, funny stories about things that have happened. If conversation lags introduce "What if," a game suggesting events that require thoughtful response. For example: "If you were given a thousand dollars, what would you do with it?" "If you could go back in time, what era would you choose?" "If you were a parent of a kid your age, what would be the first thing you'd do?"

With other families, perhaps while lunching at the park, include everyone in talk about issues of interest to all: family rules, dating, driving, racism, bullies, heroes, dreams.

 Never permit estrangements. Good advice is: "Never let the sun set on an argument." You may not settle the dispute by sundown, but you should at least be talking together.

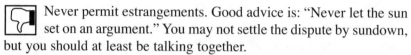 Remember the Ten Commandments for Conversation:

1. Thou shalt have at least three topics of interest to talk about at a social event.
2. Thou shalt have an ace-in-the-hole question for a time when the room becomes silent.
3. Thou shalt not give monologues, but let others talk, too.
4. Thou shalt look pleasant when talking, avoiding scowling and intimidation.
5. Thou shalt not be afraid of a pause in the conversation—a time to reflect.
6. Thou shalt treat another's topic or opinion tenderly, not putting others down.
7. Thou shalt read newspapers, magazines, and books so as to talk with facts, not rumors.
8. Thou shalt include everyone in the conversation, regardless of age or sex.
9. Thou shalt plant clues in your conversation for others to pick up and ask about.
10. Thou shalt remember that conversation is 50 percent or more listening.

COMPETITION. *See also Sibling Rivalry, Sportsmanship.*

Competition often gets a bad reputation, but not all competition is bad. Much of the business and political world runs competitively and youngsters need to learn how to handle rivalry without falling apart. Bad competition is high pressured and ignorant of ethics and the feelings of others. Good competition is based on fun and good sportsmanship and doesn't include bragging or in-your-face behavior.

See that in the competitive aspects of family life one child is not always the victor. Being the winner, always being first, or getting a prize should not be emphasized. Strive to increase the satisfaction of small successes or quiet achievements. Remember, it is perfectly normal for a child to be noncompetitive as long as this doesn't result in others taking advantage of her.

For a child who seems ready for competitive activities but is usually the loser, find those activities where she does excel and see that she has regular opportunities to build on these.

 Never permit children to compete for your love or attention. See that you value and appreciate each child for her uniqueness.

COMPLAINING. *See also Family Meeting.*

Complaints can result in changes for the better. But when friction builds and complaints multiply, it's time for a family meeting. Let all family members air their grievances, one at a time and without others interrupting. Without being judgmental, have an open discussion to look for underlying causes of the conflict and possible solutions. Share hugs when the complaint session is over.

COMPUTERS. *See also Computer Access, Computer Games.*

Just as everyone learned the 3Rs in past generations, the education of today's child must also include computer technology. While a computer is no substitute for good thinking or the ability to write and do math manually, it can perform many tasks accurately and quickly. The computer enhances the ability to concentrate, increases manual and mental dexterity, and provides educational input.

Computer use usually starts in the home as preschoolers enjoy CD-ROM play. It then continues at most grade schools. There are many fine websites for children of all ages and all you need is a modem to access the Internet.

Start early to show proper fingering, so that when youngsters wish to use the computer for homework assignments they can work quickly and accurately.

 See that both girls and boys receive computer training. Let youngsters help on computer projects at home such as writing letters, paying bills, making lists, entering data, graphing, and illustrating. Also, establish a family mailbox so that messages can be left for each family member.

Monitor the content of computer games so that youngsters do not engage in violent or satanic games. Limit the number of hours for playing games to thirty minutes or less daily, and only after homework is completed.

Ask your youngsters to agree to this simple pledge:

I will not make the computer the center of my activities and free time.

I will not give out any personal information about myself or my family.

I will not agree to get-together with someone I've met on the Web without a parent's approval.

I will not respond to obscene or threatening messages but will report these immediately to my parents.

I will check with my parents concerning appropriate sites and the length of time to be on-line.

I will be pleasant about obeying these rules and discuss any changes I want to make with a parent.

COMPUTER ACCESS.

Products are available to help parents restrict access to certain programs or activities. If you feel that inappropriate computer use is a problem for your child, installing such a program is a good idea. Products can also filter out programs based on key words believed to be objectionable.

COMPUTER GAMES.

Computer games take up far too many hours of a child's life without giving many benefits. Permit some games that provide learning or genuine fun. It is your duty and right to prohibit the purchase and play of those games that have violent, satanic, or sexual themes.

In many cases, the problem is not that the games are bad, but rather that they take up the time that a youngster should use to experience other activities.

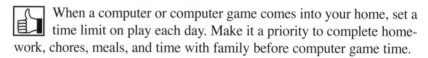 When a computer or computer game comes into your home, set a time limit on play each day. Make it a priority to complete homework, chores, meals, and time with family before computer game time.

CONCENTRATION. *See Attention Span.*

CONFIDENCE. *See Self-Worth.*

CONFLICT. *See also Arguing, Fighting, Sharing, Yelling.*

Disagreements can be healthy when youngsters are willing to be reasonable and discuss possibilities in an attempt to resolve the problem. But when disagreements become intense and a parent is not able to identify right from wrong, you may need to take other action to solve the conflict.

In the case of younger children, this action can take several forms:

- Refer the problem to the youngsters without your arbitration, saying "This is for you to settle, but if you can't, I'll do my best but I may be too strict." This indicates that you aren't taking sides and you hope they can learn to work together.
- Set a timer and state that this argument should be settled in three (or more) minutes or it's time-out for both arguers.
- Have a cooling-off period. Should the conflict become verbally or physically abusive, step in immediately, and separate the parties from each other and any play objects. Let there be a quiet "thinking time" away from each other and toys. Then bring them together and ask "How could this have been resolved in a better way." Sit quietly and wait for their answers before giving yours. It takes time and your patience at first, but it will eventually save you time since children will be learning conflict resolution skills.
- When it is difficult to understand the conflict, have youngsters use puppets to act out the problem. Facts will become more obvious and solutions will come more easily.

For older kids:

- Write down the grievance. This often shows how silly some arguments are.
- Have a re-enactment. If youngsters show exactly what happened, both you and they should be able to determine reasons behind the conflict and then discuss how it can be solved.
- Use the "court method" with each side stating the case, having a rebuttal, and then the judge coming to a decision. You might find that sometimes teens will decide that their dispute isn't worth arguing about.

Learning when to fight and when to give in is a maturing process. Learning problem solving is a skill that will be useful in all the years ahead.

CONSCIENCE.

Conscience is an inner sense of what is right or wrong, a mental tabulation of actions. Parental standards (verbalized and utilized) form the basis of a child's conscience, giving him the ability to process and recall information of moral content. This starts with toddlers who first become aware that they are "naughty" or "nice" depending on their actions.

Yearly discussions about age-appropriate rules are opportunities to talk about the many character traits that can lead to a youngster having a good conscience. As a child ages, he may try to bury his conscience so he can act in inappropriate ways (usually leading to feelings of guilt). So, it is important for a parent to continually reinforce the rules and expectations, and express appreciation when a youngster lets his good conscience be his guide.

CONSEQUENCES. *See also One-Chance Parent, Rules.*

The consequences of actions are not always apparent: good is not always rewarded and wrong is not always punished. Still, parents should set up the consequences of breaking family rules so that youngsters realize the importance of being responsible.

It is often hard for a parent to let a youngster suffer the consequences of some wrong action, but certainly in matters of safety, the parent should step in to keep the child from harm. Thus if a youngster leaves a toy animal out in the rain, she will suffer the consequences of having it ruined. However, if the youngster goes in the kitchen and plays with a knife, she is saved by a parent who gives her a nonnegotiable punishment. But, in most cases, suffering the consequences can be one of the best lessons learned since the real world does not often permit excuses for wrong action.

CONSISTENCY IN PARENTING. *See also One-Chance Parent, Parenting Skills.*

One of the issues that causes the most problems in parenting is inconsistency. Parents say one thing and then waffle, confusing the child about whether the original statement was sincere. Parents correct and correct again, remind and remind again, threaten and threaten again. And sometimes the same offense is treated differently: with no correction in one instance and an overreaction and extreme punishment another time.

Save time and energy by being a "One-Chance Parent." For example, this means that you tell a child what is expected and then give one warning (the one chance), and if the child doesn't obey, punishment comes.

Consistency also includes acting fairly between children: not tougher on the oldest and overly lenient on the youngest. Parents need to express integrity in their disciplinary dealings with children, and they also need balance—the understanding as to which subjects are important and which can be ignored.

66

Youngsters actually respect parameters; they like to know how far they can go and what will happen if they go too far.

CONTAGION. *See Diseases, Health.*

CONTROL. *See also Choices, Consequences, Mistakes.*

Learning to turn over authority to youngsters is one of the hardest parental steps. We so much want what is good for them that we often do too much to save them from mistakes, hurts, and the ensuing grief and embarrassment. Of course parents should take control when it is a matter of safety or health. Parents want to feel needed and useful but they often create the burden of dependence by the child on the parent. This is not helping a child to mature.

Remember, you will not always be right at a child's elbow suggesting the correct course to take. So, as the years pass, a parent must exchange parental control for self-control, giving youngsters more and more command of their lives. It is important to tell youngsters that you will increase their independence in proportion to their responsibility and maturity.

Don't be a controlling parent who arranges every aspect of a child's life unless you want to raise an adult afraid of living her own life fully.

CONVERSATION. *See Communication, Poise.*

COOKING.

Include youngsters in food preparation, starting with the very youngest who can tear up lettuce for a salad or peel a banana. Keep the learning going so that kids can eventually cook an entire meal. If you can read, you can cook! And cooking teaches measuring skills, orderliness, cleanliness, inventiveness, and appreciation for good food. Start a recipe file for each child so that when he moves out, he can still make his favorite dishes.

Let kids choose one meal each week, devising the entire menu. Let them have total charge from preparing food to setting the table to cleaning up afterward. Try not to interfere with the cook, just appreciate the meal!

CO-OPS. *See Preschools.*

COPPING OUT. *See also Responsibility.*

This slang term means "failing to do what has been promised." Don't permit it! Instruct children to honor their word and only "cop out" for a very valid reason (and seldom, if ever, to anyone outside the family). Some youngsters just agree to certain things to get parents off their case, and they have no intention of following through. This is a bad habit that will have dire results later in life, so stop it as soon as possible.

CORRECTING. *See Punishment.*

CRAFTS. *See Arts and Crafts Projects.*

CREATIVITY. *See also Arts and Crafts Projects.*

The ability to be creative, to show imagination and originality, is within each child. It gets stifled through overorganization (such as too many lessons and group activities), resulting in the lack of time to play without rigid rules. It can also be hampered by a controlling parent who wants to be in charge of every child activity. Creativity is magnified by having many times for unstructured activity.

When introducing ideas for play, ask questions such as "How does this work?" "What can you make from these pieces?" "How could we use this for more fun?" Then step back and let your child use his imagination. You may be amazed at the results!

Encourage creativity through crafts, scientific or building toys, or toys that can be played with several ways. Have a place where a creative project can be worked on without having to frequently clean it up or put it away.

CRITICISM. *See also Punishment, Put-Downs and Put-Ups.*

Constant criticism is depressing to both the giver and the receiver. Censure gets in the way of learning. Still, most children's mistakes shouldn't be overlooked.

Using a few large pieces of cardboard, write OOPS in big red letters on each one. Then, when you see something that you might nag about, put a sign there: by the food left out, the television left on, the messy room, the towel on the bathroom floor, the bicycle left in the driveway. Make a home for your OOPS signs so they can be returned and reused after the problem has been corrected.

Of course there are times when nonverbal correction won't work. Make sure your criticism has a positive ending, showing how the matter could have been resolved in a better way. Be clear that you are censuring the action, not the child. If you constantly fail to do this, over time a youngster will begin to feel that he is inferior, stupid, or bad and develop a hopeless attitude. But, if you zero in on the wrong action, rather than the child, you can look at the problem with some detachment, and work together to change it.

CRYING. *See also Colic.*

Crying is most often a call for attention or help, but sometimes it can be a form of baby exercise. Always determine the well-being of crying children and don't let bedtime crying become a habit. Some young children just need a few moments of your time and then they will settle down.

In most cases, crying is not the sign of a problem. Newborns cry about ninety minutes a day, and by the time a baby is six-to-eight weeks old, the crying has doubled. Then, at three months, it begins decreasing. These are just average statistics but are helpful stages to know. For some reason children also cry more in the evening hours, but this is not a concern unless it continues and becomes a habit.

To calm a baby, consider placing her on her abdomen in your lap and gently massaging her back. Sometimes holding her close to your heart or swaddling her will work.

To calm a toddler, try to distract him by asking a question or showing him something special. Or, put your hands over a crying child's eyes, then take them away quickly, then put your hands back, and so forth. Say "I see a crying Jeremy, I see a happy Jeremy" as you do this. You can do it to yourself by covering your own eyes and pretending to cry or smile.

Don't be angry with a crying child. Although you may be frantic with the continued crying, exert every effort to keep control, speaking softly and soothingly. An uptight parent makes an upset child.

Some crying babies respond to movement: rocking in an automatic baby swing, being pushed in a stroller, or even given a car ride. Try placing a warm washcloth on the back of the baby's neck. Ask siblings to comfort a crying child. A different face and voice often does the trick.

CULTURAL DIFFERENCES. *See also Bullies, Hatred, Heritage, Teasing.*

Learning to feel comfortable with people of different cultural, economic, racial, and social backgrounds is part of maturing. Parents should see that youngsters learn about people who are different from themselves. They must sincerely show respect, kindness, and tolerance.

Begin with the appreciation of the family's own culture, ethnicity, and family history. Get grandparents involved. Scrapbooks, photo albums, recipes, videos, movies, plus books on various countries provide take-off places for discussions of different cultures. A pen pal from a foreign country can be enlightening. Take part in community events honoring the traditions of others such as Octoberfest or Cinco de Mayo. As you get to know people from different backgrounds, plan informal gatherings and eventually talk about each family's traditions.

When a child has a negative reaction to a racially or culturally different person, talk about the prejudice and find the basis of the feelings. Then consider better alternatives to harmful opinions. If you suspect that a youngster harbors feelings of ethnic supremacy verging on violence (as in gangs and white supremacist groups), get professional help immediately.

CULTURAL EVENTS. *See also Dance, Drama, Museums, Music.*

Don't wait until children are older to expose them to cultural events. Start with young children, exposing them to museums, stage plays, and musical programs as often as you go to movies and amusement parks. Parents and children alike will find that culture is both educational and extremely entertaining. For very young children, choose inexpensive neighborhood theater productions that can be as short as forty-five minutes, and where the actors actually mingle with the audience. Use the resources of your library to follow up: art books, recordings of famous musical productions, and storybooks on which plays are based. Don't fear or disdain culture for yourself or your children.

DANCE.

When eating or reading, play dance music—everything from ballet to clogging. For a break in work, try jumping jacks in time to peppy march music. Start with toddlers to dance together to music. Grade-schoolers may be interested in tap or ballet lessons.

Teens like more modern forms of dance but are currently becoming interested in ballroom dancing and swing dancing. Before the first dance class or party, show youngsters how to hold a partner. Discuss how to ask (and accept or decline) for a dance. Give a child other hints on dance etiquette so he has confidence with the opposite sex long before the prom.

Watch dance programs on television, attend recitals, and introduce young children to ballet by attending a performance of *The Nutcracker*. See if your community has a line dance or square dance group as these can make for lots of family fun.

DARKNESS. *Also see Fears.*

Help youngsters to become comfortable in the dark inside and outside the home. Pretend there is a power outage and see how the family can achieve the end-of-day activities (baths, reading, bedtime) by using candles. Get accustomed to darkness outside by taking evening walks, going out to look at the stars, eating supper in the yard, or playing tag with flashlights.

If you show how to function in the dark, your youngster will follow your lead and not be fearful. Night-lights, under-the-bed checks, and a flashlight in a bed table drawer can be reassuring.

DATING. *See also Sex, Teen Years.*

Going out with the opposite sex needs advance planning, starting when children first begin to talk about dates. Parents should set an age when a child can go out on a group date (perhaps at thirteen) and when one can go out on a double date (perhaps at fifteen) and then as a twosome (perhaps at sixteen). Don't be influenced by what other families permit. Take into consideration your own child: her trustworthiness, maturity, and general behavior. If you state such rules long in advance, it will not come as a surprise and be a cause for argument. Prior to those times, give youngsters of both sexes opportunities to be together at parties and other events.

Make it clear that before going out, the youngster must give a written note of "who, where, and when" (these three Ws are the date's name and phone number, destination or destinations, time of return). Discuss and establish punishments, such as grounding, if rules are broken.

Set curfews so that youngsters come home at reasonable times. Possible curfew times are: 10 P.M. for youngsters twelve and thirteen, 11 P.M. for those fourteen and fifteen, midnight for those sixteen to eighteen years old. Week-night dating should be taboo. Occasions such as prom nights can have one-time special later curfews providing youngsters are in a safe environment. Exceptions can be made when children are with other parents.

Do not permit dating kids to be alone in the house without a parent present. Be home and available when there is a party, but not necessarily in view. Support your children in resisting stupid or illegal behavior when dating, frequently stressing your standards regarding driving, drinking, drugs, sex, and the presence of weapons.

DAY CARE. *See Child Care Facilities, Preschool.*

DEATH. *See also Grief.*

Death is not the end of life, it is only the end of what we see of it. A child's greatest fear is that a parent will die and he will be left alone.

Be frank with youngsters when a relative or friend of the family dies. Don't say "He's gone away," or "She's gone to sleep." Tell the facts in a simple way without unnecessary detail. Permit sadness or grief, then go on to commemoration. Talk about good times you all had in the past and some achievements of the person. Have your discussion in a familiar, cozy place, and with a young child, hold her and remind her of your loving care. It is important to give extra attention and love to children at such times and to listen for their questions. Don't hesitate saying that the love we felt for the person will never go away and that we will always remember him.

Regarding grief, research shows that it is normal to be depressed and angry, and it is equally normal to work through the grief rapidly with no dire consequences. Often the intensity of the grief is a matter of personal education or of religious faith.

Never force a young child to attend a funeral. Discuss the impending funeral or memorial service, explaining what the child will see and hear. Then let her decide if she wants to attend.

When a school friend dies, find out if the school would permit planting a tree in the child's memory, or giving a special book to the library.

In the case of having to euthanize a pet, avoid the phrase "put to sleep" so as not to cause fears about sleep. Allow time for a "memorial" discussion and possible burial. Sometimes losing a pet is very overwhelming to a child, especially if the pet slept on her bed through the years. Also, don't immediately substitute another pet—this belittles the life of the first one and can give a child the idea that he too can be easily replaced.

DECISION MAKING. *See Problem Solving.*

DEGRADATION. *See Humiliation.*

DENTAL CARE. *See also Doctor/Dentist Visits.*

Caring for teeth and gums is a parental responsibility but requires the child's cooperation. Brushing with a soft brush should start in babyhood when the first teeth appear. There are also brushes that play music to encourage young children to brush sufficiently. Parents need to be on the scene or set a timer so that the brushing is thorough. Starting at age three, twice a year checkups are a must and need not be fearsome events if a parent prepares the youngster and the dentist is reassuring.

DEPRESSION. *See also Self-Worth, Suicide.*

Moodiness in response to a difficult situation is not unusual, however prolonged periods of profound unhappiness should be treated seriously. Depressed children often feel ill, apathetic, sullen, and isolated—feelings that can lead to drugs or alcohol use. And many youth suicides are caused by feelings of inner chaos and low self-esteem.

Although there are antidepressants, finding the cause of the feeling is far more effective long term. Activities that build a feeling of self-worth and connect a child with others in a positive and happy way are helpful. Remind the child that he will not feel this way forever, that circumstances will change. Stay close to a depressed child and talk openly about his feelings.

Do not ignore persistent depression and threats to commit suicide. Seek professional help immediately.

DEPRIVATION. *See also Discipline, Punishment, Rules.*

To deprive a youngster of something she enjoys is one of the most effective means of correcting unacceptable behavior. It works with children as young as three and right on through the teen years. But, it is essential to know what possessions and privileges are important so that the withdrawal of them will be meaningful and memorable. (Explain that in society a drunk driver is deprived of his license, a criminal is deprived of his freedom.)

Depending on the age of a child, she can be deprived of playing with a favored toy, using the telephone or the car, the freedom to leave the house weekdays or over the weekend, television time, video games, the right to spend money, and so forth. The length of the deprivation can be anywhere from an hour to a day or to a month or more for serious infractions.

Make it known in advance that grades of C minus or worse will result in no weekday television until the next grading period and an improved grade. If a teen fails to be where she said she'd be and doesn't phone with the change of place, she can be "campused" for two weeks. If a teen gets a traffic ticket, his car keys and license are taken away.

Be sure that this type of punishment doesn't affect others. For example, don't say, "The family won't go to the circus if you continue to hit the dog." Of course deprivation saddens the child, and sometimes even the parent, but it does make a point. To be effective, don't change your mind about a deprivation, and never announce a punishment you aren't willing to follow through with.

DESSERTS. *See Sweets.*

DESTRUCTIVENESS. *See also Anger, Tantrums.*

Willfully breaking toys or other items is a cry for help. While children may sometimes unintentionally break things, persistent and purposeful destructiveness requires an assessment of the child's feelings, followed by training in how to better respond to anger.

Be specific in showing a child alternate ways of expressing frustration. Show disapproval of the destructive activity and, if possible, let the child take part in repairing the item or contribute to purchasing a new one.

 The most effective technique is to immediately take the child to a quiet area, hold him, and calmly ask why he threw (smashed, jumped on) the object and destroyed it. Was it something that was said? Did someone do something to make him angry? What was he feeling at the time? Then help him come up with several other responses to the problem.

Don't provide a child with so many toys that destroying one is meaningless to him since he already has many others to play with. Don't immediately take away the broken toy. Place it where it will be seen as a reminder that destructiveness is not acceptable in your family.

DETERMINATION. *See also Optimism.*
The "I can do it" attitude is a hopeful and optimistic approach to problems as opposed to mental defeatism and giving up. Show children that they have control over many aspects of their own successes or failures, and that positive thinking adds much to their success.

Avoid just saying "You can't. . . " " Rather couple it with "You can. . . " "You can't do fifty arithmetic problems in ten minutes but you can do them in thirty minutes." "You can't jump off the roof, but you can jump from a branch of that tree."

Encourage determination by suggesting ways in which the challenge can be overcome: waiting to do it later, doing it with help, cutting it in half. It often helps to divide a large task into several smaller ones—that way there are several successes along the way to completion. However, rather than supplying solutions immediately, ask that the youngster present one option herself.

Compliment determination, even if it doesn't result in success. And remember, some things are not worth doing now, later, or ever.

DIARIES.
Keeping a record of events and thoughts can be interesting for a youngster. Older children prefer to call it a journal and many have written daily, some well into adulthood. A gift of a small diary with lock and key can get a grade-schooler started. Formerly a "girls thing," nowadays many boys like to keep a record. Whether or not the book has a lock and key, reading it is definitely off limits to others.

DILIGENCE. *See Determination.*

DINNER. *See also Manners, Mealtime.*

The evening meal can be the most important connecting time of the day so see that it is a sit-down meal without television or intrusive phone calls. Either let the answering machine take the calls or assign one youngster the duty of answering the phone and taking messages for calls to be returned later.

Set the dinnertime for when everyone can be present and try to organize youth activities so that they don't interfere. Working parents must learn to be bold and stick up for their right to be home for the evening meal. If some family members must wait for others to come home, serve them juice and crackers to stave off extreme hunger.

Family members should help prepare the meal and also prepare themselves to take part in the dinnertime activities. These activities can be sharing events of the day (the work day and the school day), talking about current news, discussing plans for the future, listening to music (each family member gets a turn to choose what is played), and reading part of an age-appropriate book out loud.

Take turns sitting at the head of the table. It adds to a youngster's poise to say the grace, serve the food, lead a discussion, and decide when everyone can be excused. Also, vary the place where you eat: outdoors in good weather, occasionally in the living room or the family room.

A bored toddler can be kept busy in her high chair by giving her some whipped cream or yogurt on her tray, and letting her "finger paint" with it. She will enjoy licking her fingers!

When the meal is over, each person clears her own place and also has an assignment: to load the dishwasher (or to wash or to dry dishes), to put away leftovers, to wipe counters, to sweep the floor.

DISABILITIES. *See also Eyesight, Hearing, Slow Learning, Stuttering, Teasing.*

Teach youngsters to be kind about obvious disabilities of others. Tell them that everyone has some imperfections, although they may not be in view, and that they are learning how to manage them. Encourage friendship with physically challenged children who often have developed amazing talents to compensate for their disabilities. Many schools find that challenged children placed in regular classes are welcomed with interest and thoughtfulness by other students.

If a child in your family has a disability, get in touch with the appropriate national organization that can specifically provide a wealth of good ideas on care and treatment and connect you to local agencies for help.

76

DISAGREEMENTS. *See Conflicts.*

DISCIPLINE. *See also Obedience, One-Chance Parent, Punishment, Rules, Spanking, Thinking Bench.*

Discipline is training that produces self-control. While you want a child to be obedient in your presence, you are more importantly teaching him the right thing to do when he is not with you.

Consistency is the name of the game! A couple should decide even before children are born what their style of discipline will be—and that both of them will be united on this issue. Otherwise children will be quick to perceive which parent is the strict one and which one is not as insistent on good behavior, and thus they will take advantage of that information. Make it a rule that if one parent gives an answer or an order, there will be no appeal to the other. And if there is, there will be punishment.

Different kinds of correction will work for the different ages and temperaments of children. (And in some cases, discipline isn't the proper response at all—for example a child may just need help in remembering rules. But don't let "I forgot" be a constant excuse.)

An important part of discipline is teaching children to truly listen. Many parents who automatically repeat requests train youngsters that it isn't necessary to remember or take note of an adult's request. It's far better for the parent to say it once and insist on compliance. A parent speaking quietly, firmly, and consistently, and exhibiting self-control is a most effective disciplinarian and role model.

A parent needs to encourage a child to share the feelings or circumstances that precede wrong behavior. Over time, making an effort to unwind these snarls will lead to less need for punishment. Many occasions where a child had to be punished could have been averted with prior conversation and reasoning. But by not taking the time in advance, the child is punished and the parent must take the time afterward to set things right. If a child repeatedly makes the same mistake, either the punishment is not sufficient or the broken rule is not fully understood.

Discipline is also your means of keeping a child safe and at the same time teaching him values. Reckless parents encourage reckless children. Parents who don't appreciate life themselves and act in foolhardy ways often raise children who do dangerous things.

Parents need to learn when to stand back and let kids work out problems themselves and when it is important to intervene or discipline. A youngster should be aware in advance of certain punishments such as time-out for hitting, weekend "campusing" for coming home late, or loss of driving privileges for alcohol or drug use.

Write out the family rules so that there is no doubt about what you expect. These rules are *preventive discipline* while the punishments are *curative discipline*. Parents should share the discipline duties so that neither is a crabby witch or a push over. If one parent does most of the weekday discipline, the other can take over for evenings and weekends.

For older children it can be effective to write out a contract, specifying exactly what you want the child to achieve, such as an improved grade, better care of valuable possessions, or giving up cigarette smoking. Include in the contract a date of completion, the exact achievement required, and what you are willing to do as a reward for success. Do check in this encyclopedia the sections on "Rules" and "Punishment."

Make a "No P/S" Rule. Do not permit pushing and shoving that can escalate. The one who starts it gets punished and so does the one who continues it.

Start with a very young child to use the simple word "no." Turn your back and don't give attention when a child acts up. Be a "One-Chance Parent," so children learn to obey the first time or get only one warning.

Give youngsters choices: "You can hit your brother again and be punished, or you can choose to play and be happy." Or say: "If you finish your chores, you can stay up an hour later tonight or one night this weekend." Speak positively. Rather than saying "You can't play until you practice for your piano lesson," say "You can play as soon as you finish practicing for your piano lesson."

These are six important discipline points to practice:

1. Mean what you say. Don't respond to kids who beg, hoping you will waffle.
2. Before punishing, be sure both you and the child know what the wrong was.
3. Keep discipline between parent and child; don't involve other children.
4. Make the punishment fit the mistake—never too harsh, never meaningless.
5. Discipline as soon as possible, but it should not be immediate if you are very angry.
6. When the correction is over, don't talk about it again.

DISCOURAGEMENT. *See also Determination.*

Misery can be contagious. Kids say "I'll never get this done," or "I'm not as smart as Molly." But even champions feel discouraged at times, yet they know how to overcome it by not giving up.

When a child is first discouraged, acknowledge the hurt feelings and the emotions as being temporary. Listen carefully and identify the annoyance, the pressure, or the fear and talk about these. Help and encourage by gently reminding the youngster of previous successful or winning situations, no matter how small. Then, you may want to help the child get started with a project that you feel he can successfully accomplish. Don't do it for him, but give his work a boost by your interest.

Continual discouragement and depression should have immediate professional care.

DISEASES. *See also AIDS, Health, Immunization.*

Alertness is the key to keeping youngsters disease free. It is amazing that doctors report that one of the key means of preventing illness is regular hand-washing! (This should be done several times daily, before each meal, after play, and automatically after every bathroom trip.)

The common childhood diseases that a child can be immunized for are: chicken pox, measles, mumps, polio, rubella, pertussis, and diphtheria. You should discuss immunization with your doctor to ascertain just what is right for your child, since vaccinations are not always the best choice. You will also want to be on guard for colds, flu, strep throat, ear and sinus infections.

Don't smoke around children. Passive smoking (breathing the smoke from cigarettes, cigars, or pipes) increases the frequency and severity of colds and may cause long-term health problems.

Never send a sick child to school since that often results in a longer recovery period and exposes others. It may be inconvenient to provide at-home care, but that is always the best choice.

Replace or disinfect a child's toothbrush after an illness. Use paper towels or wash hand and bath towels frequently. Also, regularly use a disinfectant in the bathroom, kitchen, and diaper-changing areas. Cook eggs and poultry thoroughly and refrigerate perishables to avoid serious problems such as salmonella or E. coli infection.

Parents should be alert to environmental conditions, other than contagion, that can adversely affect children. Lead in certain paint and in water can result in lead poisoning that can be very harmful to children. The backyard environment may let dogs bring fleas and ticks into the house. Cover a child's sandbox when not in use. And, discourage the kissing of pets since, despite protestations of the cleanliness of a dog's mouth, it encourages the spread of worms and other parasites.

A parent needs to be cognizant of a child's health and not take illness casually. But, the parent should not create a hypochondriacal child who is so fearful he doesn't enjoy life to the fullest.

DIVORCE. *See also Abuse, Estrangement, Marriage, Single-Parenting.*

While the end of a marriage is rarely pleasant, it is sometimes necessary and thus both parents should work to minimize the damage to the children. Although many parents believe that the children are unaware of marital problems and the possibility of divorce, kids usually do know and are not surprised when the divorce is finally announced. Give them age-appropriate reasons for the break-up so that they do not carry the guilt of thinking they caused it.

But, whether there is or is not forewarning, a divorce is mentally and physically upsetting to youngsters — no matter what their age. Eating disorders, sleeplessness, depression, and anger are common and can add to the stress of the divorce. Fears can seem irrational — fears that losing one parent may mean the loss of the other one later, fear of abandonment, fear that bad behavior on the child's part was the cause. Good communication and one-on-one time will help to heal these fears, and parents should leave the door open for continuing conversation in the months and years to come.

If abuse is the cause of the marriage breakdown, the abused party should get out of the house *with the children* as soon as possible. The most important thing is the safety of the family members. There are shelters that temporarily protect abused families until a better living situation can be worked out. Keep good records as to dates, types of abuse, witnesses, and formal complaints made to others.

Never bad-mouth the other parent; it downgrades a child's estimation of you, and can cause loyalty problems for the child in the future.

Research shows that children who were under age six at the time of the breakup recover more quickly than older children. However, a child who has been extremely close to the departing parent may have great difficulties and become very clingy. For example, a little child who has been "Daddy's girl" and has not as yet established activities with older peers, may greatly feel the separation. Be sure to give added attention to children at this time.

Grade-schoolers openly show anger and grief but usually respond well to thoughtful communication. Teens are often the most emotionally damaged with a majority exhibiting their confusion and hurt by engaging in destructive or illegal activities.

The divorce can be expected to have least damaging effects when:

• Children are given the opportunity to maintain a good relationship with both parents.
• There is frequent contact with the noncustodial parent by phone, letter, or visit.
• Each parent can talk comfortably about the other without criticism.
• Good times of the past are referred to without bitterness.
• The child is not used as a messenger or bargaining chip between the divorced parents.
• The visiting times are frequent and closely adhered to.
• Both parents express love for the child on a regular basis.

DOCTOR/DENTIST VISITS. *See also Dental Care, Health, Pediatrician.*

Seeing a professional can often be very intimidating for an adult, so imagine how a child feels faced with such an appointment.

Never lie to a child about the visit. If she asks if it will hurt, answer that it might for a minute, but that she will feel better afterward.

Reassure youngsters that the visit is not the result of anything bad they have done. Without going into excessive detail, explain simply what will happen (for example an X-ray, a blood sample), and the end purpose of the procedure. You can even make the visit like a game, letting the child count his teeth or test his muscles.

Bring a toy and snack in case there is a long wait, and for extra comfort let a young child bring a favorite doll or animal. Play quietly together in the waiting room. During the treatment, focusing on the change for the better that will result can help a child take her thoughts off any pain. Compliment cooperation such as sitting still, and encourage questions by the child so she feels a part of the treatment.

If a child must be hospitalized, go together for a preadmission visit so that the youngster can have some familiarity with the environment. Once admitted, stay close (if possible stay overnight), see that familiar toys are available, and that a variety of friends, relatives, and activities keep the child focused on getting well.

DOWN SYNDROME.

This abnormality, caused by the presence of an extra chromosome, was formerly believed to be more common with children of older mothers. (There is no indication that subsequent pregnancies will result in the same condition.) A test for it is often done early in the pregnancy. Although it is currently deemed incurable, enormous strides have been made in giving many of these children good lives. Prospective parents of a child with Down syndrome may be so devastated by the prebirth prognosis that they consider aborting the baby. However, those who continue the pregnancy and raise the child usually find that the child brings incredible love and special attributes to the family. Support groups have been a great help to families challenged with this problem. A good book for new parents is *Hope for the Families* by Robert Perske, illustrated by Martha Perske (Abingdon Press, Nashville, Tenn.).

DRAMA.

Drama is literature made visible and audible—and often more memorable. To see a dramatic event in person is vastly different from viewing television. A good place to begin is with local productions aimed at very young children. These shows are reasonably priced, short in length, and the actors often interact with the children explaining scenery, props, costumes, and makeup. The next step is to take youngsters to a regular children's theater and to school productions, then later to appropriate adult dramatic productions, including musicals. Afterward, these visual productions are a springboard for thought and conversation.

Encourage the presentation of miniplays at home as a wonderful rainy-day project. Marionettes or hand puppets and a homemade stage are useful toys to encourage drama play. This gives youngsters poise and helps them to write and speak. Drama at home can include shadow plays, puppet theater, family play reading, and storytelling.

DREAMS. *See also Nightmares, Sleep.*

Psychologists are putting less emphasis on the meaning of dreams than a generation ago, and it is no longer thought that certain foods cause dreams. Some children dream nightly, some never recall having dreams. Even those who wake up from a dream rarely remember it moments later. However, if you note REMs (rapid eye movements that can cause the lids to flutter), the sleeper is probably dreaming.

A definite connection has been made between vivid experiences (actual or viewed on television) and dreams. Some researchers have found that subjects considered immediately before sleep often result in dreams or nightmares. Thus it is important to shield children from viewing violence, especially in the evening hours, but better to entirely ban violent television. It is wise to help children think pleasant thoughts when going to bed and to wish them "sweet dreams."

Recurring dreams may indicate an unsolved worry. If a youngster can tell you about the recurring dream, you can verbally pick up the scene and bring it to a satisfying conclusion. Then the dream is not as apt to recur. For example, if a child tells you that in his recurring dream he is being constantly chased by a bear, you can finish the story by saying: "And then your daddy and the man from the zoo catch the bear and put him back in the zoo, in a wonderful new enclosure just like the woods. And when you go to the zoo, the bear waves at you and says he'll never run away again."

DRESSING SELF. *See also Clothing.*

While some youngsters quickly master dressing themselves, others find it tedious and require much adult encouragement. For young children, choose clothes that are comfortable and easy to put on, free of buttons and ties but featuring snaps and velcro closings instead. There are cloth books available that teach all about dressing and include working snaps, buttons, and zippers.

With the child's help, select and lay out the entire outfit the night before. You can put it on a chair so that all the clothes are visible, but on top are the first ones to put on. Doing it the night before takes away the frustrating indecision and arguments that can spoil the morning when a child is still sleepy.

Provide ample time for slow dressers. Ask a youngster for a solution to the problem of not getting dressed promptly. Use a timer, or make a chart with sticker rewards, and praise success. As a child gets older, take the time to give lessons in how to tie a bow on shoes or dresses.

DRINKING ALCOHOL. *See Driving, Peer Pressure, Substance Abuse.*

DRIVING.

Driving is an earned privilege, not an automatic right at a certain age. When young teens begin to talk about driving, let them understand that they must show responsibility and honesty along with maintaining good grades in order to earn the privilege.

Driver's education classes are ideal ways for youngsters to learn the rules of the road. But your own example is the most important. Let youngsters monitor your speed, your turns, and lane changes. Explain the gauges and buttons on the dashboard. If possible, teach the proper use of the clutch. Give a learner many driving opportunities with you so you both will have confidence when she starts to drive alone.

Bad driving habits, traffic tickets, and accidents caused by poor driving should mean that the privilege to drive is withdrawn for a lengthy period of time. These infractions could include: driving without a license, illegally driving friends, failing to lock the car, cutting off other drivers, drag racing, speeding, picking up strangers, or substance abuse.

Set curfews for returning home. The penalty for lateness could be established as one weekend of being campused for each ten minutes late. (This means no car, no going out, no phone calls, no televison—just enjoying the wonders of her own home.) Be strict from the very beginning and don't let youngsters manipulate you. Mean what you say in such an important matter.

Start a fund for the youngster's first car and agree to match her earnings so that a safe used car can be bought.

DRUGS. *See Medication/Medicines, Substance Abuse.*

DUTIES. *See Chores.*

DYSFUNCTIONAL FAMILY. *See also Abuse, Parenting Skills.*

Acting abnormally/crudely/foolishly/dangerously is the status quo of many families—they just do not function in a way that supports good values or a satisfying, productive life. The problem is that many families are almost proud of being dysfunctional; they see it as modern and unique, and so they pass the problem on to the next generation. One often hears someone say "Well, I came from a dysfunctional family so I can't help it." This is just a feeble excuse, because there is help.

To break the cycle, society needs to have a better system of identifying dysfunctional families and then urging them to get help. The best solution is education, starting with parenting studies for kids in high schools, and adult evening classes for parents. Also there are many helpful books on the subject, but unfortunately dysfunctional families are usually not inclined to read them. The thoughtless acceptance of apathetic or ignorant ways is no reason for parents to fail in their duties to children and to each other.

DYSLEXIA.

This reading disability is marked by the inability to correctly recognize letters and words on the printed page. It usually results in decreased reading skills. Sometimes students reverse letters such as "b" and "d," and they also do mirror (backward) writing (for example writing "saw" for "was").

Children with dyslexia may be normal in all other ways but since reading is basic to success in most every field, the problem needs to be addressed early on. If untreated, it can lead to loss of self-esteem, behavioral problems, and aggression—all caused by the lack of reading ability. First determine if the cause is a physical one, and if it is, get treatment for it. If the problem is not physical, the nonreader can be taught through specific tutoring on a regular basis. This tutoring, plus strong emotional support by the family, can help to correct this.

EARLY LEARNING. *See also Babyhood Concepts, Hurried Child, Toddler Concepts.*

Research shows that most children who can read at age three are no further ahead of other students by age eight. And, the effort parents and some preschool teachers put into early learning may mean that there was not time spent learning important social skills. For example, a parent trying to teach words to an eighteen-month-old child on a driving trip kept pointing a finger out the window and saying "house" as they passed each building. After many tedious miles of the parent pointing and saying "house," the child responded by holding up his finger and happily saying "house!" Time that could have been used singing or mimicking interesting sounds was lost and all the child knew was that his finger was called "house."

Superbabies are often taught responses without making any connection. This does not mean that some children are not fully ready to read at three, but it does mean that the whole child cannot be ignored. There is so much to be learned in the early years, social skills that form the important basis for successful functioning in school. While early learning may increase parental pride, it can result in a child being bored and having behavior problems when he reaches school age. No matter how high an IQ a child has, he still needs to know how to share, play creatively, laugh, follow directions, handle failure, feel success, and so forth.

EASTER.

This religious holiday also unofficially marks the start of spring. Share the activities with relatives or friends: coloring eggs, planning an egg hunt, attending church, preparing the feast.

A week ahead blow out and decorate eggs, exchanging names in order to make one very special egg for each person. Create Easter baskets with eggs, candy, and cookies and deliver them to relatives and seniors who would appreciate them.

For a table decoration, create an Easter egg tree by "planting" a dead tree branch in cement or plaster of Paris. Glue small ribbons to decorated eggs for hanging on the branches.

The night before Easter, tell the adventure-filled Bible stories of Jesus' last days, his crucifixion, and resurrection. Explain the symbolic meaning of the cross, the lamb, colored eggs, rabbits, and chicks. Then have a unique Easter morning egg hunt: along with eggs and candy, wrap and hide breakfast items: orange segments, coffee cake, a soft-boiled egg, and a container of juice.

Consider introducing new dishes into your Easter feast, but always serve the traditional dessert cake in the shape of a lamb or rabbit with white frosting and coconut. Stores and catalogs have these specific cake molds that you'll use for many years to come.

EATING. *See Breakfast, Dinner, Eating Out, Manners, Mealtime.*

EATING DISORDERS. *See Anorexia, Bulimia, Mealtime.*

EATING OUT. *See also Manners.*

Advance planning and gentle control can make eating out a pleasure. Show youngsters how to read a menu, evaluate prices, make acceptable table talk, and not gorge on crackers before the meal comes.

For a more peaceful meal, tell them in advance that they are permitted only one complaint at the restaurant and that they should have at least three topics of conversation. Go over proper manners on the way and also remind them about "restaurant voices." And, firmly tell youngsters that they will be expected to remain seated during the meal and during the before-meal wait. Take along a little bag of small toys to use should a toddler become restless, but don't give it before needed.

Gradually help youngsters learn special culinary and foreign terms on a menu. Older children can learn to read the right-hand column of the menu and compare values, figure the total cost and the tip.

A quiet table game is "I Spy." A parent says "I spy with my little eye. . ." and names an object (clock, hat, flower) and a child looks around to try and see it. The first to see it is the next person to name something (not someone) in view.

More and more fast-food restaurants are featuring interesting healthy choices instead of only the traditional high-fat foods, so eating out can still include interesting nutritional foods.

EDUCATION. *See also Computers, Gifted Children, Grades, Home Schooling, Homework, Learning Skills, Parent/Teacher Relationship, Schools.*

Properly educating children so they can function effectively in the world is the task that will take most of the parent's time. It matters little what the educational background of the parent happens to be—an uneducated parent can learn right along with a child or connect the child with tutors and mentors.

Going to school is the child's duty and he should approach his education with the same dedication that an adult conducts his career. Make interest in and appreciation for good school work more important than sports successes.

Never skimp on education. If a school lacks a certain subject, lobby for it. If it needs equipment, help the school to get it. Support the public school system if at all possible and only as a last resort, or in matters of safety, put a child in a private school.

See that first lessons are studiously learned. There is nothing archaic about the 3 Rs. A child who can read can do anything! Of course computer literacy is important, but not more important than reading well, writing intelligently, and mastering numbers. Competence in these skills is basic to computer excellence. Support education with truly worthwhile books at home. And, if necessary, get workbooks and tutoring if a child is falling behind.

Be a watchdog concerning school subjects beyond the 3 Rs. Art, music, science, history, civics, and physical education are other essentials. Unfortunately some of these are the first to go when budgets are cut. Fight for these classes.

Parents should fully take part in school activities, volunteering in the classroom as chaperones, on committees, and faithfully attending student assessment interviews and parent-teacher meetings.

Oppose the "dumbing down" of the curriculum and, in most cases, oppose social promotion. Make a high school diploma symbolize the mastery of certain skills. A good high school education can lead to a good college and graduate school experience.

The newspaper can be a great learning tool and an encouragement for reading and learning. Ask family members to bring an interesting news item to the dinner table each night. A young child can bring a picture. These items will start interesting conversations. The Educational Testing Service (the group who prepares the SAT tests) has found that children who are talked to and regularly asked by their parents about their activities are much more knowledgeable on tests.

 Forget the myth that "some children just don't test well." In most cases tests are indicators as to what is being learned. Don't let poor test scores discourage you or your child, give or get help.

Insist on excellence in your schools and especially in the teachers who will be major influences on your child.

EMERGENCIES. *See Safety.*

EMPATHY. *See also Caring.*

Empathy is not often discussed but it is very important. Empathy is the ability to understand how others feel and to respond appropriately. Research shows that empathetic people do better in school and career because they can put themselves in another's place. Even young children can be taught to think how others would feel if hit, if left all alone, if lost, if constantly criticized, if called names, if ignored, or if mistreated at play. Show how inappropriate words ("Look at that man's big nose!") can make others feel bad.

Parents are the best teachers of empathy, referring to feelings that underlie many daily events. For example, a parent can say that she feels sad when a child fails to feed the cat because the cat is so hungry. When a child complains that his baby brother gets so much attention, the parent can comfort the child and explain why it is necessary at certain times. Why we do certain things and how we respond to those things gives us good or bad feelings. A parent can point out how we should understand those feelings and thus be empathetic. It is important for a parent to show empathy when a child is frightened, disappointed, hurt, or out-of-sorts.

Often when a child sees someone with a disability, she may fear that "this could happen to me," and because of the fear she lacks empathy. While young children are quick to accept people with disabilities, teens have a more difficult time since their perceptions of worth are more often linked to appearance. Mainstreaming physically challenged youngsters with their peers has somewhat alleviated this problem. However, there are many varieties of disabilities and a physical handicap is often easier for youngsters to accept than a mental handicap. Insist that teasing is never an appropriate response to someone who happens to be different.

Sensing how others feel makes for kinder children, and empathy is a character trait that is endearing to others. It also gives the child a sense of being part of the larger picture of humankind.

EMPTY NEST. *See also Marriage.*

Although the time may seem distant, the children usually do move out, leaving the parents to each other. Life changes when the nest is empty and wise parents are always preparing for that time so as not to be at a loss when it happens. A new career, hobbies, service groups, sports, self-improvement classes, and other activities can fill the void. But it is best to begin some of these activities during the child-rearing years so that the sudden transition to an empty nest isn't such a challenge but is pleasant and fruitful.

ENCOURAGEMENT. *See also Appreciation, Self-Worth.*

Home life is much happier when family members are encouraged to do the right thing. Unfortunately, many parents are very vocal when children do wrong, and rather silent when all is going well.

Use these words of encouragement: "Hey, you're catching on." "It's your choice." "I respect what you're doing." "You've got the winning solution." "That's using your imagination." "Keep trying, you'll get it." "I trust you."

You will find that a few sincere words of encouragement can overcome discouragement and the stress of too much to do with too little time.

ENTERTAINING. *See also Neighborhood Activities, Parties.*

Enjoying the company of other children and adults should be encouraged at an early age. Teach children how to be polite to your friends and able to share some bit of information without shyly hanging the head.

When parents are entertaining, let kids taste-test and give opinions on party foods in advance. Young children can also show guests where to put coats. Older youngsters can serve and clean up at a party. When children are helping at your parties, indicate just how much you want them to be involved, and when it is time to absent themselves from the adult activities. It is vital to their social growth to enjoy the company of others on this more formal basis.

For the children's own entertaining, such as holiday or birthday parties, they should be instructed about how to be a good host. Do this as role-playing the day before the party and go over it again on party day. The role-playing examples should include greeting and speaking to each guest, taking turns in an activity, being gracious during games, using good manners when eating, thanking for gifts, and saying thank you to each departing guest. These are not too difficult to teach to a child of four or five, and such good manners will make him a welcome guest in the parties given by others.

So you don't overlook certain people or repeat certain refreshments, keep a record of parties, attendees, food served, activities. Make a time schedule for the day of the party to help you accomplish everything without stress.

Don't be a taker and never a giver. If you are entertained, be sure you entertain in return. After that, don't accept invitations from people you don't enjoy and don't wish to invite back. You should explain this concept to your children and how to decline an invitation without lying.

Involve children in planning their own parties, letting them choose the theme, whom to invite, and the activities. And, include them in the needed cleanup afterward. For many entertaining ideas, see *The Family Party Book* (Caryl Krueger, Abingdon Press, Nashville, Tenn.).

ENTERTAINMENT. *See Cultural Events, Dance, Drama, Movies.*

ENTHUSIASM.

Don't live a bland life and raise a dull child. Have games and activities where there is excitement that you can respond to with joy and exuberance.

Words such as these show a child your enthusiasm: "Hooray!" "Wow!" "Great!" "Terrific!" "Superb!" "Excellent!" "Remarkable!" "Fantastic!" "Incredible!" "Marvelous!" "Perfect!" "Amazing!" "Spectacular!" If you use these on suitable occasions, you will soon hear youngsters using them, too.

ENVIRONMENT (HOME). *See also Babyproofing, Order.*

A child's room is his castle—an important place he should enjoy. That's why you don't send kids to their rooms as punishment.

A child's room should be more than just a place to sleep. Do make it kid friendly with good storage for games, books, and clothes. Simple shelves can be made of bricks and boards. Plywood on legs can be a low play table for a train, dollhouse, or building blocks. Provide a cozy chair and lamp for enjoying book reading. Let a youngster choose his own wall decor and provide a bulletin board for displays. When the youngster starts school, equip a desk area for homework with a good lamp, dictionary, and writing supplies. If a youngster shares a room with a sibling, make some division such as a shelf unit, and provide separate storage areas.

Youngsters also need an area for projects such as crafts, and these can be in his own room, the family room, or the garage. If possible, a child should have an outdoor area of his own—a place to dig without upsetting the garden and places to pitch a tent or make a clubhouse out of boxes.

Visit a child's room daily, knocking first if the door is closed. This "turf" is a good environment for both tender and serious conversations. It's an ideal place to remind a youngster of your love.

 Don't insist on room neatness each day. A once-a-week clean-up is sufficient. No one's résumé says "He keeps a neat room."

Help a youngster rearrange the room each year, getting rid of outgrown toys, books, and clothes. Hold your tongue if you don't like the arrangement plan because what the child likes is most important. Matching spreads and draperies are not as important as a comfortable place a child can call his own.

ENVIRONMENTAL ISSUES. *See also Nature.*

Enjoying and protecting the outdoors begins with taking baby on a nature walk and just looking at trees and flowers. Later, let a toddler place a garbage can lid on the lawn for forty-eight hours, then lift it and see all the worms and other insects that have chosen to reside in the dark, cool place. Encourage youngsters to collect interesting rocks or use field glasses to observe birds and small animals up close. Make a booklet of tree leaves and learn to identify them.

At the seashore, lake, or river, turn over rocks to see what's under them. Observe tide pools and moss. Identify fish and shells. On a clear night, stretch out on a chaise or the grass and look at the heavens. Later talk about and identify certain constellations.

Bring nature into the home through a piece of driftwood or a rock collection that could be a table decoration. Be sure that youngsters don't spoil nature by taking living things such as bugs away from their environment.

Above all, teach the appreciation of nature and the importance of conservation. Be an example by not littering, by planting drought-resistant trees and shrubs, and by supporting responsible conservation activities. Let your youngsters take part in these activities and also in setting up a recycling plan for your house.

 Make it a family event to celebrate Earth Day each April by helping to improve a park, combat graffiti, or plant a tree.

ERRANDS. *See Excursions, Shopping.*

ESTRANGEMENT. *See also Divorce, Parenting Skills.*

Once there has been an unpleasant separation between parent and child, it takes work to repair it. While it is best to see that estrangement never occurs in the first place, it can be cured. Estrangement can be caused by misunderstandings, breaking family rules, using hurtful words, or a lack of love. Do your best to avert these!

Avoid lines such as "I never want to see you again!" "I can never love you!" "Don't talk to me—ever!" These phrases only incense the other person and you don't truly mean them.

When the other party is upset, be calm by contrast. Be conciliatory, looking for ways to work out the problem or compromise. Keep talking, telephoning, writing—making sure that the lines of communication remain open for that time when you will need to use them for reconciliation. Use lines such as "I'm sure there's an answer." "I love you no matter what!" "We both feel sad, so what could I do to help?"

Sometimes it helps to have a third party serve as a mediator: to bring the combatants together, talk through the problem, find where each side can give a little, and then make up. Life is too short to let family problems come between you and those you love.

ETHICS. *See also Honesty, Morality, Religion, Rules.*

Ethical behavior has been described as "what you do when no one is looking." Parents set ethical standards for youngsters in truth-telling, in strictly abiding by the law themselves, in acting democratically in the home, and in following the family rules. Parents must avoid sending mixed messages by saying one thing and doing another. For example, a parent may preach "Never tell a lie" and then at the theater say "Act like you're only eleven so we can buy you a cheaper ticket."

It is difficult for a child to honor ethical standards when she sees what is going on in much of the world. So, it is important for parents to point out ethical behavior by other people the family knows or in news stories.

 Don't give in just because "everyone is doing it." Your response can be "I know their family does it that way, but we do it this way."

 Praise and praise more when a youngster takes a firm ethical stand. You should be very proud of a youngster who puts ethics before power or money.

ETIQUETTE. *See Manners.*

EVENING ACTIVITIES. *See also Activities.*

The time between dinner and bedtime can be useful or wasted. It should be far more than reading the paper, doing homework, or looking at television. Each weekday have one evening activity for the entire family—it can be as short as a ten-minute walk around the block. For young children, it can be floor play with a parent. For grade-schoolers, it's an ideal time to play a box game or cards or share a craft. Teens might enjoy shooting a few baskets, making popcorn, or having a snack in the middle of the homework session. No matter how short the time available, make the connection because this can be one of the most important togetherness times during the week.

EXCURSIONS. *See also Shopping.*

Pleasant little trips can be memorable highlights in the middle of routine days. Consider these places to visit: library, park, swim club, ice-cream store, garden shop, boat harbor, thrift shop, garage sale, humane society (to get educated about what pet to own), or a small airport to watch planes take off or land. While these small trips can take as little as twenty minutes, they chase away the feeling of weekday dullness.

EXERCISE. *See Fitness, Sports, Team Sports.*

EXTRACURRICULAR ACTIVITIES. *See also Activities, Classes, Lessons, Sports.*

Many schools provide after-school opportunities that are both educational and enjoyable. Some are free, some require a small fee. Schools offer sports teams, music and drama groups, debate teams, science and

94

rocketry clubs, and so forth. Take advantage of one or two of these during each school term but don't sign up a child for five days a week of organized activities. Consider together which of the activities will help make for a well-rounded youngster. Be cognizant of the importance of commitment—both that of the participant and the parent.

EYESIGHT. *See also Disabilities.*

A parent may not be aware of a child's faulty eyesight and may attribute poor schoolwork or lack of sports ability to other causes. Even the child may not realize that he is not seeing clearly. During the annual physical exam, have his eyes checked. Glasses for young children and contact lenses later, or even corrective surgery, can make a huge difference in how he views both himself and the world.

FADS. *See also Appearance, Clothing, Haircuts, Teen Years.*

Every generation has some unique fad or craze such as certain words, music, clothes, games, or dances. Just remember the fads you had and how interest in them eventually passed. But be alert to fads that are ghoulish, dangerous, or illegal. Long hair may not have been attractive in the eyes of a parent, but it never was harmful if it was clean. However, a metal button punched in the middle of the tongue can impede good speaking habits and also can become infected.

Don't refuse to allow fads unless they violate your family principles. Give teens a clothing budget so they can decide if they wish to spend it on fadish clothes or more-lasting purchases.

Be alert to fads in music and games that are violent, satanic, or unacceptable in other ways. Actually listen to your children's music and discuss songs with sexual or vicious words or themes. Look at the games and computer games they play. Don't permit youngsters to spend allowances on such unacceptable materials or bring them into your home.

FAILURE. *See also Self-Worth, Success.*

Along with successes, youngsters often experience failures. A team loss, a bad grade, a mistake at the recital—such happenings can bring on a defeatist attitude as self-worth plummets. When a child feels like a failure, it is important to remind her how much you love her and perhaps share an example of a previous success. As soon as feasible, arrange for her to do something that will provide a sense of achievement. Through your own example, show that failures can be stepping stones to more positive experiences.

Fear of failure can be overcome by challenging youngsters to try new things when others aren't watching: to climb a tree, or to give a book report first to you and then to the family. Share the fact that Babe Ruth struck out 1,330 times, but also hit 714 home runs. Tell a youngster not to worry about failure, but to worry about the chances she misses when she doesn't even try.

FAILURE TO THRIVE. *See also Touching.*

The problem of lack of progress in babyhood years is often the result of less than normal interaction between the baby and the parent or other care-giver. It can result in low weight in early years, unresponsiveness, slowness in learning skills, and poor eating habits. Sometimes parents are unintentionally permitting malnutrition by watering down the formula or by looking at the quantity of formula/food offered, rather than what is actually consumed. It can also be the result of an undiagnosed medical condition, such as the malabsorption of food. At the same time, some parents don't recognize the importance of stimulating activities for babies.

Failure to thrive can also result from conditions in care facilities where there is not sufficient trained staff to hold and speak to babies. Or, it can happen when a baby is consciously or subconsciously ignored because of an unwanted pregnancy, or because of other pressing conditions, such as substance abuse, that prevent loving care.

Investigate both medical and practical ways of encouraging physical and mental growth. Failure to thrive does not need to lead to lifelong problems but overcoming it requires hands-on parenting that will include stimulating activities and expressions of loving interest. Social service organizations can help.

FAITH. *See also Prayers, Religion.*

Today's youngsters are becoming much more interested in spirituality and faith than their parent's generation. (Although the word God is used in this section, you can use whatever term you choose for the Supreme Being.)

Religious study can be a backbone in difficult times so give children this training even if they don't appear to be vitally interested at present. Then when they are young adults they will be able to benefit from it in many wonderful ways they never thought of before.

God is shown to us in many ways. While we do not see the wind, we see the result of the wind whipping the water, we hear it rustling the leaves, we feel it on our cheeks. The same is true of God's presence—we can see, hear, and feel it in our lives.

Point out opportunities for a youngster to use his faith to rely on God for safety, good ideas, or comfort. Then reinforce his faith by mentioning those good things that God has done. Be a good example of relying on God for guidance in difficult situations, and don't hesitate to ask youngsters to join in your prayers.

FAMILY BED. *See also Bedtime Routine, Nightmares, Sleep.*

The idea of having children sleep with parents, so popular a decade ago, is gradually dying out. If sleeping is the only time for family closeness, the family is in a sorry state and should carefully look over its activities for other ways to connect.

Of course it helps to have new babies nearby for the first few months. A cradle next to the parents' bed, or the new cribs that butt right up to the bed like little bay windows, are good, safe answers. Too many babies have been smothered by parents who take them into bed and then, while sleeping, accidentally roll over on them.

Family members go to bed at various times and have varied sleep habits and research shows that children sleep more soundly in their own beds. A child sleeping in his own bed on his own mattress is not affected by heavier parents who weigh down the mattress making it not level, thus causing a child to sleep on a sloped surface. Most important, family bed deprives a youngster of independence and the enjoyment of his own space.

Another gigantic problem with family bed is that it inhibits the parents' loving and sexual relationship. After a busy day, parents enjoy snuggling together without fear of waking others in the bed.

Of course there are those occasions when a child is fearful and comes to the parents' bed in the night. It's certainly acceptable then for the parent to take the child back to his bed and stay a while, or to have him in the parents' bed until he is calm and can return to his own room.

Establish good sleeping conditions for young children in their own rooms. Mobiles and music boxes will help soothe a fretful child. Older children enjoy the company of a radio, tuned to a music station, at their bedside.

FAMILY HEADQUARTERS. *See Home Management, Organizational Skills, Parenting Skills.*

FAMILY HISTORY. *See also Heritage, Traditions.*

In the very busy early years of marriage, learning family history often isn't a priority. Then, as older relatives pass on, the younger members of the family wish they had learned more about their family roots.

Use a tape recorder to collect stories from the senior members of the family. Make a copy for each youngster to have when he establishes his own home. Keep family photo albums up-to-date with dates and names of those in pictures. When you go on a trip, let family members take turns being the reporter for the day, writing up the highlights. When you return home, turn these reports into a scrapbook with photos and other trip memorabilia.

For your own personal family history, establish a drawer or box where anyone in the family can place items that help tell the story of the year (a good school report card, the program from an event, a loving letter or card, photos, baby announcements, and so forth). At the end of the year, flip the drawer or box over and the contents will be in chronological order, ready to be put into a scrapbook. Let youngsters add comments on the pages. A good time to assemble it is during the New Year's Day parade and football games, then look at it together as a new year starts.

FAMILY LIFE ESSENTIALS. *See also Parenting Skills, Togetherness.*

Among the many elements of family life, certain components bring about a lifetime of good relationships. The following concepts will help to create a viable, vital family life, not just a situation with disinterested people living together:

• **Create family ties.** Be a close-knit family by spending time with one another. Plan creative activities and reunions. Never let a period of no communication get a foothold. Make the investment of truly understanding each person in the family, even at the expense of being rebuffed. Come to an understanding or compromise when there is a problem.

• **Respect diversity.** Look for and appreciate the precious individuality of each family member. Don't expect clones of you—expect improvements on you! Try to understand another's point of view, especially when it is different from yours.

• **Cultivate communication.** Remember how much you loved your little baby and how you spoke comforting words even before the baby comprehended the meanings of those words. Now, when that person may be too big to hold, but certainly can comprehend your meaning, engage in conversation—both serious and lighthearted. Practice speaking with patience and consideration. Provide many opportunities to talk each day and week. For faraway family members, communicate regularly by phone, letter, or e-mail.

- **Love unconditionally.** Be sure you express your love each day in actual words, and also in actions. Practice many ways of showing your love. Get comfortable with the words "I love you." If love doesn't seem to be returned, never give up. Remember, you may not always like what a youngster does, but you will always love him.

- **Practice giving.** Volunteer. Vote. Contribute. Serve. Be sure you have a balance of activities—for yourself and family and activities that include others.

- **Develop a circle of friends.** Don't be an island or a cold fish. Enlarge your circle each year, no matter what your age. A lonely old age comes from failure to reach out to new friends on a regular basis. Even if you think you don't need them, they may need you.

- **Try new things.** Sameness is easy but it can get boring. Whether it is the food you eat, the music you listen to, the books you read, the sports you engage in, remember to try your wings on things that are different. You may be in for a pleasant surprise.

- **Act with humility.** No one knows everything. Realize that you are just one part of creation. Keep your ethical standards and religious beliefs active. Talk to God (or the Supreme Being of your choice) well ahead of those times when you are forced to do so out of fear or grief. Listen for guidance and don't always bull ahead with your own preconceived notions.

- **Believe in yourself.** Mentally make a list of all your good qualities and don't let others belittle you. Act with confidence and speak up for what you know is right. If you make a mistake or misjudgment, acknowledge it. Learn to laugh at yourself and remember, it's not the end of the world.

- **Respect the law.** We can't expect to be protected by the law if we cut corners when it suits us. Know right from wrong, and don't support the idea that the end justifies the means. Be law abiding and just in your thinking and in your actions.

- **Be a good-news bearer.** Share positive ideas, not negative gossip. Contrary to the evening news, there truly are good things happening. Search them out, share them with others, and think of them through the day and as you fall asleep at night.

- **Appreciate people who are different.** Don't bad-mouth teens. You probably had some wild times, strange songs, and odd clothing habits in your youth and you turned out fine. Don't judge those who are different from you and don't write-off senior citizens as having nothing to offer. Ask questions. Listen and learn.

- **Keep control of stuff.** Amassing things is selfish. Remember that things unused deprive others of their use. Give away what you don't need. If you haven't used something in a year, pass it on to family, friends, or social service organizations.

- **Have a working home headquarters.** Running a home and family is truly big business so have a desk or counter with necessary supplies. Don't let undone projects stack up. Get rid of junk mail. Answer letters at least once a month. Keep a list of things to do today, this week, this month, later. On a bulletin board list things to buy, problems to solve, chores, people to entertain, and a calendar of events.

- **Use your home.** Don't let it become a hotel with restaurant. Make it the family center, not the circumference. Give it a new look by rearranging it, rather than spending more money. Have an area for home crafts, a cozy place to read, a table for games. Share your home with others and encourage parties and informal gatherings.

- **Know your neighborhood.** Become friendly with neighbors. Keep a list of local places to visit and revisit. Consider inexpensive ways of improving your neighborhood, making it safer and more beautiful.

- **Get smarter and better.** Keep growing mentally. Have a basket of things to read. Investigate a new sport. Attend cultural events. Go for walks. Take a class. Eat wisely. Look sharp even when you're going to be home alone.

- **Be a happy person.** Don't be a complainer, a judge, or a constant arguer. Do what you feel is right and let others do the same if they're acting within the law. Sure, life has some lumps, but don't let them overshadow the good. Don't dwell on what you don't have. Rejoice daily over all you do have.

FAMILY MEETING. *See also Arguing.*

Regular family gatherings can be informative and happy times. Some families have an apple/popcorn/cocoa supper every Sunday night and talk over important family matters and the events of the previous week. Let youngsters take turns being in charge of the meeting.

Occasionally the family meeting may be a bit like a court case when there is a complaint between family members. Listen to both sides, determine the motives for the argument, and then what can be done to set it right. On topics where parents are willing to let the entire family decide, vote in secret so there will not be hurt feelings.

FAMILY TREE.

Learning who's who in the family can become an interesting project. Of course you can draw a simple family tree (oldest known relatives as the roots or lower branches, your generation as upper branches with kids as leaves), but a photo tree is more fun. Look in photo albums for pictures of relatives or write to everyone for a current head shot. Paste them on a very large piece of cardboard showing one generation on each level. Write full names, home towns, and birth places of the relatives under their photos.

At family get-togethers or reunions, be sure to show the family tree so everyone will see just how they're related.

FANTASY. *See Make-Believe.*

FATHERS. *See also Mothers, Parenting Skills.*

A dad or father figure should be an essential part of almost every family. Single parents need to be alert to the need for the influence of both male and female role models. Mothers in two-parent families should be sure not to take over the parenting duties to the extent that the father doesn't feel needed. Sometimes fathers may abdicate their role because they think they are too busy, or because the mother appears to be capably in charge.

So as not to deprive a child of this important influence, a father must plan the time for regular and special ways to connect, such as taking on the bedtime routine or the morning carpooling. And on weekends, dads can organize kids for errands, work projects, and family events.

It is not unusual today for fathers to take on special assignments such as being a leader for a Scout group or other activity. Fathers are totally capable of nurturing and there has been a recent increase in fathers being the stay-at-home parent and the mother working outside the home. Even if dads do this for only a year, they will certainly have greater appreciation for the hard work of stay-at-home moms.

FATHER'S DAY.

To honor the important influence that dads have on family life, celebrate this day every year. When children are young, the mother should help organize it.

Using shelf paper, make a banner with an appropriate message and tack it up in a special place before dad wakes up. Serve him breakfast in bed. Surprise dad by taking him fishing or to some special place he likes, perhaps with another family. Good gifts are books, golf or tennis balls, bright socks, a new tool. Before bedtime gather for hot chocolate and chat about dad's dad and granddad.

This day can be awkward if the parents are divorced, but if possible, there should still be a celebration. This may require the graciousness of both parents. In those cases where there is no known father, youngsters may feel ill at ease with school preparations for the day. A good solution is for those youngsters to consider the day "Family Day" or "Brothers and Sisters Day" and celebrate those good connections.

FAVORITISM. *See also Competition, Sibling Rivalry.*

Evenhanded dealing with children is not always easy. Some seem sweeter, smarter, more responsible, and cuter than others. But a parent must not play favorites. The one that seems to have less charm often needs the parent's love even more! Find something special, lovable, or commendable about each child and make a point of mentioning it daily. You never want a child to say later "You loved him more than you loved me!"

FEARS. *See also Bedtime, Darkness, Fears at Bedtime, Nightmares, Separation Anxiety.*

Loving, reassuring parents are the best antidote for fear. Remind children what is real and what is fantasy. Most fears are normal and a parent needs to show youngsters how to cope with them and how to gain control over them.

One of the most common fears is of the night. Start with very young children to help them be comfortable in the dark. Talk with them in the dark, sitting by their bedside. Choose partners and play hide-and-seek in the dark. Take children on evening walks as the sun sets and show them how magical the dark can be. Show that darkness is not a "thing" but just the absence of light. Ask a child where the darkness goes when the light is turned on.

Many children fear failure in school. When you sense that a particular subject is difficult, get special help to allay the fear. Fear of failure in sports activities can be a large problem if coaches and parents focus on winning rather than on good sportsmanship and fun. If a child has done

103

his level best, he has not failed. Before special events (recitals, games, tests) where a child is expected to perform well, give her extra attention, extra rest, and extra love.

Children also have fears of being alone, of dying, or of getting lost. You allay these fears through reason and reassuring conversation. Make being alone a special event (playing alone at home, even with an adult in the house). See that youngsters have activities they can enjoy when by themselves. Counteract a fear of dying by talking about your great love and care for her, and all the wonderful things ahead in her life. In going to public places, have a plan about what a child should do if lost and role-play how this will work.

Avoid reading scary stories to young children. When you know there is something in a book or movie that might frighten them (like the trees reaching out for Snow White), talk about it in advance. In a scary movie, you can relieve the pressure by getting up for a drink or popcorn. This reestablishes safe reality as opposed to the scary fantasy of the movie.

FEARS AT BEDTIME.

About half of all children have bedtime fears of darkness, monsters, or other animals. With young children, cut out scary television or stories at any time during the day as the visions can be retained and recalled at bedtime. When tucking a child in, anticipate fears by having a night-light, checking for "monsters" under the bed, and reminding kids that you will be looking in on them. (And then see that you do.)

On rare occasions, such as during a violent storm, you can take a youngster into your bed. Don't make this a regular practice as it is not safe for children and not fair for parents. An alternate approach is to go into the child's room and sit in a chair near the bed until he is calm.

See that there is a working flashlight in each youngster's bedside table. Some younger children like having a bell they can ring when they wake up in the night. The bell is a comfort that can remind them not to cry but rather turn over and go back to sleep, to go and seek a parent, or to ring the bell for someone to come to their aid. A tape of a parent's voice singing or reading a story can also allay bedtime fear.

FEMININITY.

Emphasis on the qualities of womanhood starts early in a little girl's life. She is dressed differently, given different toys, and often treated much more gently than a son. However, bravery, ingenuity, and strength are also feminine qualities just as kindness, nurturing, and gentleness can be masculine qualities. Some parents unconsciously keep girls from having certain experiences and even from pursuing certain academic classes. Teach girls that they don't need to be inhibited by their sex and that they have the same opportunities as their brothers. Don't degrade tomboyish girls. Give girls a wide variety of activities and let them be astronauts, mechanics or doctors or whatever they choose.

FIGHTING. *See also Arguing, Disagreements, Problem Solving, Yelling.*

With a greater number of parents working and consequently not having as much time to oversee children, fighting with children and between children has become far more common. This is because family members (children who often feel they've been neglected and parents who feel stressed) assume that they just deserve to have their way. This usually happens near the end of the day, a time when everyone is tired and tempers are short.

Parents may have been permitted as children to argue over every tiny disagreement and so they now think it better to expect unquestioning compliance with their orders. And when this doesn't happen, there is war. Kids quickly pick up on this inferior method of problem solving and totally forget to talk over challenges. Instead, in frustration, they just insist.

Fighting with children and between children is an emotional response that can, with a little effort, be replaced by a reasoned response. First, parents and youngsters should determine the trigger for the fight: failure to share, lack of time, messiness, need for attention, meanness, forgetfulness, disobedience, and so forth. When you get to the reason for the fight, you find that it is often quite trivial. Then ask how the problem could be resolved without the fight. This procedure takes time, but if you do it after each confrontation, kids will soon decide that they can avoid trouble by negotiating before fighting.

Fighting between youngsters can take the form of hitting, pinching, teasing, arguing, biting, spitting, tripping, stealing toys—certainly not the material of the old sitcoms when it appeared families never bickered! Birth order, age, sex, family rules, and parental influence generally influence how much fighting goes on. And it is interesting to note that there's less fighting when parents are not right on the scene!

 Never physically fight with a child. Corporal punishment doesn't solve the basic problem and hitting only further hurts feelings.

No pushing, no shoving, no spanking, no finger in the chest, no in-your-face threats.

Make some strict rules about physical fighting. The one who makes the first punch gets the most punishment; the one who responds also gets punished. If possible, outlaw fighting words that only incense.

There may be occasions when a parent senses that a fight is brewing between youngsters. Before it gets physical, the parent should insist on everyone sitting down for a quiet time of information sharing and suggestions.

By the time kids reach the preteens, their arguments are more in keeping with their desires for maturity, symbolized by independence. At this age, preteens should have been introduced to problem-solving skills to make it a fair fight: no name calling, no switching topics, but instead a clear statement of the problem followed by ideas for alleviating it. These may seem like adult methods, but they are valuable skills for youngsters to master. You may be surprised at the kids' suggestions and how fair they are. For fights where the parent must step in and negotiate, try voicing a number of solutions—some very oppressive, some funny, some realistic.

An important ingredient in averting fights is a parent who frequently spends time alone with each child. This helps to recognize the individuality of the child and thus avoid giving labels such as "feisty" or "stubborn," which can become self-fulfilling prophecies. This special time together lets a parent understand the child's method of thinking and point of view that in turn removes much of the criticism a parent feels toward a physically argumentative child.

FILE FOLDERS. *See also Home Management, Organizational Skills, Parenting Skills.*

Introduce children to the wonders of keeping paperwork under control. As soon as a child can read and starts to collect things, provide her with a desk and a few file folders for special school papers, awards, membership cards, toy and game directions and guarantees, pet care and feeding instructions, wish list, and so forth. Keep this up during all the school years, suggesting the addition of more files on pertinent topics, and you will have started youngsters on a good habit that will help them for a lifetime.

FIRST AID. *See also Safety.*

Every family member needs to know the location of first aid supplies and how to use them. If you live in a two-story home, have a first aid kit on each floor. You also may want one in the garage or basement. Some of these can be small, with the largest one in the kitchen. See that a pair of scissors is included in each and that emergency numbers are taped inside the cover of the kit. Along with these, provide ipecac syrup, which is useful to induce vomiting.

Let youngsters practice cleaning and bandaging a make-believe wound. Explain the use of a tourniquet. Older youngsters should know how to give CPR and also the Heimlich maneuver. Make the training calm, factual, and not scary.

FITNESS. *See also Cleanliness, Health, Nutrition, Sports.*

Make well-being a natural part of growing up, not something that is beyond one's control. Practice wise, balanced eating, good posture, regular athletic activity, good dental habits, bodily cleanliness, and skin care. Don't wait to make fitness an issue. Start with young children who can learn to scrub their fingernails, brush their teeth long enough to name something for each letter of the alphabet, and brush their hair so that tangles don't build up.

Exercise is the movement of body parts in ways they were designed to move, not unnatural or forced movements. Physical exercise should be fun for youngsters, not grueling long-distance running or boring sit-ups. If at all possible, let exercise be an integral part of the day: walking or bicycling to school, enjoying a team sport or backyard games, or playing on a doorway chinning bar in bad weather. See that children have some exercise daily, even if it is just a game of tag after dinner each night.

FLAG AND FLAG DAY.

Flying the flag is a wonderful family tradition and it promotes feelings of patriotism in youngsters. As soon as a child is able, let one of her chores be to raise and lower the flag each day. How to care for the flag, its history, and traditions is a subject that can be learned at school, in youth groups, or from an encyclopedia.

Flag Day is celebrated each year on June 14, the anniversary of the adoption of the stars and stripes in 1777. Look at pictures of all the United States flags and see how they have changed through the years. Also consider flying the flag of your state.

FLEXIBILITY. *See Spontaneity.*

FOOD. *See Nutrition.*

FORGETFULNESS. *See also Discipline, One-Chance Parent, Organizational Skills, Reminding.*

Unless there is a diagnosed mental problem, forgetfulness is just a form of mental laziness. A forgetful child is often one who has little reason to remember. His parents continually remind, and there are no repercussions for forgetting. Tell him that there will be a new system: he is going to be told just one time what to do, given one chance, and then punished for forgetting. Discuss methods for remembering such as writing it down or setting out an object as a reminder. Compliment him when he does remember.

FORGIVENESS. *See also Apologizing.*

Learning how to forgive and not hold a grudge is a lesson usually taught by parental example. Once forgiven, forget the incident and don't bring it up again.

When a child has done something wrong, and understands that it was wrong, he should apologize and expect a parent's forgiveness. The words "I'm sorry" are welcome ones in most households and should be used between parents and children and between one child and another. They should usually be followed with the words "I forgive you."

When a child sincerely feels he has not done wrong and finds it hard to say "I'm sorry," teach him to say, "I'm sorry you feel I was wrong." "I'm sorry you thought I was rude." "I'm sorry I hurt your feelings." Those are acceptable truthful statements that adults can also use in confrontations. Talk with children about how certain of their actions can appear to others as thoughtless or naughty when they weren't meant that way, and how they can avert these misconceptions.

Explain that there is no mistake or injustice that cannot be forgiven. It may take time, reparations, or learning new ways, but the matter must eventually be settled with the final step being forgiveness.

FOSTER CARE.

On any given day in the United States, there are over half a million foster children and that number is constantly climbing. In California alone, there is hardly a public school that does not have foster children enrolled. Your children should know the basics of the foster care system, especially that the foster child has not been bad, is not being punished, and should be embraced in every possible way. This is an excellent opportunity for parents to discuss substance abuse, since more than 90 percent of children who have been removed from homes are those where parents are substance abusers.

Many of these children have been saved from neglect, abuse, and a lonely life through the work of foster families. This is a good lead in to adoption, as most county adoptions are by foster parents. While caring for a foster child is not always easy, it is certainly one of the finest ways that adults can give back to the community and enjoy the blessings that a child can bring.

Compare for your child his own stable life with caring parents to the life of a foster child, removed from parents he loves because they have not cared for him, and living in someone else's home while the foster-care system tries to reform and teach his parents in order to reunite the family. If the parents fail to reform, or are jailed for long periods, the court will terminate their parental rights so that the foster child can start a new life as the adopted child of his foster parents or another family. Above all, foster children need the support of love, consistency in parenting, stability, and security.

FRIENDS, FRIENDSHIP. *See also Cliques, Gangs, Popularity.*

Friends are an important part of growing up, but while making friends comes easily to some youngsters, it is very difficult for others. Young children can make friends by having a new acquaintance (from play school, church, or the neighborhood) come over to play and have lunch. Backyard play is ideal and parents should see that there is safe and attractive play equipment. Indoor play can be games or make believe, never television viewing. Sometimes a parent will need to make a suggestion of something to do.

Never reprimand your child in the presence of friends. If you need to correct something, take your youngster aside for a moment. As with siblings, there can be disagreements with friends, but a wise parent will encourage youngsters to come up with ways to settle problems through compromise, sharing, or changing the activity.

Let this be a rule for younger children: When it is fifteen minutes from the going home time, a parent will tell them that there are ten minutes more to play, then five minutes to tidy up. For teens, it's

109

the responsibility of the host (not the parent) to tidy up with the help of friends or alone.

Teens often meet potential friends through activities and clubs. The next step is to invite them over to do homework, make pizza, play games, just talk, or to go out for a sport event or movie. Adding new acquaintances to a group activity or party can also widen the circle of friends. Parents can help by making the home an attractive place for youngsters to congregate. A supply of games and other activities, readily available snacks, and comfortable but unpretentious furniture combine to make a home where kids feel welcome and safe. Parents need to be aware that there are friends in the house, but the parents should not be intrusive.

When friends come to the house, a youngster should introduce them to a parent and the parent should make the visitor feel welcome. When the guest leaves, a parent should say "good-bye" and express pleasure at having had them at the house. These small touches are important in cementing friendships as youngsters like to feel the approval of other adults.

Parents are responsible for the safety of other youngsters at their home or in their car. They should know the full names and phone numbers of visiting youngsters. Teens can prepare a list of friends and their numbers each semester. This can be vital in case of a change of plans or an emergency.

Early on, make a rule that youngsters are not to be part of gangs. Show the wrongness of the gang or clique mentality. Exclusiveness can separate a youngster from a wide group of diverse friends.

At dinner, talk about the qualities that make a good friend: cheerfulness, agreeability, the ability to share, honesty, a sense of adventure. Talk about words that harm friendships and phrases that make friends feel comfortable.

FRUSTRATION. *See Anger, Patience, Time Management.*

FUN. *See also Activities.*

Having fun with *all* the family together is on the brink of extinction. Spontaneous, joyful times are rare when parents and children have overfilled schedules. Parents need to reestablish those small things that make being a loving group worthwhile: talking around the supper table, baking cookies and eating them immediately, long summer evenings in the yard, camping trips, anticipation and preparation for a holiday, or walking in the rain.

Parenting is not something to get through. A child's journey from baby-hood to age eighteen should be one that parent and child can look back on with affection. If most all your time together is spent instructing, remind-ing, and scolding, make some basic organizational changes that get you through the work routines and on to the fun.

Researchers surveyed successful law-abiding college students about how they spent their free time when growing up. Comparing these activ-ities with those of troubled youngsters, they found that the successful ones had played games, were active in sports, did household chores, and had many playful activities *with their parents*. The troubled youngsters had minimal togetherness time with the family, spent little or no time playing games or working together, and spent a majority of free time on video games and television.

Include something in each day that's fun, even if it is just for a few minutes. Play tag outdoors after supper, do stunts on the liv-ing room carpet, go outside and look up at the cloud formations when it's stormy or the stars when it is dark, tell a funny story, play a quick card or box game, do a puzzle, spend a little time on a craft or other interesting project, have a backward supper, make s'mores for every-one to eat.

GAMES. *See also Activities, Party Games and Icebreakers, Sports.*

Games shouldn't be reserved for party times. Families can have a short game each night after dinner. Here are three very simple ones to get you started:

1. **Mirror pictures.** Players sit in front of a large mirror with paper and pencil (and a lap board or magazine to write on). While looking in the mirror, not at the paper, each tries to draw a simple thing such as a pig or a house, working up to a bicycle rider or letters of the alphabet. Even parents are challenged!

2. **Silly Sardines.** This is a good bedtime game. One person hides, others look for him. When one finds the hider, she quietly joins him in the hiding place. This continues until the last person has found the group. In game two, the first one to have found the hider is the next one to hide.

3. **Mystery Timer.** This fast-moving game is played throughout the entire house. Players stay in one room while a parent hides a timer set for about three minutes. Everyone starts to search and the first to find it (before or after it buzzes) is the next to hide it.

For hundreds more game ideas see *1001 Things to Do with Your Kids* and *1001 MORE Things to Do with Your Kids* (Caryl Krueger, Abingdon Press, Nashville, Tenn.).

GANGS. *See also Bullies, Cliques.*

Youngsters have a need to belong, to be cared for, to be respected, and to be loved. For many young people, gangs fill the void of an absent family. Unfortunately, gangs cannot and should not replace even the most dysfunctional family. Gangs hold on to youngsters through fear and intimidation. They are noted for illegal activities, terrorism, and substance abuse. Alert police to suspected gang activities. Although the authorities may not be able to act on your information immediately, it may be a piece in the puzzle of eventually controlling and eliminating gangs.

As a family, talk about gangs when the subject comes up in the news or at school. Do not permit children to wear any gang-related clothing or colors. Take the time and effort to search out alternate groups, such as Boys and Girls Clubs or the Y, that can take the place of gangs and offer caring leadership and age-appropriate ties. Help youngsters to make friends who are not members of gangs.

When a parent suspects that a youngster is becoming interested in joining a gang, it is time for even more serious discussion. School or professional counseling, proper alternate activities, and lots of parental love can help bridge the gap. If your child is already in a gang, sometimes a non-gang member will be able to influence him to leave the group. Be alert to the ramifications of leaving a gang and protect your youngster. This may require getting some tips from the police about the safest course of action.

Work together with others in your area to make a gang-free neighborhood.

GARDENING. *See also Nature.*

Teach youngsters the joy of growing things. Even if you live in an apartment, your family can enjoy gardening. The selection of plants is important and you should help kids to choose plants that are fun, grow quickly, or are useful. Here are some suggestions:

- **Indoor plants:** Amaryllis can actually be seen growing daily! Or plant morning glory seeds in pots and let the vines race up strings to a curtain rod.

- **Plants that attract birds:** Most birds like asters and coreopsis. Hummingbirds like phlox and honeysuckle.

- **Plants to eat:** Nasturtiums, violets, bean and pea flowers (be sure they haven't been sprayed with insecticides) go great with cream cheese in a sandwich. Radishes, carrots, lettuce, and zucchini are easy to grow.

- **Colorful plants:** Choose yellow or pink tomatoes, blue potatoes, purple beans, yellow beets, or white pumpkins.

- **Plants to play with:** Hollyhock blooms make good dresses for small dolls. Gourds make bird houses, loofah gourds make sponges, hosta leaves make good masks. Pumpkins can supply jack-o-lanterns for Halloween.

• **Monster plants:** Plant beans with tall poles and see if they get big enough for Jack to climb. Sunflowers rapidly shoot skyward and provide seeds that can be roasted and eaten or left for the birds.

You will be pleasantly surprised at how interested youngsters are in growing plants in the garden or in pots indoors. But, do remind young gardeners that their help is required in cultivating and weeding before the fun of harvest.

GEOGRAPHY.

As the world "shrinks" and communication becomes more instant, knowledge of world geography becomes more important to each of us. Start educating youngsters with a globe or map to show where relatives live, where stories in books take place, or where world news is happening. See how geography affects crops, population, even wars.

Place a globe in the center of a table where it can be seen by all family members. In advance, make a list of about ten countries or cities. Call out the name of one and see who can locate it first. Make other lists of ten places to use another time but keep the lists for use again to see how much the family remembers.

Stamp collecting is a good hobby that ties in with geography. Locate on the globe the countries of the stamps. Consider the picture on each stamp and use an encyclopedia to learn more about why a particular person, object, or building is featured.

When traveling, always have maps so youngsters can follow, noting the special words and coloring to indicate geographical elements such as mountains and rivers. Don't always race along freeways, occasionally take the smaller roads and really see the country, the towns, the special geographical and historical sites. Point out the geography and elevation of your own county, the highest hills or mountains, or the places adjacent to bodies of water.

Buy a large world map and hang it on a wall. Using different colored push-pins, let the family identify locations in different categories: where you now live and your state capital, where you have visited, where each family member was born, where parents went to school, where relatives live, where older family members came from in this country or other countries, where news is currently taking place, and eventually the capital of each state and country.

Schools may provide day excursions and even longer trips that teach geographical lessons. Opening your home to foreign exchange students is another way to learn about the world, and your youngster may eventually visit other countries in a reciprocal arrangement.

GETTING EVEN. *See also Arguing, Fighting, Hatred, Revenge, Self-Worth.*

There are some wrongs in family life that are not worth the time and effort to retaliate against. Of course you will stand up in major matters of principle, but most occasions for getting even are petty.

Often a child feels an irresistible need to get even and does so without much thought. Then when he has acted inappropriately by paying back, a parent finds himself in the position of judge and jury with only half the facts, just one side of the story. (Children who strike out like this as a first response to a perceived injustice usually learn this knee-jerk reaction from adults.)

When one child says something mean to another child, train youngsters to refrain from mean words in return. Point out that this kind of escalation would have gotten *both* youngsters in trouble. Take the original offender aside and ask what happened to cause him to say mean things, and ask how he would feel if such words were used against him. Don't fail to tell the child how unhappy you are to hear those mean words. Then, take the other child aside, the one who did not get even by saying mean words as a response. Make his praise lavish so that he will recognize the importance of keeping cool.

Some youngsters seem to truly enjoy the process of getting even. When they feel dissatisfied with their own achievements, they find joy in spoiling things for someone else. They tease, interfere, or hit because they feel stymied. This desire to pay back because of their own inadequacies is an immature response, even though it may seem logical to them. The offending child needs occasions of success to lift his self-worth. If the parent looks for these and comments favorably on them, it should bring improvement.

When children are playing, be aware of times when there have been fifteen minutes of pleasantness. Make a point of noticing it and compliment the children. And, when a child feels the need to get even, suggest the alternate of forgiveness.

GIFTED CHILDREN. *See also Education.*

The signs of a gifted child include:

- curiosity and thoughtful questions
- extensive vocabulary and complex sentences

- a good memory, or the ability to retain and recall information
- talent in the arts or music
- ability to discuss ideas and show humor
- quick learning of new concepts
- initiative and persistence regarding challenging tasks
- ability to work independently, combined with a sustained attention span
- special interest in how things work
- enjoyment in reading and creating stories

The highly intelligent child needs many of the same things as other youngsters: love, playtime, challenges, and, especially, unstructured time. Don't let her think that her only value is a good mind. For valuable information on living with and educating a gifted child, read *Your Gifted Child* (Smutney and Veenker, Facts on File, New York). A motivating home environment, letting youngsters choose activities and interests, and vitally interested (but not pushy) parents are essentials for those labeled "gifted."

Most schools nowadays have enrichment programs for gifted children that permit them to remain in some classes with their peers. Social development is just as important as intellectual development for these youngsters. At home, a gifted child should be nurtured with time to read books, do research, write stories, and enjoy activities that satisfy the need to know how things work.

GIFTS. *See also Christmas Gifts, Mother's Little Store, Wish Lists.*
Gifts are just symbols of love, and when you know and love someone you should know what he'd like as a gift. You may want to ask for a wish list that keeps some element of surprise but still lets you choose a gift that is really wanted.

Don't just give cash. It is all too often frittered away. If cash is your only gift, make it special by buying a big card and tying a balloon to it. Inside the balloon put rolled up bills, inserted into the neck of the balloon before inflating.

Occasionally surprise a child with a "just because" gift. It needn't be expensive to be meaningful.

Good gifts for birthdays and holidays include: bike speedometer, kick ball, set of felt pens, label-making machine, radio, world globe, wall picture, bag of plaster of Paris, box of batteries/wires/buzzers/bells, plastic cabinet with many drawers. More expensive gifts can be sports equipment, doll house, musical instrument, scientific equipment, automotive toys, outdoor play equipment, wrist watch, walkie talkie, tape recorder, telephone, bedroom furnishings.

GIVING VERSUS GETTING. *See also Service.*

Giving is an aspect of loving and the antidote for the "What's in it for me?" attitude. Encourage youngsters to give to others through church-related and social-service projects or specific kindnesses to friends and neighbors. Each year help children select some of their possessions for giving to charitable groups. At gift-giving occasions, emphasize the giver of the gift and insist on thank-you notes or calls afterward.

When a youngster goes to an event, a parent usually says "Go and have a good time." How much better to say "Go and *give* a good time." Research shows that children who generously give to others are happier and more successful than those who live selfishly.

GOALS. *See also Resolutions.*

Talk often about the long- and short-term aims of each family member. Lack of goals, not lack of ability, is a chief reason for lack of achievement in school, sports, and social life. Goal-setting meetings bring the family together to look ahead to new experiences and to gradually make some changes in family life.

At the meeting provide each family member with paper and pencil in order to write a "wish list" of fun things she'd like the family to do in the next six months. Share these ideas, letting everyone be heard. Then, list the ideas the majority agrees on. These could be a vacation destination, building a backyard tree house, or a plan to go hiking once a month.

Next, list goals that are not recreation oriented, yet generally important to family health and welfare. These could be to cut down on eating junk food, to clean up family language, to reduce the electric bill by 10 percent.

Finally, each person writes specific goals for himself, and a suggested one for another family member. These are private but can be discussed one-on-one with a parent unless the youngster wishes to make them public. Depending on the age of the youngster, the goals could include: to save for a new bike, to raise a grade, to redecorate a bedroom, to make a new friend, to have a special party. And ones suggested for other family members could be: to read fifteen minutes each night, to teach the dog a trick, to get along better with a younger sibling.

Parents' goals could be: to join a civic group, to spend daily one-on-one time with each family member, to laugh more, to make a vegetable garden, to ask (not order) others, to read a book each month.

After considering all their possibilities, encourage each person to put a star in front of two of them, ones they'd like to strive to achieve in the next two months. Set the example by getting going on your own goals and ask family members how you can help them with theirs. While parents should not nag or chide, a friendly "how is it going?" comment is acceptable. Be very complimentary when a goal is achieved.

GOLDEN RULE. *See also Caring, Service.*

In most every religion and philosophy, some form of the golden rule is a standard for civilized living. Encourage youngsters to follow the words "Do unto others as you would have them do unto you" or "Love others as you would like to be loved." Following the rule makes family life much more harmonious.

GOD. *See Religion.*

GOODNESS.

Everyone hopes to have a commendable child—a child that is good, not out of fear of punishment but because he understands that goodness is his right and natural state. Don't label little children good or bad, naughty or nice, as that can become a self-fulfilling prophecy. Look for the good things that a child does each day and reinforce these with praise.

GOSSIP. *See also Lies.*

Half-truths, speculation, and innuendo have no place in family life. Squelch gossip the first time it is voiced. Set an example not to gossip yourself, and don't take pleasure in gossip about public figures. When children share gossip, ask bluntly how they know it is true. Explain that your family deals in facts, not fantasy, and that it is cruel and dishonest to gossip.

GOVERNMENT. *See Business.*

GRACE. *See also Prayers, Religion.*

Giving thanks for good received doesn't have to be just before dinner, but that's a good time since it may have been overlooked during the day. Avoid routine rapid-fire words that can be meaningless. Let each family member take a turn giving a brief, heartfelt grace. You will be pleasantly surprised at the many things your family is grateful for.

GRADES. *See School Grades.*

GRADE-SCHOOL-AGE CONCEPTS.
Here are some skills that younger children should grasp for use in first grade and beyond: listening and following instructions, telling time, using coins, speaking in front of a small group, cutting and pasting, writing the alphabet, working with another student, making a phone call, dressing, bringing home assignments. Older youngsters who have learned to read should also know how to do research, use reference books, make an outline, take notes, print or write legibly, and work with a group. While these are just a sampling, mastering these concepts will help a student excel.

GRAMMAR. *See also Language, Speech.*
Although grammar is taught in schools, most children learn to speak correctly (or incorrectly) by listening to their parents and peers. In order to be at ease in public, children should be comfortable speaking correctly without having to think about it. Thus, bad grammar should not become a permitted habit, tolerated in the home. Be alert to problems such as the proper use of *I* and *me*, *lie* and *lay*, *don't* and *doesn't*. Also discourage the use of profanity and slang or pop phrases that often include bad grammar. Giving children opportunities to speak in front of others, at school or within the family, will help them to perfect their grammar skills.

GRANDPARENTS. *See also Caregivers, Heritage, Love, Travel.*
Family living can be greatly enhanced by active grandparents who are willing to be loving resources.

Encourage grandparents to be more than free baby-sitters! These ideas will encourage some one-on-one activities between the generations that grandparents can easily do. Make suggestions such as these to the grandparents:

• Communicate through letters, postcards, e-mail, audio and video tapes, letters including clippings of interest and photos, phone calls (although more expensive, you may want to tell faraway grandkids to call collect).
• Get together for more than just Sunday or holiday dinners. Attend youth events, take youngsters to plays, museums, and sports events.

- Plan visits and trips. Let your home become a second home for grandchildren, equipping it with toys and activities and storage places for possessions. And, take them along on your trips. Plan special trips to celebrate a child's becoming age six and twelve, and for graduating from high school or college.
- Pay for "firsts": first bike, first earrings, first long dress, even part of the money for a first car.
- Teach certain skills: photography, cooking, computer, sewing, woodworking, driving, tennis and so forth. Some grandparents even serve as coaches and group leaders, sharing their expertise.
- With parental approval, supervise the religious education of children, taking them to Sunday school and teaching them the importance of good values.
- Be a historian. The family heritage is not dull when told in firsthand accounts by elders who may be the custodians of scrapbooks and photo albums. Start youngsters on their own albums and work together to make a video family history.
- Plan reunions to mark anniversaries or serve as yearly get-togethers of relatives from far and near.
- Give gifts. Perhaps your resources can supply funds for monetary gifts to grandchildren to help pay for large expenditures such as cars and college. But on lesser occasions, the gifts should be personal, not just money. Grandparents who truly know their grandchildren also know what they would enjoy and take pleasure in surprising a youngster or going on a shopping trip together. Start with young children to ask for wish lists. And, be sure that what you bring when you visit grandchildren is yourself and your good ideas, and only occasionally a gift. Don't fall into the habit of bringing a gift at each visit.
- Be a no-strings-attached source for love and support. Use words of love. Do acts of love. Love no matter what!

When baby-sitting or caring for grandchildren, grandparents should ask the rules in advance and adhere to them, not changing rules to suit their own agenda. The important purpose of baby-sitting is to enjoy the youngsters, to talk and play together safely, never to undermine the parents' standards.

Grandparents should endeavor to be nonjudgmental about their grandchildren. While grandparents can use well-timed, gentle remarks about values, each youngster must make his own way without criticism. Appearance, career choices, lifestyles, mates—all these issues are very important but not as important as loving support.

Families can celebrate Grandparents' Day in September with phone calls, cards, useful gifts, and a celebration. Let youngsters plan the event. A useful gift from nearby grandkids is a homemade book of coupons for services they are willing to perform: cutting lawns, cleaning cupboards, washing a car, serving at a party, or running errands. For faraway grandparents, make an audio or video tape that shows family activities and an interview that tells what the youngsters would like to do when next together.

More grandparents than ever before, actually 3.4 million, are serving as full-time parents. Even though they have already reared their own children, they have accepted this job out of loving concern for their grandchildren. These heroic, selfless individuals deserve much support and love.

For further ideas, read *The Ten Commandments for Grandparents* (Caryl Krueger, Abingdon Press, distributed by Belleridge Press, Escondido, Calif.).

GRATITUDE. *See also Appreciation.*

A grateful child is a social winner! Practicing verbal thanks within the family is a good place to start. Then, extend it to friends and relatives, teachers, coaches and other helpers: practice what might be said when thanking for a meal out, a movie, or a gift. Remind children in advance of an event so you don't have to use the hackneyed phrase "What do you say?" to prompt a thank-you.

Insist on written thanks. Those too young to write can draw a thank-you picture. Children should write a line for each year of their age, with ten being the maximum required. Be sure you set the example of written gratitude yourself.

GRIEF. *See also Death.*

Grieving over a serious mistake, a death, or other disturbing activity can, if not properly considered, fester in children for months and even years. Grief is best handled by not ignoring it or figuring it will just go away, but rather by talking about it: why it happened, what comes next, how to handle similar tragedies, what one does to be forgiven a mistake, or what the family religious beliefs are about life and death.

In helping a child to eventually overcome the grief, you may have to return to the subject many times. While the feeling may never be totally obliterated, a child should eventually feel satisfied that she has thought it through, done what she could, and if needed, been forgiven.

A grieving child needs comfort from family and friends, a sense of acceptance, and an understanding of his place in the world. When a dear person, or a pet, has died, it is important to keep the memory of that relationship alive in a positive way, not going over the separation but focusing on the good qualities that can never be lost.

GUILT. *See Conscience.*

GUNS. *See also Killing, Safety.*

Ideally, guns should have no place in a family. The purpose of a gun is to maim or kill. Target practice is not a necessary skill! However, if you feel the need for guns for hunting or protection, be sure that they have safety locks and that ammunition is carefully locked up separate from the weapons. Far too many youngsters are accidentally killed or injured by guns that were easily accessible.

Explain to children that they are never to play with guns, even if they think they are not loaded. Teach that there is nothing funny about guns and that jokes about them are inappropriate. When someone has a gun, instruct children to quietly and quickly leave the area.

Toy guns are not necessary for child's play. Why should children even pretend killing? Work with your neighbors to outlaw the outlaws and have a violence-free neighborhood. As children start playing video games, prohibit games based on guns and killing.

HABITS. *See also Character Building.*

Things we do automatically, with little or no thinking, are habits. There are some good habits such as cleanliness, politeness, and honesty. Just as parents would protect their youngsters from bad influences on the body, they need to also protect children from bad influences on the mind: watching violent or deviant entertainment, or dabbling in mind control, satanism, hatred, racism, and so forth. These can become bad habits just as easily as lying, procrastination, sloppiness, and laziness.

Bad habits get established when parents fail to speak against the habit the first time it occurs. Sometimes it is viewed as cute as when a little child takes a sip from an adult's alcoholic drink. Don't permit what you don't want to be exhibited. If a bad habit such as swearing is entrenched, you may have to set up some form of punishment to show the youngster that you're serious about his stopping it. Let the youngster know in advance what will happen if he continues the bad habit. And remember to celebrate when that habit disappears!

HAIRCUTS, HAIRSTYLES. *See also Fads.*

The trauma of a child's first haircut can be alleviated by letting her sit in your lap while your hair is cut. Don't surprise a child with a visit to the salon, rather build up the visit as something special, tell how it doesn't hurt, even offer a reward for good behavior. Give the child an attractive little box in which to put a piece of the cut-off hair so that she can show it to others.

To alleviate any stress, start reading a story at home, then take the book along and finish reading it during the haircut. Take along something such as a favorite toy animal that a youngster can hold on to during the process. Be sure to take before and after photos.

As youngsters get older, they develop strong opinions on hairstyles. As long as hair is clean and kept in good condition, don't make a huge issue out of the style. It is often a way of showing independence, and although you may think it looks ludicrous, it is usually not permanently damaging. There are far worse fads and you'll find that most of the weird ones are gone by the time a teen goes to college or seeks a job.

HALLOWEEN.

Halloween has taken on a ghoulish turn, so try to downplay death in favor of the fun of dressing up in happier costumes. Rather than begging for candy door-to-door, have a party that celebrates autumn and features bobbing for apples, square dancing, making small scarecrows of straw, carving pumpkins, and stringing popcorn. For an interesting costume party, ask everyone to come as a pumpkin, you'll be amazed at the inventiveness!

HANDSHAKES.

Politeness requires that children shake hands when introduced to some people. Practice at home, showing a child how to make eye contact while firmly grasping the hand. Although not important on most occasions, many people think that a limp handshake shows poor manners.

HANUKKAH (also called Chanukah).

This Jewish holiday honors the Feast of Lights and celebrates the defeat of the Syrians about 165 years before Jesus' time and the miraculous way one cruse of oil let the holy lamps burn for eight days. Today the eight candles of the menorah (candelabrum) are lighted in honor of that event, along with giving ceremonial gifts and serving special foods.

HAPPINESS. *See also Appreciation, Self-Worth.*

One of the character traits we all hope to attain is happiness—a joyful and cheerful attitude. Many things contribute to a happy attitude; it isn't something you can force. Research shows children are happiest when they understand what they can do: what is acceptable to do, what can be achieved, and what is not possible at present. That's why smart parents work together to set parameters, accepting the fact that even good families sometimes have unhappy times, but they bounce back. Happy families set reachable priorities, have good manners, respect innocence, find many opportunities to talk, and enjoy good humor.

Caring parents provide opportunities for fun, make light of silly mistakes, create a home atmosphere that is flexible, plan surprises and adventures, and speak with hope. They realize that children are happier when parents applaud a child's special effort or achievement, increasing the feeling of self-worth. Some parents help youngsters create a list of good things they have achieved—small and large.

Don't use words that tear down happy feelings: "You never do anything right!" "It will never work!" "What a dumb thing to do!" When bad things happen, say "Let's see what we can do about it," "I love you no matter what."

Make a child feel special by commenting each day on something good that he's done. Once a month have a dinner to honor one family member, toasting him, letting him sit at the head of the table, and asking that everyone say only good things about the honoree. Provide regular opportunities for enjoyable activities each weekday and especially on weekends. Talk with youngsters about the times they were happiest in the past, and see if you can recreate some of these good times.

HARASSMENT. *See also Bullies, Cultural Differences, Hatred, Teasing.*

Harassment is defined as causing trouble and annoyance continually to another and making repeated attacks on another. Harassers may be wrongly motivated by their own feelings of cultural or racial supremacy. They may target their victims because of their appearance or talents or sex. Whatever lame excuse is given, it is a vicious behavior and should not be tolerated. Parents should not permit even mild harassment in the home, and school administrators should be put on notice by parents that it is not acceptable behavior in the classroom or on the playground.

HATRED. *See also Anger, Cultural Differences, Getting Even.*

Hostility to others is contagious: parents teach it to children, children teach it to other children. We may hate others for their superior talents, their costly mistakes, their different appearance, race, or religion, or for some perceived injustice. Hate groups build on fears of one group losing control to another group. If not curbed, hatred can lead to violence, and hateful people are rarely happy people.

Start with young children to teach that hateful discrimination has no place in family or community life. Praise diversity. Appreciate good qualities regardless of outward appearance.

Help children recognize hateful words by making a list and posting it on the bulletin board. Some common hateful words that hurt feelings or start fights are: "I hate you." "You stink." "I never want to play with you again." "You're a baby." Other words are "Fatso," "Four Eyes," and "Dumbo." Start by encouraging your children to get through one day without using any hateful words, then try for two days, and so forth. Set an example in your own life of being accepting and welcoming of those who act in different ways and whose backgrounds are different from yours by including them among your friends. Talk about times when people have expressed hatred toward you and how you handled the situation.

HEALTH, SICKNESS. *See also AIDS, Diseases, Fitness, Healthy Habits, Nutrition.*

A parent's approach to health issues usually sets the tone for children. If a parent is overly fearful of every sneeze, the youngster may become a hypochondriac at an early age and every cut and scrape will be seen as life threatening. However, if the parent remains calm, shows a caring attitude, and tends carefully to the child's needs, small health problems will not be blown out of proportion.

Ignoring health questions is a major fault of some parents as they think the illness will just go away. Parents need to be alert to health problems that do not quickly diminish, and seek professional help. Choose a doctor who is up-to-date on the latest techniques and agrees with your comfort level on giving prescription medicine to children. Never hesitate to get a second opinion.

For young children, keep the explanation of a health problem very simple. And, if medicines are to be taken, the parent must strictly supervise and remind youngsters that they are never to take them on their own. Older children can be included in the discussion of how to handle the condition and given some responsibility for their own health care.

A child's health can affect her ability to play and learn, so preventing illness is as important as curing it. Help a child to follow a healthy regimen that includes good nutrition and proper exercise. Be alert to problems that linger such as a continually stuffy nose. In case of a contagious disease, be strict in following all the requirements to protect others. If the child must be in a hospital, use age-appropriate language to explain what has happened and what is probably going to happen.

126

When a child is ill at home, see that the time doesn't become mindless television viewing. Staying home from school should be taken seriously with time for resting and sleeping, eating wisely, reading, doing some homework, and focusing on getting well. An ill child may feel lonely and abandoned, so supply him with the security of a bell to ring when he needs attention. Provide in-bed activities and eventually other home activities that tie in with the normal routine. Getting partially dressed, eating some food at the table, playing with the dog, and telephoning a friend, can be the first steps in recovery.

A nice project is making the "Get Well Pillowcase." Give the child a plain pillowcase, some indelible marking pens, and a tray to work on. Put thick newspaper pages inside the pillowcase to absorb any ink. Let the child draw pictures and words on one side, then let family members put get-well messages on the other side.

Another in-bed activity is fort building. Use blankets or pillows to make a barrier across the middle of the bed. Make balls out of tissue paper or newspaper. With the child on one side and a parent on the other, throw the balls back and forth. This provides a little excitement in an otherwise placid time.

The Internet offers many sites that give up-to-date information on child health issues.

When a parent is very ill, children often find this disturbing and hard to believe. To young children, illness can seem almost magical: something that can be treated with the wave of a fairy's wand or an alien's laser beam. It has little reality as something permanently damaging for they think that they and their parents will live forever. Thus, when a parent has an extended illness, it shakes a child's faith in the perfection of life. Even teens cling to irrational fears and sometimes even believe that something they have done has caused the illness. Or, to the contrary, they may refuse to believe that anything is wrong. Parents need to be very honest with children, sharing information in terms they can understand, and suggesting some ways they can contribute to the recovery: being extra quiet, fixing a meal, or reading to the ill parent. As much as possible, continue the normal family routine so that youngsters don't fear that everything is changing.

Keep good health and immunization records on every family member. They may be needed for schools, camps, or travel, and will be appreciated when your children have children of their own.

HEALTHY HABITS. *See also Health, Fitness, Nutrition.*

Start with babies to establish good health habits such as cleanliness, exercise, and good nutrition. Tell children you love them too much to let them fall into bad health habits. Certain good habits should become so routine that a child hardly has to remember them: brushing teeth after meals, washing hands after going to the bathroom, eating fruits and vegetables, taking part in active play. Making these a normal part of every day when children are very young will make their lives much healthier as they grow.

Each year on Child-Health Day in October, give your family's health a checkup. Spend the dinner hour talking about how you can improve family health. Have everyone give suggestions of improvements you all can make, and put a list of these on the family bulletin board. Then regularly promote them.

HEARING. *See also Disabilities.*

Learning difficulties can stem from poor hearing. If you think your child is not hearing clearly, get professional help as soon as possible. See that a hearing test is part of a yearly checkup.

Many youngsters today are sustaining permanent high frequency hearing loss. Testing shows that many are so damaged that they are unable to hear sounds higher than 4,000 hertz. Parents should work with kids to prevent this hearing disorder by avoiding prolonged exposure to loud noise such as the sounds of amplified music and drums, heavy machinery, and some fireworks that greatly damage the inner ear. Loud music heard at concerts and through head phones is the biggest concern, and a strong appeal emphasizing the youngster's own future well-being may help to curtail the problem.

HELPFULNESS. *See Chores, Service.*

HERITAGE. *See also Family History, Family Tree, Grandparents, Reunions.*

Keep alive the family heritage without it becoming a matter of superiority. Making a family tree, visiting ethnic neighborhoods and festivals, learning national dances and songs, taking part in storytelling with older relatives, keeping photo albums and scrapbooks, and talking about patriotism will help youngsters understand their roots and appreciate the roots of others. Involve grandparents in sharing the family heritage. Plan a family reunion that includes stories, photos, and foods from the past.

Help youngsters learn to enjoy ethnic foods typical of the country of your family's origin. Copy favorite recipes and start a recipe file for each youngster to take when she goes off on her own.

HIGH SCHOOL CONCEPTS. *See also Grade-school-age Concepts, Teen Years.*

In addition to those concepts listed for grade school youngsters, teens should know how to give an oral report, do research, write a simple résumé, change a car tire, write checks and keep a checkbook, fill out a job application, cook a nutritious meal, make a budget and stick to it, manage time, clean a house, care for his clothes, care for his health and hygiene, and talk easily and politely to adults.

HISTORY AND GOVERNMENT.

History is the record of the progress of humankind. See that youngsters have a positive view of political, governmental, geographical, and historical changes. Follow one topic in the news or of general interest, consider how one would act as a head of state, look at maps, talk about pivotal dates in history, discuss what is learned in school history classes. Connect the history of the past with the political present. Consider what events in the past decade will eventually be considered as important historical events.

While dates mean little, they do indicate turning points in history. See that youngsters know what happened in years such as 1215, 1440, 1492, 1776, 1914, 1941, 1944, 1946, and 1969 (Magna Carta signed, invention of moveable type for printing press, arrival in the new world by Columbus, signing of the U.S. Declaration of Independence, World War I, Word War II, first digital computer, television era begins, man walks on the moon).

Encourage participation in school government. Managing a political campaign, working on "white papers" or discussion points, writing ads and flyers, counting ballots, and helping to augment new ideas are practical lessons for the future.

Parents can set an example by taking part in local government, having an interest in local issues, and either speaking out or writing about them. Tell youngsters that they are welcome to write "letters to the editor" on topics of interest to youth.

HOBBIES. *See Arts and Crafts Projects, Collections.*

HOLIDAYS. *See also specific holidays, Entertaining, Parties.*

Celebrations, large or small, are the stuff from which memories are built. Create a celebration each month, even if it's not an official holiday. A calendar will list other occasions that give you reasons to celebrate events such as Australia Day, Saint Patrick's Day, Secretaries Day, May Day, Columbus Day, United Nations Day, and Election Day. Invent your own holidays: honor the last day of school, the first day of school, a new neighbor, a friend moving away, the dog's birthday, and so forth. Ask a youngster to plan the celebration of such events.

HOME HEADQUARTERS AND MANAGEMENT. *See also Time Management.*

When you consider the cost of shelter, food, clothing, education, health care, and entertainment, you see that managing a home is big business. Create a family headquarters that has these essentials:

- a desk or counter and drawers well-equipped with supplies
- a file drawer with files for each family member, including education information and grades, activities and hobbies, health information, and photos
- files for directions and warranties for household equipment, budget and bills, financial investments, insurance, wills, correspondence, charge card receipts, vacation ideas, shopping, entertaining, community activities, and so forth
- an expanding bring-up file to keep items that must be available during the month: bills, letters to be answered, tickets, reminders to clean carpets, invitations, and so forth
- monthly family calendar, posted where the family can see it regularly, showing all activities
- a bulletin board for important lists: emergency phone numbers, often-used phone numbers, approved television shows, repair list, grocery list, loaned-out list, menus, chores, photos, and good school papers

This headquarters is also the place for phone messages. Encourage each family member to use the headquarters desk daily.

HOMEMAKING AND HOME MAINTENANCE. *See also Chores.*

Many parents feel that they are being kind to children by not teaching them how to manage a home. Actually, they are crippling them. These are the skills you should teach: cooking and baking, housecleaning, laundry, sewing, gardening, auto maintenance, home repairs (fuses, lightbulbs, paint touch ups), simple health care and safety, and giving parties. If you assign chores in these categories to children, they will learn the skills to live successfully on their own.

HOME SCHOOLING. *See also Education.*

The option of home schooling has greatly increased in the last decade. Many parents believe they are protecting their children from vulgarity and violence by teaching them at home. (Of course, it is still important to show youngsters how to handle these situations.) Materials supplied for home schooling vary greatly and a parent should investigate the programs and choose the most comprehensive plan with the most suitable backup materials.

Home schooling works best when the child is motivated to learn and the parent is sufficiently educated and able to supervise the work using top-notch teaching guides. Home schooling requires daily interaction between parent and student.

Some home schooled children do not have opportunities for social interaction so be sure to include this through activities and excursions with other youngsters. Other problem areas may include courses that require lab work and extensive equipment. And, participation in physical education classes and on sport teams may also be missing elements, although some programs provide for the student to take part in these at a nearby school.

A parent choosing home schooling must be committed to spending the time, providing opportunities outside the home, and seeking out options for special learning such as science lab work and athletic training. Computer connections are available for some class work and also for advanced placement classes for students who live too far from higher education facilities.

HOMESICKNESS. *See also Separation Anxiety.*

A temporary feeling of illness, panic, or anxiety may cloud a youngster's first time away from home and parents. Unlike separation anxiety, it usually doesn't last long. It can happen at school, camp, the home of a relative or friend, or even in a child's own home when the normal routine is interrupted by a parent's absence. Take many little steps to prepare a child for going away to camp. Work up to it through a backyard camp out, then an overnight at a friend's, then a weekend at the grandparents' home.

131

👎 Don't make fun of a homesick child. It is an intense feeling and in many cases it indicates how connected a child is to home and family, so it is actually a compliment. Still, it is not funny to the child experiencing it.

👍 Derail homesick feelings by adequate advance preparation (telling the child about the separation, its length, who will be caring for her) and also by setting up special connections. These can be as simple as a phone call, or an audio tape of a bedtime story, a family picture or favorite toy to hold, a collection of one-a-day short messages sealed in small envelopes, or a secret token that indicates the family bond. One such token that is successful is the presentation (with explanation) of a small angel pin, fastened inside a jacket pocket, that gives comfort without anyone else knowing of it.

HOMEWORK. *See also School Grades.*

Homework is the "work" of the child. The student's duty is to do it without complaint. The parent's duty is to create an atmosphere conducive to study, to be aware when help is needed, and to encourage and praise good work.

In general, there will probably not be homework given until about second grade, although a younger student may have easy home assignments such as to bring a picture to school or collect egg cartons for a school project. A good guide is fifteen minutes of homework for each grade in school. (Thus a fourth grade student has an hour and a high school senior three hours of homework. This gradual increase prepares students for the greater amount of homework required during college.)

Research shows that children who get regular homework assignments in the early years of grade school do better schoolwork and are not as overwhelmed as youngsters who don't get homework until the junior high school years. Grade school students usually do the best work in the hour before dinner and after some vigorous play. Older students may have to spend additional time after dinner.

Keep a studious atmosphere for homework. It should not be done in front of television or lying on a bed. Provide a desk or table, a straight chair, good lighting, and the necessary supplies. Be willing to help drill on facts and spelling words. If you need to give more help, see that the child is working *with* you, not you merely correcting the work.

Find out how much input the teacher expects of the parent. Know the teacher and attend as many meetings as possible. At the first sign of a

132

child's apathy or misunderstanding of the work, contact the teacher. It is much easier to catch up if the problem is caught early.

For a student having trouble with schoolwork because of laziness or inattention, consider making a written contract with him—that specifies what is expected of him concerning a particular course. The terms of the contract should include exactly what is to be achieved and when, what will be granted for success or removed for failure, and that there will be no nagging by the parent and no grumbling by the student.

The field of research is one aspect where a parent can help: teach how to find answers at home, at the library, or on the Internet, using reference books and the computer, and how to restate information without plagiarizing.

For most students, experts suggest the order of homework should be math, writing, nonfiction reading, science projects, fiction reading.

Establish the 48-Hour Rule: Two days before a large project or book report is due, it is to be shown to a parent. When a youngster faces this type of in-depth project, encourage him to work on it a little each week, rather than try to do it all in one night.

Don't let homework time be a dreary time. Recommend a midpoint break for a game, shower, or relaxation (not television). Surprise a child doing homework by bringing snacks (such as hot chocolate and crackers) to her room.

HOMOSEXUALITY. *See also AIDS, Sex, Teasing.*

When youngsters begin to mature, they sometimes experiment with a friend of the same sex: holding hands, kissing, fondling, and so forth. This does not necessarily mean that you are rearing a gay or lesbian child. However, these prelude activities to sex are topics that parents must discuss with youngsters. Religion and ethics play a part in approving or disapproving of homosexual activities. A child needs to know that a parent will always love and support him but this can be a hard road for a parent to follow.

In talking about this subject, parents should also point out some of the dangers of escalating these relationships, dangers that include sexually transmitted diseases (STDs) and rejection by some members of society. Sometimes school or religious counselors can provide factual information on the subject. But above all, a parent's loving concern for the well-being of the child should come first.

Parents should not hesitate to share their personal opinions on subjects such as premarital sex. And they should rear children to be tolerant and free from hatred of anyone.

HONESTY. *See also Ethics, Lying.*

Honesty is one of the most important character traits for a successful home and business life. For preschool children, lies and fantasy are closely related—wishes can masquerade as reality. Only when youngsters are older do they learn how to employ the manipulation of an out-and-out lie.

Start with toddlers to reward honesty and lightly punish dishonesty. Explain that telling the truth is part of being a good person. Compliment the courage to tell the truth when a fib might cover the situation. When you must punish, make the point that punishment is always less when the truth is told. Encourage children to abide by what they say they'll do by using the phrase: "I give you my word that I'll do it."

Older youngsters need stiffer punishments for lying since it becomes more prevalent in the preteen and teen years. By now, they are aware of the dishonesty in the world that goes on unchecked, some of it even by their parents. A parent's word should be truthful. Don't live with a double standard; both parents and children need to be completely honest. Sloppy ethics by parents is mimicked by children.

Discuss these hypothetical cases and what kids might do in these instances:

- Finding money on the sidewalk
- Seeing a friend copying another student's homework or cheating on a test
- Seeing parents bringing home office supplies or items from work or from hotel stays
- Telling white lies so as not to hurt another's feelings
- Shoplifting, even when dared to do it
- Lying about age when buying tickets or looking for a job
- Making a plan on how to buy drugs and use them secretly
- Exceeding the speed limit or going through a red light, when no one is around
- Pretending to put money in the church collection but instead keeping it
- Sneaking out of the house or lying about where one is going to be when out

 When you sense that you are not being told the truth, ask the youngster to tell again what happened, or write it out. This often brings the facts to the surface. Get to the cause of a lie and you can remove the need to lie.

Don't magnify the guilt of dishonesty by bringing it up again and again. When the incident is over, it is over. However, do say "I trust you not to do that again." Don't make a child promise to never tell another lie, but do express the hope that he will be more honest in the future.

HUGS. *See also Love, Touching.*

Teach and use a variety of hugs. Sometimes just being held close is all that is needed to heal a hurt. Hug arms, knees, heads, and bodies.

Teach children to use the symbol for a hug. Clench the fist (closing your fingers) and then tuck the thumb behind the little finger. Make hugs a part of your family greeting and parting all through time. Hugs are low energy with high yield, pesticide free and inflation-proof, nonfattening, nontaxable, and fully refundable!

HUMBLENESS. *See Humility, Pride, Self-Worth.*

HUMILIATION. *See also Abuse, Shame.*

Degrading a child has no place in parenting; it is really a form of child abuse. Conversations and actions that put down and erode self-worth can cause depression. A child can be corrected or punished most effectively without humiliation because shame takes the focus off the wrong that was done and turns it inward.

For example, if a young child wets his pants, making him remain in that condition is degrading. While the child's mistake can be frustrating to a parent, the humiliation only compounds the problem and solves nothing since the degradation overshadows the cause and possible solution. A parent should employ patience and turn the focus to some positive activity until steps are found to correct the problem.

Never use words or actions that make a child feel unimportant, terribly embarrassed, or unloved. Your job is not to goad, but rather to guide, and humiliation has no part in it.

HUMILITY. *See also Bragging, Gratitude.*

This term includes modesty, the ability to apologize, and gratitude. How refreshing to have a child who doesn't vaunt her achievements. A humble child knows who she is, what good things she has done, and doesn't need to have them validated by others. Cultivate this admirable quality in your kids by giving them opportunities to excel. When she has done something successfully, ask her how she feels. Tell her that this good feeling is hers, even when others don't notice. However, as her parent, do try to recognize each of her triumphs.

Teach children that they are each different from others, that they excel in some areas, but are not superior to all others. As an example, tell when you have achieved something good and acknowledge the help and inspiration you received from others.

 A humble person does not brag, take all the credit, put down others, or insist on always being first or right.

 A humble person makes others feel good, shares their glory, and shows her concern for others.

It takes great humility to say you're sorry when you've done something wrong. And it takes even greater humility to apologize when others say that you've made a mistake when you honestly believe you have not.

Contrarily, when a youngster has achieved something good, don't let him get by with the saying "It was nothing," when it really was something. He should quietly acknowledge the good that has come to him and also say thank you. And, when youngsters are downcast, play the "Glad Game," taking turns sharing good experiences from the past.

HUMOR. *See also April Fool's Day, Fun.*

The things that youngsters find funny indicate their level of development. While toddlers giggle over funny words and young children adore riddles, some teens unfortunately prefer off-color jokes.

A good, clean sense of humor lifts mental health. More than entertainment, it helps youngsters weather sad or discouraging situations. We love to see babies smile and laugh and should encourage humorous occasions as kids get older: funny faces, silly costumes, corny riddles and jokes, satire and mimicry, and the repetition of funny situations. Be sure to laugh about things you do and encourage others with your laughter.

Don't permit a child to be a tease or a smart aleck. Most teasing is degrading, but some poking fun can be funny if the recipient can poke right back. Profanity is never funny despite the fact that certain comedians make a good living from it. It is still a cheap and degrading form of humor.

Make fun moments in the everyday routine. Singing off key in the shower, hopping like a bunny to the breakfast table, telling a funny story at supper, friendly tussling before bed are simple but amusing activities.

Keep foremost in thought that family life should consist of happy times and those times can be occasions for good humor.

HURRIED CHILD. *See also Early Learning, Gifted Children.*

While most children grow up achieving walking, talking, toilet training, bike riding, reading, sports skills, and so forth at age-appropriate times, others are encouraged to accomplish these things early, sometimes earlier than any other child. Often this is the work of a proud parent with a first child who wants to prove that his child is the most talented.

Unfortunately, this child is hurried through childhood, always pushed to higher goals, and in many cases not enjoying important activities suitable for his own age. Research shows that most hurried children don't remain ahead of their peers for more than a few years. While there are some child geniuses, an average child's progression allows for him to bring together physical, mental, social, and emotional skills so that he is ready for the next step of progress. The hurried child may miss some of these essential developments.

Parental expectation should not push a child to the point where he does not have the time to enjoy life right where he is on the time continuum.

HYPERACTIVITY. *See also ADD/ADHD.*

Overactivity can be a problem in itself, or one that accompanies attention deficit disorder (ADD) or attention deficit hyperactive disorder (ADHD). Not every very active child should be labeled ADD or ADHD. Although children vary in their level of physical activity, all young children, and especially boys, can be very active to the point of distressing and exhausting their parents.

Some youngsters however are so excessively active that it exceeds the natural exuberance of childhood. These children are in constant motion, never staying with one activity for more than a few minutes. They often fail to stop when requested and their actions are independent of parental suggestions or punishment. Teachers find it difficult to direct their activity or get them to focus on one task for a length of time sufficient to learn. And often their busyness is disruptive to other children trying to learn.

Behavior modification techniques and restructuring home and school activities will do much to bring this under control. A change in diet can also be helpful, especially cutting back on excessive sweets. While medicines can be prescribed to reduce overactivity, calm directions, nonstimulating projects and games, and extreme patience can also bring lasting results without the side effects of drugs. Be alert and get professional help if you are not succeeding in conquering this challenge.

"I" STATEMENTS. *See also "Me Time," Parenting Skills.*

Parents often zero in on how children are acting and feeling and they overuse the word "you." "You were naughty." "You need to eat your spinach." "You must pick up your toys." Most children will better respond if you turn these into "I" statements that show how *you* feel: "I was sad when you hit your sister." "I worked hard to make that vegetable taste good." "I would enjoy playing a game with you when you've tidied the play room."

Remember, the child is not the center of the home; the entire family of parents and children together is the focal point.

IDENTITY. *See Individuality.*

ILLNESS. *See Diseases, Health.*

IMMUNIZATIONS. *See also Diseases, Health.*

Certain immunizations are often required for infants, school-age children, and for foreign travel. If you are going to have these, choose a time when the family schedule is not busy in the days that follow. Reactions can occur and one or more days of illness may result. Certainly check any unusual reaction with your health care professional. There are also exemptions available on the application forms for those who do not wish (or should not have) these immunizations.

INCENTIVES. *See Charts for Chores.*

INDEPENDENCE. *See also Choices, Rules, Self-Government.*

Independence is not a one-day declaration made as a youngster goes off for college or career. Parents sometimes impede the desirable progress toward independence by kindling unnecessary fears about the first day of school or the first date.

Youngsters learn how to act independently when parents give toddlers to teens opportunities to be in charge of specific activities. A child will become independent if given an environment that has some routine to it, but also has opportunities for adventurous choices—decisions that can result in mistakes. The opportunity to safely make a mistake, assess it, and come up with another choice fosters independence.

Involve youngsters in developing family rules and parameters so that they feel they have a say in how independent they can be. Gradually teach the skills of money management, care of possessions and clothing, house maintenance, minor car repairs, and simple cooking so that you are not sending a naive babe out into the world.

Let each child practice independence by being a "parent" for a day. Let her choose what foods to eat, games to play, chores to do, television shows to see, time to go to bed. Being in charge teaches the youngster to be fair, since she knows a sibling will be in charge another day.

INDEPENDENCE DAY.

One of the happiest holidays, July 4, features food and fireworks. If your neighborhood doesn't have a parade, organize one with bicycles and buggies, dogs and drums. Make the food special by making red/white/blue potato salad (add red pimientos, and use food coloring to make the celery blue), add a thin slice of cooked steak in the bun beside each wiener and hold it in place with cooked bacon, serve red and blue Jell-O squares with whipped cream, and end with a birthday cake with candles in honor of the nation. Be sure to have a good speaker tell the dramatic story of how our country became independent.

INDIVIDUAL EDUCATION PLAN—IEP. *See also Education.*

For children who are average in some areas, but are behind in others, the school will devise an Individual Education Plan. This may involve mainstreaming in many subjects but tutoring or special education in others. If your child is falling behind in some classes, inquire about an IEP that can bring him up to par.

INDIVIDUALITY.

The uniqueness of each person, adult or child, is exciting because of the myriad possibilities. No two people, not even identical twins, are exactly alike. Discovering the individuality of your child is one of the adventures of parenting. Sometimes it is obviously apparent; sometimes it is well hidden.

This is why you give children a variety of experiences so you and they can discover their distinct talents, likes, and dreams. Refrain from verbally or mentally using labels to describe a child, labels such as "Clown," "Princess," "Genius," or "Macho-man." Quietly observe individuality and how it evolves (and over time you may note that the clown becomes the genius). Never underestimate a youngster's ability to grow and develop, since some children are early achievers while others are late bloomers. Whichever they are, they deserve a parent's loving, nonjudgmental support along the path to maturity.

INQUISITIVENESS. *See Intelligence.*

INTEGRITY. *See Character Building, Ethics, Honesty.*

INTELLIGENCE. *See also Gifted Children.*

Creative thinking, inquisitiveness, and wisdom combine to make an intelligent child. Teach youngsters that a satisfying and successful life is usually based on diligent study and work. Amassing knowledge is not as valuable as applying knowledge.

Youngsters develop intelligence at different rates, and often in spurts, so never put down a child's intelligence. Don't ever label him (in your words or your thoughts) as slow, as this can be a self-fulfilling prophecy that may take years to overcome. This doesn't mean that you ignore a child's educational problems, but be patient and get help when needed. Early tutoring is important since problems are easier to solve before they become ingrained.

Research shows that children who are talked to, touched, and questioned develop intelligence 40 percent faster than those who grow up in an atmosphere that lacks caring and stimulation. Negative communication can destroy intellect, so avoid verbal put-downs such as "It was dumb to do that." "Figure it out yourself." "Don't argue with me about it, just do it." "Put away this game since you're not following the directions." Instead, help youngsters find answers, show the reasoning behind your commands, and permit creative play that may not be according to the so-called rules of the game.

To nurture intellect, consider these important points:

141

- Teach a love of reading—the single most important skill for a smart child.
- Communicate—ask questions that require more than a yes or no answer.
- Encourage a youngster to think through problems and suggest solutions.
- Cut back on television viewing by offering attractive alternatives.
- Carefully select gifts that foster creativity—drawing materials, chemistry sets, or building sets.
- Purchase a current encyclopedia and dictionary and be eager to look up topics.
- Provide a quiet atmosphere for doing homework.
- Take children to the library, plays, museums, and musical events as often as to movies and amusement parks.
- Encourage a variety of lessons in sports, music, and drama, leaving free time for creative play.
- Make learning fun by working together each week on an all-family project such as building a tree house or putting together a puzzle.
- Be a good example—keep learning yourself by reading, taking a class, doing creative activities at home.
- Show you value your child's intellect. Make grades important and help a youngster improve them, support school activities, be aware of large school assignments.
- Be alert to signs of boredom or discouragement and take action.
- Talk about the value of a good education and a strong intellect.

INTERACTION. *See also Conflict, Sharing.*

Life is a series of interactions between people of all ages and personalities. From toddlerhood onward, show youngsters how to effectively deal with others with respect and interest. With very shy children actually practice meeting and talking with pretend guests. Talk about how to solve conflicts and teach how to work together as a democratic group. Unless you want your youngster to grow up to be a hermit, teach the ability to interact effectively.

INVITATIONS. *See also Manners, Parties.*

One of the signs of boorishness is the inability to handle an invitation. Starting with the first birthday party invitation, show children the importance of responding. The response should be timely and definite (never "I'll *try* to come"). If a written response is expected to a more formal invitation, do so within five days of receiving it or definitely before the requested RSVP date. And, if you have said you will attend, do not change your mind if you suddenly get a more attractive invitation. Entertaining is expensive and no-shows cost money. Of course, if an emergency arises, the youngster should notify the host as soon as possible.

Accepting an invitation usually means that the child will extend an invitation in return. If your child finds she does not wish to entertain a certain child in return, she should not accept any further invitations from that child. People who never entertain in return are uncouth freeloaders.

Invitations are usually only to the person addressed, and if the recipient wishes to bring additional people with her, she must call the host for permission.

 Never let a child take party invitations to deliver at school unless the entire class is being invited.

IRREVERENCE. *See Respect.*

JOBS. *See also Career Choices, Chores.*

With homework, family activities, and work around the home, few teens should have the time for a part-time job. However, circumstances may make it necessary for a youngster to work. Many families find that they can save money by hiring their own child for home maintenance tasks (beyond regular chores that are done free of charge). If possible, a weekend job, or a job that allows time for daily homework is better. But best is a full-time summer job that provides the needed funds for the coming school year. Summer job experience is good preparation for joining the workforce later as it teaches working with others, promptness, responsibility, following orders, and when to use initiative.

JOURNALS. *See Diaries.*

JOY. *See Happiness.*

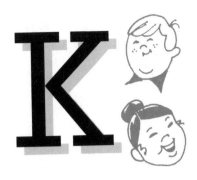

KICKING. *See also Anger, Conflict, Fighting.*

Kicking is good exercise for babies, but it is a bad habit for older children who lose their tempers. When a toddler first kicks at a playmate or parent, take him aside and explain that this is unacceptable behavior. Find out the cause and explain other ways of achieving his aim. If it continues, initiate strict punishment so that the child sees that kicking is not worth it.

KILLING. *See also Guns, Video Games.*

Teach the value of life, whether it is of a bird or a person. There is no need for killing activities or play in a child's life. And, there is no need for killing toys or equipment. Since the mind can only absorb so much, see that your child does not fill it with violence. Prohibit playing video or arcade games based on killing. Speak up against the casual approach to ending a life as shown in many movies and television shows.

Parents in many neighborhoods are now working together to provide a neighborhood free of violence, war games, and make-believe killing toys. If all families prohibit these, they will not become a "normal" part of a child's life.

KINDERGARTEN. *See also School: First Day, Separation Anxiety.*

Kindergarten differs from preschool which focuses on physical care, play, and socialization. Most kindergarten training emphasizes very basic learning skills, listening, working as a group, following orders, and recognizing numbers and letters. This education leads into the important work of first grade, which centers on learning to read.

Ease children into kindergarten by visiting the school in advance, seeing the classroom and playground, and meeting the teacher if possible. Talk eagerly about starting kindergarten and provide a comfortable first-day outfit and all the requested materials. Some youngsters find it easier to start kindergarten if they can go with a friend. Plan a special dinner that night to celebrate the first day.

KINDNESS. *See Caring, Service.*

KISSING. *See also Love, Touching.*

It seems normal to kiss babies, but kissing family members and others lessens with each succeeding year. (Romantic teens are the exception when they become interested in the opposite sex.)

Don't let strangers give wet mouth kisses to babies; hugs or a gentle closed-mouth kiss on the cheek are much better. Never force youngsters to kiss aunties or others. Show them how to give good hearty hugs, cheek to cheek.

Family kisses can become a natural and normal way of saying hello, good-bye, and goodnight and a response to exciting news.

LABOR DAY.

This holiday that often falls at the start of the school year can be a sad time since it signals the end of summer. Change this into a special time honoring both work and play. Decide on one large family labor project for the weekend—for example fence painting or garage cleaning. While working, talk about labor and professions, trade and trade unions, the kinds of jobs that friends have, and the job aspirations of the youngsters in the family. Then, when the work project is finished, it's time to play.

One family celebrates Labor Day with a traditional activity. They consider the sunrise as a symbol of the dawn of a new school season. With a breakfast picnic prepared the night before, they gather on the highest hill in their area in advance of the sunrise. Sitting in the dark on blankets, they watch for the first sign of light and then give a shout as a crescent of sun appears. When the sun clears the horizon, they picnic on foods the colors of the sun: orange segments, hard-boiled eggs, sweet rolls, and pineapple juice. Then it's home for the great Labor Day barbecue or beach party.

LANGUAGE. *See also Profanity, Speech, Words.*

Language is a mirror of one's education, culture, background, and interests. Language mastery is an educated skill and starts with day one of a child's life. Even to babies, speak clearly and pronounce words correctly. Children learn what they hear, whether it is bad grammar, profanity, street slang, hurtful phrases, or caring and distinct speech.

Teach your young child this basic twenty-five word/phrase vocabulary: yes, no, maybe, please, thank you, now, later, today, tomorrow, come, sit, stop, help, ask, tell, share, give, follow, pick up, quiet, up, down, hello, good-bye, and I love you.

When children grow older, draw a firm line between slang and acceptable language. See that the school teaches good grammar and pronunciation and does not permit trash talk in the classroom or on the playing field.

Encourage the early study of a second language that will be useful in daily life. The study of Latin is becoming popular once again as it greatly increases vocabulary. Practice kindness in speech within the family, language that helps rather than hurts.

 Parents should avoid these lines:
You never do anything right!
Who do you think you are?
Because I said so!
You think you're so smart!
Can't you see I'm busy?
How stupid!
Where did you get those clothes?
I never change my mind.
How many times do I have to tell you?
That's final—you can't go!
Just see if I ever let you borrow it again.
No one loves a naughty child.

 Instead, practice these lines:
That's okay, you tried.
Here's a little extra cash.
You have our permission.
I'm glad you're mine!
We trust you.
I couldn't wait to hear your voice!
Let's see if we can fix it together.
What a great idea.
You don't have to clean up tonight.
I miss you.
How do you suggest we do it?
No one else could have done it as well!
You can stay out thirty minutes later tonight since you've been so responsible.
I love you no matter what.

 Youngsters should avoid these words:
You never understand!
How come I never get to?
I hate you.
I could never learn that.

I'm telling!
Why do I have to do all this stuff?
It's going to cost more than I said.
I know something you don't know.
Shut up!
It's not my turn.
I hate this food.
But everyone else is doing it.
Not now, I'll do it later.

 Better are these lines from kids:
What can I do to help?
I like just being with you.
Thanks a lot.
I'll think about what you said.
I guess you're right.
Yes.
I love you.
You look nice.
I have a nice surprise for you.
I understand what you mean.
I want you to see my report card.
That's a good idea!
I'm willing to try again.
This isn't as bad as I thought it would be.
Thanks for your help.

Find opportunities to use these good lines each day and see how quickly your family can improve its language skills when they rule out the bad lines.

LATCHKEY CHILDREN. *See also After-School Activities.*

Youngsters who return from school to an empty house need guidance and reassurance. Research shows that latch-key children tend to waste time, feel bored or lonely, and have lower self-esteem. So it is important to be specific in your instructions about what to do along with your safety instructions. Make it an everyday practice to call home and make sure that your youngster is confident and happily occupied.

If at all possible, don't leave children under twelve alone after school; find a neighbor, friend, or club that can safely care for them. Maturity and responsibility is a better gauge than age.

149

Leave a detailed written or recorded message about things to do: play, homework, chores, starting supper. Your message might say: "See if you can finish the jigsaw puzzle! Get a start on your math. Please exercise Fido. Put the potatoes in the oven at 5 P.M., 375 degrees. Love, Mom." It only takes a minute to make a new message for each afternoon.

If you are an at-home parent, include latchkey children in play at your house.

LAUNDRY. *See also Chores.*

Show young children how to put dirty clothes in a hamper or in the laundry room. When they are about eight, teach them how to use the washer and dryer, sort clothes, and with your supervision treat some hard-to-remove spots. Let younger kids fold clean clothing and deliver it to bedrooms. Show preteens how clothes are ironed and talk about the importance of selecting clothes in fabrics that require minimum care.

As a regular weekly chore, let one responsible youngster be the chairman of doing laundry. As a lesson to family members, give permission for him to keep or dispose of any items left in pockets: candy, tissues, money, and so forth.

LAUGHTER. *See also Humor.*

Laughter is essential to happy family life. Share stories of funny happenings and retell them through the years. Tell good jokes, and if you don't know any, borrow a joke book from the library or buy a joke-a-day calendar. Keep it at the breakfast table and start this meal with laughter. When you do something silly or stupid, share it with the family and be ready to laugh at yourself. Laughter can smooth some of the lumps in daily life!

LAZINESS. *See also Apathy, Boredom, Determination.*

Unless there is a health problem, don't permit a child to adopt lazy habits such as daytime sleep, living in rubbish, forgetting assignments, and so forth. Withdraw desired privileges (such as a later bedtime, telephone use, car borrowing, computer game play) until the laziness is corrected. Attack apathy early and often with young children so it does not become a serious problem when they are teens.

LEADERSHIP. *See also Character Building, Choices, Poise.*

A child learns to be a leader by following good examples of people who are dynamic, yet still willing to listen to the ideas of others. Give youngsters opportunities to be leaders in groups such as Camp Fire and Scouts, but most of all at home.

Let a youngster be the leader on a family hike, in organizing a game to play, in planning a party, in seeing that all family members complete their daily chores, in training the dog, in making an audio tape for the grandparents, or in teaching computer skills to younger siblings.

Part of being a good leader is understanding the important place of followers, so also give youngsters chances to work under the direction of others who lead with creativity, orderliness, and kindness.

Children who are constantly told and reminded what to do never learn how to lead responsibly. Nor do they learn respect for leadership since their experience is limited to domination or bossiness. Parents can correct this by offering fair guidance and by sharing leadership opportunities in the home.

LEARNING SKILLS. *See also Education.*

Support the school by reinforcing at home the skills of how to concentrate, how to pick out facts, how to retain knowledge, how to recall it, and how to access knowledge sources. As soon as a youngster can read fluently, show him how to use a dictionary, encyclopedia, and thesaurus. Have up-to-date books or computer disks in the place where he studies.

Practice memory work by learning words to popular or patriotic songs as well as well-known prose and poetry. Provide time for creative thinking. Insist on good grammar and spelling in homework and in written projects at home. Keep learning skills honed during vacation times so going back to school won't be a huge struggle.

LEFT-HANDEDNESS.

Since the media has emphasized the great number of lefties who have excelled, it is no longer a stigma to be left-handed. The chief disadvantage of being left-handed is bumping elbows at a crowded dining table!

Do not force a child to prefer one hand over another. Simply observe which hand she favors when picking up a toy or a spoon. Never permit educators to attempt to switch a left-handed child to be right-handed as this can cause speech problems.

While there are shops with equipment created just for left-handers, most of this is unnecessary. As an example, most lefties are able to use regular scissors and many can switch to the right side when playing golf rather than purchase an expensive set of left-handed clubs. Schools are gradually providing desks with writing arms on the left side that are more comfortable for lefties.

LESSONS. *See also Dance, Extracurricular Activities, Music.*

Be aware of the many different kinds of lessons available, not just piano and ballet. Before starting lessons of any kind, investigate carefully, talk about commitment, practice time, and cost. If you thoroughly discuss these with the student-to-be, the instrument or special shoes will not be gathering dust in the attic six months later. Consider renting instruments or joining a school group that provides instruments. Sometimes letting a child pay 10 percent of the cost will bring about greater dedication.

For practice time, supply a timer so that kids know how long to practice. Permit one day off during the week, but no more. Ask for a recital the day before the next lesson so you can observe what has been learned.

An important aspect of lessons is recitals—giving youngsters the opportunity to express poise while showing their accomplishments. Be sure that family members attend major recitals. A nice touch is to present the performer with one rose after the program.

LIBRARY. *See also Books, Reading.*

A weekly trip to a library plus a minimum of thirty minutes of reading each day will provide youngsters with wonderful views of both real and imaginary worlds. As soon as a child can read and write, make it a special occasion to apply for his own library card. Provide a special shelf in a child's room for borrowed books and see that they are returned on time and in good condition.

Encourage attendance at library storytelling hours and other special events for children. If the library is within biking distance, permit an older youngster to borrow and return books on his own. Most libraries will provide a list of recommended books for various age groups. Look over this list together, see what books he has already read (and any you have read) and note what books he wishes to borrow next. A library trip can be enjoyable for several youngsters going together with one parent.

It is sometimes hard for a youngster to start a new book, but once he's started reading, he's eager to continue. To start a book, let him begin reading it at the library before going home; or, have him read the opening chapter to a parent doing a household task.

LISTENING. *See also Communication.*

The taller the child, the less she listens or so goes the saying. Some parents even begin to wonder if the youngster has a hearing problem. (And if you truly suspect this, get professional help immediately.)

Even when we listen to a child, the words we hear may not be the real message a child is sending. A sharing/listening/responding relationship is indispensable to a child's confidence in her identity as a member of the family and the community. While child/peer listening often includes judging, child/parent listening should include perceptiveness and love. Just the willingness of an adult to listen bolsters a child's sense of worth.

When talking with a child, try to maintain eye contact since that helps both of you focus on the subject. When you are talking to a small child, get on her level by sitting on the floor or holding her. Avoid the "I'm bigger and more important than you" stance since this intimidating position can blot out the message being given.

Teach children to listen by giving verbal instructions, simple ones at first, and then build up to more complicated ones. It's simple to get the frying pan out; it's more complicated to fry an egg. It's simple to put the broken toy on the work bench, it's more complicated to glue it. Start with just one instruction and then increase the number of steps in the instruction. It helps if you have a youngster repeat the message you've just given to show how well she listened to everything you said. Don't remind her of your message unless she asks you to repeat it. Encourage her to fully listen the first time.

Show the results of listening: "Because you listened you finished on time and have time for play." Or, "Because you listened you didn't have to pay a library fine." Or, "Because you didn't listen at breakfast, you didn't know we were going to meet for ice cream after school."

 Vow that during your parenting years you will never use the phrase "Shut up."

 Do say, "That's so important and since I'm busy now, let's talk about it after supper." Or, "I'm interested in what you have to say." Or, "I'm always willing to hear your side of the problem." Or, "I'll listen as soon as I'm off the telephone."

LITERATURE. *See Books, Library, Reading.*

LIVING TOGETHER. *See also AIDS, Parenting Skills.*

Living together before marriage is a fad that has failed to bring about better relationships. Breakups are just as difficult. A sense of loyalty is lost. Health is endangered in cases where there are multiple sex partners.

The excuse for cohabitation used to be "We want to see if we're compatible." Well, there are many ways to find out how well a couple gets along without moving in together. And there is more to "getting along" than sexual compatibility. There is love, friendship, comfort, loyalty, and experiencing both similar and separate interests. While society seems to accept cohabitation, research doesn't back it up as a smart alternative. Living together increases the risk of divorce by 46 percent and also greatly increases the risk of domestic violence and abuse. Unfortunately, living together often produces children who grow up confused as to the importance of marriage and fidelity. Compared to children of parents who married before they were born, children born of cohabiting couples who later marry are twice as likely to face the trauma of seeing their parents divorce. Thus, the risks of marriage are much less than the risks of not being married and living together.

If your teen and her boyfriend want to live together, suggest some alternatives to try first, such as waiting six months. "Playing house" sounds attractive but paying the bills and doing the dishes is best when a couple has a commitment based on a reasonably long history of working and playing together.

Hesitancy about getting married seems to stem from seeing and hearing so much about divorce and figuring that a "test-drive" might be an option. Actually the best solution is far greater marriage education, teaching that covers the subjects of compatibility, solving problems, rearing children, money management, equality, and life goals.

LONELINESS. *See also Only Children, Self-Worth.*

Loneliness can be the result of fear of rejection, failure, or ridicule. Still, children need socialization to succeed in school and career. This is taught in the family and also in groups such as Camp Fire and Scouts. Encourage a shy child to choose one group activity, with the idea that the trial will be for just six months. Make the surroundings familiar (at church, school, club, or by having meetings at your house so the child is familiar with at least one other child in the group).

Be watchful of a youngster who prefers being alone. While some loners are deeply intellectual, others are apathetic about making relationships. But worst of all, some loners have dark and dangerous inner feelings of resentment against certain people or groups. If you know a youngster who seems to manifest unhealthy loneliness, see what you can do to get him professional help.

A pen pal, or a *carefully chosen* e-mail friend, can ease loneliness.

While not a substitute for a friend, a parent can frequently soothe the lonely child by doing a craft together, reading together on a regular basis, or planning an excursion on which a child can take an acquaintance.

While a sense of loneliness can be cured, learning to be happily alone is a valuable asset for any child. A child needs a "do nothing" time each day when he can get away from everyone and enjoy his own room, a secret hideout in a tree, or a quiet time in a hot tub. Parents need this alone time, too. Having time alone teaches self-sufficiency to a child. Of course, you want children to interact with others, but learning to be content when alone is a great asset.

See that the daily schedule allows time alone and encourages a youngster to take time to just think or read. Consider these other alone activities: writing a letter, making a scrapbook, putting together a model kit, trying a new recipe, rearranging a bedroom, sewing, composing a poem, repairing something broken, experimenting with a hair style, jogging around the house, teaching the dog a trick, painting, planting seeds, making popcorn, reading a magazine, reorganizing a cupboard or desk, looking at a photo album, listening to a recording, looking up at the clouds. (Note that watching television is not listed.)

LOVE. *See also Hate, Hugs, Kissing, Sibling Rivalry, Touching.*

Love is affection with principle. Don't confuse love with permissiveness. When a baby is born, parents usually find it easy to love the child. But, the physical expression of this love decreases a little each year, to the point that it can be almost nonexistent in the teen and adult years. So, it is important to keep love alive through everyday words and deeds and by asking friendly questions about what a youngster is doing and feeling. In books and movies, point out examples of kindness and love. Don't overlook these lessons learned about consideration. Let your love radiate outward through caring activities in the community to seniors, those not feeling well, and to others in need.

Teach youngsters from the time they are little to be caring of others. In teaching this important quality, don't hesitate to use the word "love." Don't be ashamed of love. Giving and receiving love is the most important aspect of parenting.

Start the day by holding hands around the breakfast table and squeezing the hand next to you three times for "I love you!" Don't let a day pass without expressing love to a child.

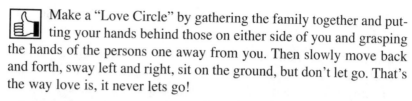 Make a "Love Circle" by gathering the family together and putting your hands behind those on either side of you and grasping the hands of the persons one away from you. Then slowly move back and forth, sway left and right, sit on the ground, but don't let go. That's the way love is, it never lets go!

Suggest love names for family members, ones they can use within the family. These could be names like: honey-bun, dearie, cutie baby, love-bug, darling, little one, bunnykins, doll, hubby-bear, sweetheart, or sweetie-pie.

Consider adopting a child by mail through one of the many organizations who can connect you with a child who needs your care. You will give money each month, but also send letters of love and encouragement.

Family bands (flat rings) can be symbols of unconditional, unbroken love. Take youngsters to a shop that has good but inexpensive rings. Let each pick out one. A girl may want to wear hers on a finger, a boy will usually prefer to put his on a key chain or notebook ring. If asked, a child can say, "It's our family ring." The simple band will represent an everlasting bond.

When family members are going to be separated, choose a specific time for each of you to send loving *thoughts* to one another—a convenient time during the lunch hour or before bed. Or, in the evening, the two separated people can look up at a certain star and remember the love of the other.

Have a secret word to use on letters or over the phone. One such word is RILY, which is an acronym for "Remember I Love You."

Encourage good deeds done in secret. Exchange names and be a secret friend for another family member: putting a cartoon in a lunch bag, making someone's bed, taking out the trash without being asked. See who can do a secret deed each day without getting caught.

Utilize "Warm Fuzzies," the name for notes of love and encouragement from parent to child. These can be as long as a sonnet or letter or as short as a phrase. Leave a "warm fuzzie" in a drawer, on a mirror, in a pocket, or under the bed pillow.

156

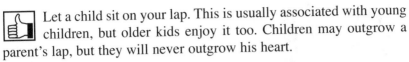 Let a child sit on your lap. This is usually associated with young children, but older kids enjoy it too. Children may outgrow a parent's lap, but they will never outgrow his heart.

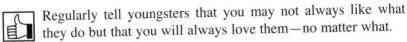 Regularly tell youngsters that you may not always like what they do but that you will always love them—no matter what.

For more ideas, read *365 Ways to Love Your Child* (Caryl Krueger, Abingdon Press, distributed by Belleridge Press, Escondido, Calif.).

LOYALTY. *See also Character Building.*

Being true to oneself and one's family is admirable. Loyalty includes not sharing private family business with others, putting family first in most cases, speaking positively about family and homeland, and expressing love, no matter what. A steadfast person is not only loyal when things are going well, but also during difficult times.

LULLABIES. *See also Music.*

Singing soothes, whether the babe is still in the womb or fretting on your shoulder. Soft music (in traditional, pop, country, or soft rock style), along with rocking or swaying helps calm a baby. Later, let toddlers sing lullabies along with you.

LUNCH. *See also Mealtimes, Nutrition.*

The midday meal is important since it provides the energy to accomplish all the varied afternoon activities. Actually it's a healthy idea to have a substantial lunch and a lighter supper, but this is usually not possible for a school child.

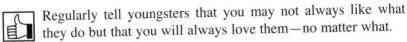 Consider these lunch ideas that also pack well: A tuna-stuffed tomato with crackers and cheese, a fruit smoothie with oatmeal cookies, a thermos of soup and cornbread, veggies with different dips. For school lunches, add a surprise: a cartoon or comic strip, a small puzzle, a caring message inside the paper napkin or on it, a small heart carved in the apple skin, a little person made of marshmallows and gum drops.

LYING. *See Gossip, Honesty.*

MAGAZINES. *See also Reading.*

The thrill of getting mail is enhanced by a magazine subscription that comes each month and provides good reading and activities for youngsters. Specialized magazines for younger children have stories, photos, contests, and games. Several fine ones focus on the outdoors. For preteens and teens, a parent should be alert to magazines that encourage growing up too fast, that feature impractical clothing or diet fads, and tout depressingly thin models. Before subscribing, get a single copy and look it over carefully together.

MAKE-BELIEVE.

Creative play knows no age limits. Make sure young children know the difference between make-believe and reality—this will help allay some of their fears of giants or flying bicycles. Encourage make-believe with a dress-up trunk or box by assigning parts and helping them act out a story. Pretend that dolls and animals can talk. Create a city of blocks, vehicles, and figures and then create situations to play out. Let older children write simple plays to act out with puppets.

MAKEUP. *See also Appearance.*

Set an age when a girl can wear makeup—possibly at age twelve. But well before that time, talk about what looks natural and what looks cheap or bizarre. Read magazines together to see how makeup is carefully applied. Look at the effect of makeup up close and also at a distance. When a youngster starts to wear makeup, talk about how to remove it in order to keep the skin clear and blemish free. If a child has a skin problem, get professional help on how to clear it up, but also on how to safely cover it up in the meantime.

 If you permit any makeup for young girls, see that it doesn't make them look older than is proper for them. And, if you permit fingernail polish, insist on it being removed as soon as it chips.

Stores will give complimentary makeup advice and some will even refund the cost of cosmetics that don't result in the desired effect. Help your teen set a budget for cosmetics so that purchases are not just left idle in drawers. Show how makeup differs in everyday situations as opposed to stage presentations when the viewers are farther away.

And remember that sunblock is one of the best products to apply to the skin for a lifetime of beauty and protection.

MANIPULATION.

Learning how to "manage" a parent starts as young as toddlerhood. Youngsters often try to make a deal to ease rules, punishments, or other parameters. It may seem cute at first and a parent can be amazed at how clever the tiny toddler is, but after a while, the parent realizes that the youngster is gradually taking over the job of parenting. Of course you want to give kids choices, but there are some areas that are not open to manipulative negotiation no matter how sweet the smile or how pitiful the protestations.

Be sure to give youngsters some areas in which you feel comfortable in giving them total charge, and be sure you do not manipulate their decisions in these situations.

Don't give in to wily methods. Perhaps a parent has told a child to eat a reasonable amount of a vegetable. The child dawdles, then tries to make a deal to eat only half of it. The parent gives in and soon the child is bargaining to eat only one-quarter of it. Stand by your original request. Or perhaps, a youngster comes home later than the designated time and has some lame excuse. Merely say "I'm sorry the traffic was heavy; you should have allowed for it."

Some youngsters refuse to do anything without wheedling, whining, or procrastinating in hopes the parent will give in. This manipulation results in a lazy, selfish child and an already busy parent who ends up feeding the dog, picking up the toys, correcting the homework.

If you feel a youngster should be able to accomplish a certain task or requirement, don't permit his bartering it down to some lesser goal. Once you start giving in, it will become the chosen way of acting for the youngster. Manipulators don't make good students, good friends, or good employees.

MANLINESS.

With the entire family, explain the difference between masculinity and macho. A man can be caring, appreciative, and loving without being wimpish. Good manners, a well-modulated voice and descriptive vocabulary, and considering others are manly attributes as opposed to a big-mouthed, show-off, big-timer attitude.

MANNERS. *See also Eating Out, Invitations, Poise, Rudeness.*

Good manners help a youngster to be comfortable in social situations. These are the most common good manners for parents to instill in kids:

- Using the words "please," "thank you," and "excuse me."
- Writing thank-you notes for gifts—one sentence for each year, ten being the maximum. Until notes are written, display gifts in the center of the dining table for all to see but not to use.
- Responding to compliments and questions (such as "You look pretty" or "How are you?") with more than a one-word grunt or answer.
- Asking permission to borrow something and returning it promptly and in good condition.
- When away from home, asking to use the phone, never asking to stay for a meal, helping to pick up toys, thanking for meals or snacks.
- At the table: Placing the napkin in the lap, waiting for the host/hostess before starting to eat, using the correct silver, keeping elbows off the table, taking a proportionate amount of the food from a dish, passing serving dishes around (not across) the table, not speaking with a full mouth, coping with bones and disagreeable foods in a nonoffensive way, cutting food a little at a time, breaking off a small piece of bread and buttering it (as opposed to slathering the entire slab on the palm of the hand), keeping the salt and pepper shakers together, making conversation, thanking for the meal, asking to help clear the table.
- Helping at doors and elevators and with heavy chairs.
- Making conversation without interrupting and contradicting others.
- Introducing people to each other.
- Remembering the obligation of entertaining someone who has entertained you.

A parent may need to brush up on these himself in order to set an example.

Before attending a social event, talk about how to be a pleasant guest: expressing interest in others including loners, joining cheerfully in activities, contributing to the conversation, willingly trying new foods or games, helping to set up or clean up, enthusiastically thanking for gifts, telling the host how much you enjoyed the event.

👍 It's fun to have a "Bad Manners Night" at the dinner table when family members see how many gaffs they can purposefully make without being caught.

👎 Eating out is not an occasion for bad manners and loud talk. Show youngsters who first follows the waiter or maître d' to the table (the hostess or wife of the host), how to read the right-hand column (the prices), how to order, what to do while waiting for the food (not stuffing oneself with crackers), and how to make table conversation.

MARIJUANA. *See Substance Abuse.*

MARRIAGE. *See also Divorce.*
A successful marriage greatly enhances parenting and family life. Before planning children, husbands and wives should have a general understanding about the size of the family, the division of parenting duties, how discipline will be handled, and the role education, culture and religion will play in everyday family life. Deciding on these issues will save many arguments later on.

Growing up in a home with two loving parents (less common nowadays) does add to the stability of the family and the confidence and self-worth of the child. Bickering, violent arguments, lack of loving interest by one or both parents, can lead to childhood depression and also sour a child on the whole idea of marriage. Strong families are built on marriages with these assets:

Good communication. Parents need time to connect with each other in the morning, once during the day, and a private time after the children have gone to bed. This conversation needs to go beyond sharing information—it should include talk about aims, emotional needs, and love. The word love needs to be part of their everyday conversation.

Private time. Whether it is a back rub or meeting for lunch, time-for-two keeps the bonds strong. Certainly "date night" should be planned for every week, even if it is as simple as a pizza and rental movie to share one evening at home.

Trust. The marriage vows need to be kept alive. An extramarital affair takes its toll. Rekindle the love that brought the husband and wife together in the first place. It is difficult to manage a busy life and family if one parent is worried about the dedication of the other.

Caring deeds. Show love through helping each other, and by remembering special times such as anniversaries and birthdays with cards and small gifts. Create surprises and occasions to show loving care.

Growing together. Don't stagnate mentally. Always be learning new things through reading, classes, and excursions. This includes service in the community that brings new insights and appreciation for marriage and the family.

A circle of support. Cultivate friends with compatible interests, people that you can be with on the spur of the moment and without elaborate preparations. Youngsters should also get to know these "near relatives" who may be more fun and helpful than some blood relatives!

Getting along. While every marriage has disagreements, *how* you disagree is important. Avoid idle threats, name calling, and abuse of any kind. Don't let arguments linger—set a time to settle them or to forget them if you can't agree. The leading causes of arguments are money and child rearing (followed by sex, politics, religion, and use of social time). Take time to talk about, settle, or compromise on these issues.

Money. Make a realistic budget that includes money for a family vacation, and then stick to it. See that each partner has some discretionary funds. Start saving for costly items. Cut up all or most all the charge cards.

Child rearing. Be united as to methods of discipline. Divide disciplinary duties equally. Set goals for discussion of important age-appropriate topics with children, such as sharing, saving, and substance abuse. Plan a family event for every weekend. Insist on respectful conversation, care of possessions, and genuine concern for one another.

Managing the home. If both parents work outside the home, the in-home duties must be fairly divided. And youngsters definitely need to be included in home duties. Work together to complete projects such as washing dishes, cleaning, folding laundry, car upkeep, and gardening. An orderly home is easier to maintain than a messy one. Work quickly so there is still time for family fun.

Fun. Marriage should be enjoyable, not a constricting ritual. With the children, create traditions, play together, eat together, and travel together.
For specific, tested ideas read *222 Terrific Tips for Two* (Caryl Krueger, Abingdon Press, Nashville, Tenn.).

MASTURBATION.
This stimulation of the genitals is not uncommon—in fact, babies do it almost unconsciously. Some youngsters feel guilty about doing it because they've been told it is dirty or wrong. Never shame kids for the practice. For some youngsters, it is a comfort habit that provides release from sexual tension, gives pleasure, and curbs impulses to engage in inappropriate sexual behavior with others. Often youngsters outgrow the habit when they discover other acceptable ways of gaining comfort.

Excessive masturbation can also be a symptom of sexual abuse and should be carefully monitored. Talk casually with a youngster about it, and make it very clear that it is definitely inappropriate in public places.

MATURITY. *See also High School Concepts, Privileges, Responsibility, Security/Success/Satisfaction, Teen Concepts.*
Maturity doesn't just happen all at once. A youngster gradually reaches the point of demonstrating adequate mental and physical powers that let her function in society in a way that is useful, and not harmful to herself or others. Some youngsters who live in an apathetic environment do not reach maturity except through hard times.

Master these skills as steps toward maturity: knowing right from wrong, being able to keep one's word, demonstrating the follow through to complete a project, having good personal hygiene, being able to solve problems amicably, and caring for others. Being a mature person also involves these abilities: eating nutritiously, caring for clothes, entertaining comfortably, shopping intelligently, doing home repairs and cleaning house, maintaining a yard and auto, and understanding money management.

See which of these a teen is weak in, and help her to mature in these areas before setting off on her own.

MAY DAY.
This date is celebrated as a time of renewal or a symbol of freedom. In Hawaii it's called Lei Day and everyone wears flower leis. Bring the encyclopedia to the table and see what it says about May Day in Russia and other countries. Pick a small bouquet of flowers, tie them with a ribbon, leave them on a friend's doorstep, ring the bell, and then hide. Phone later to end the mystery of the May Day bouquet.

"ME TIME." *See also Parenting Skills.*
Often parents fail to teach themselves the important things they provide to their youngsters. "Me Time," the time when a parent sees to her own

needs and builds a feeling of self-worth, is a precious time that must be both scheduled and also fitted spontaneously into spare moments. Parents should support each other's desire to be free of stress by having this essential time for renewal. For greater happiness and stress-free living, a parent needs:

- Space: a place to call her very own where little hands can't interfere.
- Good health: time to eat nutritious meals, exercise, and relax.
- Money: discretionary funds for small extras, and the feeling of being in charge or co-charge of family expenditures.
- A regular time for leisure activities, some with spouse, some with friends.
- A time to grow and learn, accomplished by reading, attending classes, being part of social or civic clubs.
- Quiet time. This is the most important "Me Time" and is preferably early in the morning. One way to get it is to rise just ten minutes ahead of everyone else. This isn't the time to make pancakes or iron shirts, it is a personal and reflective time enjoyed in a comfortable chair or other cozy spot. Let your mind be a blank piece of paper, don't plan the day, rather think about the good things already in your life. Perhaps read something inspirational, look out the window, listen for birds, and just see what good ideas come to mind. Then remind yourself that in the next busy hour you are going to keep your temper, overlook arguments and whining meanness, and be grateful you're alive and have a healthy family. At first you'll probably have to force yourself to do *nothing* for ten minutes, but once you get the hang of it you'll want to do it every day.

MEALTIME. *See also Breakfast, Dinner, Eating Out, Lunch, Manners.*

Mealtime for kids usually has nothing to do with nutrition, love of the cook, or pleasant conversation. It's just a time to satisfy hunger. Some youngsters seem to be hungry on a different schedule from parents and it is acceptable that they eat alone, providing they eat at a table, with the television off, and then join the others, perhaps eating a little while contributing to the conversation. Sometimes picky eaters will do better if they help plan meals and go shopping with a parent at the market.

Mealtime is not a battle time! Eating should be pleasant with a few simple rules and reminders given at the start and not repeated. Give youngsters small portions and explain what you expect. Try to eat together as a family at least five nights out of the week.

164

Do not use mealtime as an occasion for reprimanding children as it can be physically and mentally upsetting. Correction is best done away from the table on a one-to-one basis.

Encourage good conversation, questions, reading from a book or newspaper clipping, or sharing news and plans. Let one person answer the phone and take messages so the dinnertime is not disturbed (or use an answering machine). Eating by candlelight brings out better manners and conversation. Also, let children provide the table centerpiece such as a flower, shell, leaves, or a toy. Several times a year, have a special supper where everyone comes in costume.

During a vacation, let one child help to organize a restaurant, acting as waiter, seating others and taking orders by offering choices (a good way to use up leftovers). Eventually the cook and waiter can sit down with the family. At the end, a "bill" can be presented.

MEDICATION/MEDICINES. *See also Diseases, Health.*

There is a tendency to overmedicate children. Of course you should take immediate action when a child is not well, but you also need to be an informed parent. When complicated treatments are prescribed for a child, it's best to get a second opinion since the quick fix is not always the best solution to a health problem. You may want to become better informed about the condition by researching it on the Internet or in a medical book from the library. Be alert to side effects and the problems of long-term drug use by reading the information flyer that comes with the drug or is explained by the doctor or nurse before the injection.

Do not permit children to take their own medicines until they are older teens. Until youngsters are very responsible, always oversee to be sure of dosage and timing. When permitting a caregiver to administer medications, be sure to write out explicit instructions and keep this information with the medicine.

See that young children do not have access to medications. Keeping them in a medicine chest or on top of the refrigerator is not sufficient. Keep them under lock and key (in a cabinet chest or drawer) until youngsters are responsible enough not to take any without permission.

Be alert to the overuse of medications not professionally prescribed.

MEMORABILIA. *See also Family Tree, Photography, Scrapbooks, Traditions.*

Keeping valuable family memorabilia is somewhat time consuming but definitely worthwhile since it records history on a personal basis. Early in marriage, make a system for keeping important material. Certainly birth certificates, social security information, and other documents deserve a file. But beyond that, discretion must be used about what to save. The items usually fall in two main categories: visual records and written records.

Visual records consist of photos, slides, and video tapes. A photo album needs to be kept up-to-date with pictures dated and identified—a good task to do when watching television. Videos should also be dated. Many parents record milestones in *each* child's life on a separate tape so that they eventually have a continuing story. Others prefer to make a video of the family's high points of each year.

Written records can include a simple chart of each year showing the home address, work location and job titles, activities and volunteer work, children's grade level and teachers' names, family trips, and special achievements of all family members. In addition, many families make a written family history in story form or on audio tape.

The family scrapbook is another important piece of memorabilia. Establish a drawer or container into which all family members contribute items: a sports program, report card, party invitation, a child's special drawing, an award certificate—all those items that tell the story of the year. Then once each year all this material is pasted into a scrapbook in chronological order (easy since you just turn over the container you've been keeping it in). It can be a family project to do the pasting, then adding comments to each page.

MEMORIAL DAY.

Parades and ceremonies at cemeteries make this an unusual holiday of joy and sadness. Its original meaning, to commemorate those who have died, should be discussed and family members who served in wars should be honored. Give a deeper meaning to the day by looking at old photograph albums and memorabilia honoring those who have passed on. Many families use flowers and flags to decorate graves of loved ones on this day.

For gardeners, it is the time to start planting flowers in the yard. For outdoor cooks, it signals the first barbecue of the season.

MEMORY BUILDING. *See also Memorabilia, Scrapbooks, Traditions.*

When youngsters are grown, they may not remember an expensive trip or a fabulous birthday party. Instead, they may remember many small, seemingly insignificant activities such as the day you all played in the puddles following the rain, or the time the power went out and you roasted hot dogs and marshmallows in the fireplace for dinner.

Don't let a day pass without doing or saying something that will stick in your child's mind. Memories are built when families spend time together—doing work projects, making a special cake, learning to ride a bike without the training wheels, or feeding the birds in the snow.

Simple family memories may include measuring everyone's height yearly, making and burying a time capsule to open in ten years, putting handprints in new cement, making the fifth Sunday (which comes four times a year) into a special holiday, making taffy each summer, or repeating certain silly sayings.

To keep good memories alive, regularly look at family scrapbooks, photo albums, or videos. Once a month have "Nostalgia Night" and, along with older relatives, tell interesting stories about times past.

MESSINESS. *See also Order, Organization Skills.*

A certain amount of clutter is part of family life. But when the mess gets to the point that you feel like calling the Sanitation Department, it's time to set some rules and see that youngsters understand that you are serious about not letting them grow up as slobs.

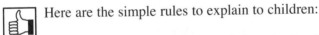 Here are the simple rules to explain to children:

• No clothes on the floor or furniture. They belong in the closet, in dresser drawers, or in the dirty clothes hamper.

• No dishes or old food left in the bedroom. Take them to the kitchen, rinse them off, put them in the dishwasher or stack them neatly on the counter.

• Toys played with in a bedroom should be picked up once a week. If a parent or cleaning person has to pick up toys on cleaning day, there will be a twenty-five cent to five dollar charge, depending on age.

• Place trash in the wastebasket, and empty the wastebasket as often as needed.

• Leave the bathroom in an orderly condition: a clean wash bowl and tub, towels picked up, soap and tissue refilled as needed.

Let younger children learn how to clean up after themselves. If they play in a room used by all the family, they should pick up toys daily. And when older kids make snacks in the kitchen, they should leave that area in good order.

MISTAKES. *See also Control.*

When a child does the wrong thing, it is not automatically a time for severe repercussions by the parent. Some mistakes deserve punishment, others may not. However, important ethical or illegal lapses are *not* mistakes and should be dealt with firmly.

Teach kids to say those difficult words: "I was wrong" or "I made a mistake." Youngsters should be shown how to repair the damage (or give help). Then the mistake should be forgiven and forgotten. When a child freely admits a transgression, pour on the love. Make it easy for her to tell the truth. And don't forget to admit your own parental blunders.

One of the best ways for youngsters to learn is by letting them suffer the consequences of their own mistakes that are not dangerous ones. If they fail to finish a chore, they can do it while others play. If they continuously fail to get up when the alarm goes off, let them be late for the school bus and charge them a fee to drive them. If they don't come home on time, they can't go out the following weekend. Such mistakes are teaching the youngster that she has control of her choices: to act appropriately or do otherwise and suffer the consequences. Thus the parent sets loose the child to make the decision, rather than control every aspect of the child's life. While we love our children and want to protect them from missteps, sometimes the best lesson comes from a mistake.

MODESTY. *See also Privacy, Shyness.*

Two meanings of the word are pertinent to parenting. First, you want a child to have composure without being boastful or vain about his accomplishments. And second, you also want him to have regard for conventional decencies. Home example and training can cover both aspects of the word. Do not confuse modesty with shyness, which is usually the inability to function in public situations.

To have modest composure, help a child keep his activities in perspective and also provide him with adequate opportunities for excelling, followed by suitable praise. Also, be very specific about your family values concerning proper dress in public, and comments on bodily functions (hence no audible burping at a party). Youngsters should always honor the privacy of the bathroom or any room with a closed door.

168

MOLESTATION. *See also Abuse, Safety, Sex Education.*
This most serious form of abuse can often be lessened and even averted if children are taught early to be alert to situations that could be dangerous and how to wisely avoid them. Should it happen, don't make the child feel guilty since the rape or molestation is certainly traumatic enough. Get immediate professional counseling for both parent and child. Be supportive and especially caring of the victim. It need not be a forever imprint on the child if she has been taught to be resilient enough to carry her through bad experiences.

Role play so youngsters know what to do when strangers approach them. However, molestation is often from people the child already knows. Encourage children to be open about such contacts and tell them never to let anyone touch their bodies in places that a bathing suit would cover.

Use common sense: meet young children at the school bus, let them play on the neighborhood sidewalks with a buddy rather than alone, accompany them into public restrooms, hold hands in crowded places, and have an emergency plan if a child gets lost or separated from the family. Help youngsters think their way through possibly dangerous situations.

MONEY.
Don't raise a financially naive child. Until a child understands the value of a dime or dollar, don't give her money. (Funds given as gifts should be kept by a parent until spent or saved.) By age six, a child should have an allowance that includes a very small amount for her discretionary spending. This allowance is for being part of the family and not contingent on the behavior of the child or on doing chores. The amount should be small enough that it takes several weeks to accumulate enough to buy an inexpensive desired toy. The allowance will be a variable amount and should cover regular expenditures such as school lunch, church contribution, club dues, movie admission when going with friends, gifts to family members, and a small discretionary-spending sum.

For young children, pay the allowance weekly, for older ones, a monthly allowance gives them the challenge to carefully manage their money. Until good money sense is established, check that kids have not misspent their lunch money or church contribution money on toys.

When a child misbehaves, do not take away his allowance. However, do not permit him to spend money on anything but the essentials.

Saving money in a special account can start with money gifts to babies. Encourage older youngsters to save 10 percent of any money gift. Help them set saving goals and enjoy the results of achieving a goal and spending the money. When youngsters are preteens, help them set up a budget that covers their clothes and recreational needs, but also helps them save. For a large purchase, such as the first car, make a deal that you will pay for half if the youngster earns the other half. Sometimes grandparents will provide matching funds.

Don't hesitate to talk to older children about family finances, especially when there is a loss of income. Enlist their help in holding down expenses such as electric bills. Youngsters are usually resilient if there is a calm discussion of the family budget and the need to cut back. During this serious discussion, parents should be sure to answer a child's silent questions: "Will we still have a house to live in together?" and "Will there be food to eat?" Youngsters may surprise you with their helpful ideas on how the family can manage with less income.

Part-time jobs have benefits and problems. While they do give a youngster some business experience, they may not be at all related to the ultimate job. They do however teach responsibility and working with others. On the other side, youngsters who have regular paid jobs after school, in general, have poorer grades, are more apt to drop out, and are more likely to become involved in drug use. However, students who serve as volunteers develop competence and feel useful to the community. (A comparison of youngsters doing volunteer work as opposed to fast-food jobs found that the volunteers gained more useful skills, were better at problem solving, were more reliable, and had a better feeling of self-worth.) So, parents and teens must balance the minimum wage (or no earnings from volunteer work) versus the loss of study time and free time.

Include youngsters in talk about investments and their risks, buying on credit, and interest rates. As a learning experiment, let a youngster pick a stock that is attractive to her and make a pretend purchase of 100 shares. Show her how to keep a log of its ups and downs, splits, and dividends. Then after one year, compute the pretend profit or loss.

MOODINESS. *See Depression.*

MORALITY. *See also Conscience, Ethics, Honesty, Religion, Sexuality.*

Parents need to keep current on youth challenges to the family moral code. Decide what the standards will be for your family and stick to them. Instill them in children starting at a young age by talking about honesty, loyalty, and the responsible and caring side of sexuality.

Keep the lines of communication open and your shock threshold high! Use the library to become informed on sexual diseases, safe sex practices, and substance abuse. Regarding sex, talk about emotions and strong feelings and the best option of abstinence. Set an example by having a marriage that is caring and faithful. But, should there be a divorce, don't think that youngsters are too young to understand. Share simple, nonjudgmental reasons for the break up, and show how divorced parents can still have high ethical standards.

Rather than lecturing kids on morality and ethics, ask "what if" questions that let youngsters think of how to act in advance of the situation. Typical questions could be: "What if your best friend asked to copy your homework?" "What if you were dared to shoplift just an apple from a sidewalk fruit stand?" "What if a boyfriend asked you to come into a bedroom and close the door?" "What if you were offered a drug or alcohol at a big party?"

See that your youngsters have a strong religious foundation from early years to help them combat temptations as they grow to adulthood.

MORNING ROUTINE. *See also Breakfast.*

Create a morning routine that frees you from nagging and gives a child a sense of accomplishment. Make breakfast an absolute essential, using that time to go over the day's plans, establish good feelings, and express love.

Make a picture chart or word list of these seven morning essentials:

1. Going to the bathroom
2. Washing or showering
3. Dressing in clean clothes
4. Making the bed
5. Tidying the room
6. Doing one chore
7. Brushing teeth after breakfast.

Play peppy music (such as Sousa marches) in the morning to speed up activities. Give a child his own alarm clock and let him learn independence.

171

MOTHERS. *See also Fathers, "Me Time," Parenting Skills.*

Mothers are usually the main nurturers in the family, possibly because they spend more time with youngsters than fathers (who are equally capable of nurturing). Both parents contribute to the well-being of a child but mothers are often the ones in charge of nutrition, health, safety, and education. Even mothers who work outside the home still end up with a disproportionate amount of time spent on child and home care.

Mothers need to take good care of themselves since most families would fall apart if the mother could not function.

MOTHER'S DAY.

This special day should be honored by the family every year. When children are very young, it's dad's job to plan the event. Start with breakfast in bed and include on the tray a cupcake with a candle and a flower. Homemade cards can express love and appreciation. Make it a no-kitchen day for mom—others should cook and clean up. Plan a park picnic or a family movie. Gifts could include a plant for her desk, a new jogging shirt, or tickets for a special event. A cozy dinner out in the evening can top off the day.

MOTHER'S LITTLE STORE. *See also Christmas Gifts, Gifts.*

Little children often don't have the money to buy gifts or the skills to make them, yet they want to participate in gift giving. Mother's Little Store provides the opportunity for youngsters to gain the satisfaction of picking out and paying for a gift, then wrapping it.

When there is to be a gift-giving occasion such as Christmas, mother or father will have bought several gifts for each family member. These are placed on a big surface, such as a bed, and a very reasonable price tag is put on each—something youngsters can easily afford. One at a time, children are admitted to the store to inspect and select their gifts, pay for them, and then (for a penny) purchase the wrapping paper. This is also a good exercise in learning to keep secrets since children will have seen many gifts (but not their own).

MOVIES.

Going to a movie should be a special treat with preparatory conversation in advance. Don't rely on reviews and ads that show just the best parts of movies. Note the ratings and avoid those movies that contain violence, sex, profanity, and other inappropriate subjects. If you see something objectionable, be sure to discuss it afterward. Be alert to the content of movies that older kids see with friends or videos that they rent for home viewing.

Help older youngsters to assess the merits of movies. At Academy Award time, have a party combining friends of teens and adults to celebrate this gala event. Serve movie-style refreshments such as popcorn, candy, nachos, and sodas. Provide ballots for each person to fill out in advance, picking who he thinks will win in each category. Take special interest in costuming, set design, music, and other artistic elements. Award points for each win (more in the major categories) and present the winner with a king-sized bag of popcorn or a certificate for two theater tickets.

MOVING. *See also Separation Anxiety.*

Children often feel left out and lonely when the family is moving to a new home. A child is further overwhelmed if the move is caused by divorce, death, or a change in family finances. Certain ages take moving more dramatically than others: toddlers are just getting used to the routine and environment of home and preschool. Grade-school children can be confused by the changes (even if it is an upscale move), while older children resent being separated from friends and wonder if they will ever be happy again.

However, the more a youngster is prepared and participates in the move, the easier the move. Seeing the new home or pictures of it, helping to pack and being reminded that his possessions will be at the new home, getting information about the locality (schools, parks, entertainment, friends)—all these can allay fears.

At moving time, spend extra time (even though you are busy) with children to reassure them that parents, siblings, friends, toys, school, and good times are ahead. Talk about the move, asking these questions: "What do you think will be the best thing about the new house?" "What are you happy to leave behind?" "What should be the first thing we do at the new house?" Sort out possessions and pack together, talking as you work. Suggest that older children put funny messages in the packing boxes that will be read when they are opened at the new home. Be sure that in a new larger home, you still have the coziness that was comforting in the smaller home.

Encourage memories by taking photos of the old house and of friends. Be sure you have addresses and phone numbers so youngsters can keep in touch. After a month or so, plan a time to revisit the neighborhood.

After you move in but before school starts, arrange for a same-aged youngster (find one in the neighborhood or ask the school to put you in contact) to show your child the ropes at the new school, and then invite her to your home for play and lunch.

MUSEUM TRIP. *See also Cultural Events, Drama, Music.*

A museum is a warehouse of knowledge and a trip to a museum needn't be a dismal experience for parent or child. Visit a museum as often as you visit a recreational facility. Visiting an outdoor art fair is a good prelude to a museum trip.

Follow these easy steps to make a trip to an art museum an enjoyable experience:

- Visit the library and look together at art books.
- On the way, talk about favorite colors and subjects in anticipation of seeing them.
- Sit outside the museum and enjoy a snack, looking at the different kinds of people going into the museum.
- Go into the museum store and let the child buy a postcard of a picture he likes, one that he will later see.
- On a first visit, don't sign up for a scholarly museum tour. Go leisurely, looking at subjects, colors, and looking for the child's postcard picture.
- Show where an artist signs the picture and also explain the other information posted next to the picture.
- Ask youngsters to find "themselves" in pictures that have children in them. Encourage the making up of stories about what they think is going on in the picture.
- Sit down and let youngsters sketch a picture using something he sees in a nearby picture. (You'll need to bring along tablets and crayons.)
- Play the game "I'd Like to Live There." Let kids point out places that look interesting for play, living, working, or visiting. Or play "If I Were a Millionaire" and let each child point out a painting he'd like to take home if he could afford the huge price.
- After about an hour of viewing, have a bathroom and lunch break. See who has found their postcard picture. Then enjoy more viewing before returning to the museum shop to look at art books, games, and other items that could be holiday gifts.
- On the way home, talk about the most interesting things seen. Look out the car windows and point out scenes that would make good paintings.
- Put the postcards on the family bulletin board or send them to grand-

parents, telling them about the trip. Encourage art projects in the home, and plan another art museum trip for the future.

MUSIC. *See also Lessons, Lullabies, Singing.*
The sound of music starts with a baby's music box and lullabies. For toddlers, a collection of simple instruments (tambourine, bells, maracas, kazoo, sticks) can become a basic orchestra. An older child will enjoy a recorder as a first instrument.

Use music as a background for naps, baths, homework, dinner, and story time. Family members should be willing to listen to a variety of music. Sing-along tapes make car trips more pleasant as they teach riders the favorite songs of others. Whether or not a child learns to play music, show her how to read music so that she can know the notes and timing when singing hymns or in a chorus.

Music lessons should not begin until parent and child have investigated the wide array of instruments available, the cost of lessons, and the youngster's commitment (to practice for a prescribed amount of time without being nagged, and to continue for at least six months). Be open to more than piano or violin lessons; consider wind instruments and even drums.

Introduce classical music through works such as "Peter and the Wolf" or the "Grand Canyon Suite." Attend live music events, preparing youngsters in advance for what they will hear and how they should behave. (Many parks have free weekend band concerts that are a good beginning.) Also attend summer stock musicals, and work up to children's opera productions. Before attending an orchestral program, use the encyclopedia to identify the various instruments. Before attending a choral production, learn the various voice ranges.

Popular music is acceptable providing the decibels are not ear damaging or the words inappropriate. As a parent, it is your right to ban from your home music with obscene lyrics. Widen the range of your own musical interests by listening to varied radio stations while you work.

NAGGING. *See also One-Chance Parent, Pests, Questions.*

Both parents and children can be naggers. A parent's constant griping and reminding makes the mood of home life ugly. Better, let youngsters know what is expected of them. Write it down. Post it where they can see it. Tell them what happens if they fail to do what is expected. Then be quiet and let them choose to do the acceptable thing or be punished.

Children who are constantly nagged do not feel the need to remember important things; a parent will remind them. This is no way to teach maturity. Instead it keeps youngsters as dependent babes. It also increases the number of unpleasant words heard each day.

Nagging by children is equally objectionable. Kids try this because they have found that parents don't always mean what they say, so pestering them may bring about a more desirable result. Unless you have made a mistake, don't give in to naggers and you'll find they soon quit.

NAME-CALLING. *See also Bullies, Teasing.*

Rude and crude name-calling can be damaging to any child, young or old. Don't permit this within the family and see that teasing friends or relatives refrain from this cruel act. In your own family, charge fifty cents for any name-calling and have the name-caller hand the money to the other child with an apology.

Help youngsters to withstand taunts of peers by pretending not to hear the words. Sometimes a youngster can merely say "I think you're not hearing right—my name isn't Dopey, it's Davey."

NAMES.

A child's name is very important. It should not sound like or rhyme with something objectionable. Check out what the initials spell out or say and consider how a name will probably be changed into a nickname during school years. Unusual names can often serve as middle names so as not to cause embarrassment. So that a youngster feels more distinctive, try not to choose the most common names (which can result in the teacher having four Roberts in the class). It's fun to look up original meanings of names to see the qualities they stood for.

NAPS. *See also Bedtime Routine, Sleep.*

A short rest can be beneficial to children of all ages when tired or cranky. Never make naps a punishment and don't hesitate to take one yourself if you need it.

By about age one, a baby is usually ready to gradually move from two naps to one. If the morning nap is his preferred one, little by little move the start time later until it finally becomes an afternoon nap.

When preschoolers begin to fight a nap, turn it into a quiet time of play in bed. This quiet time can be refreshing and some youngsters will actually fall asleep (don't tell them!). Set a timer for about thirty minutes and see that the child has books and other soft toys to occupy her. You can name it "quiet time," "book time," or "pillow time" so that it is not associated with baby naps. Just like night bedtime, this resting time needs a ritual: a trip to the bathroom, a drink of water, selecting a special toy, or reading a short story. For children in toilet training and wearing pull-ups only at night, naptime is a good time to try to remain dry.

In general, the end of naptime coincides with the start of kindergarten where there may be a "heads down on the table" rest, but not a time to sleep on a mat or cot.

NATURE. *See also Environmental Issues, Gardening.*

Encourage activities that show an appreciation of nature: looking at the stars, visiting tide pools, snorkeling, keeping a rain gauge, watching birds and bugs, and growing plants. Aquariums, planetariums, botanical gardens, and animal parks and zoos make enjoyable and educational excursions. For comprehensive information, look up www.eNature.com.

Let children select nature objects as dining table centerpieces, things such as fallen leaves, a dandelion, an interesting rock, a bird feather. Bring nature into the home with flowers, shells, drift wood, and fish tanks.

Good gifts that help kids become nature lovers are a bird feeder, a worm or ant farm, field glasses, garden seeds, or a magnifying glass. Provide nature magazines and pocket-sized identification books available for birds, insects, flowers, and trees.

NEGLECT. *See also Abandonment, Abuse, Evening Activities, Love.*
Childhood neglect comes in many forms and crosses all social and economic barriers. Affluent, intelligent parents can be so busy with their own lives that they fail to connect with their children and are content to let other caregivers take over. Busy parents need to realize that weekday neglect is harmful to children, resulting in poor grades, bad attitudes, and health problems. A weekend excursion can't make up for a week of failing to connect with children.

NEIGHBORHOOD ACTIVITIES. *See also Entertaining.*
If at all possible, choose to live in an area that has a strong feeling of neighborhood. This can happen in a house or apartment complex. Along with children playing together, encourage an annual toy exchange, an outdoor sports day, a progressive supper, a block party, and a neighborhood summer camp. A weekly meeting of mothers (or dads) with children playing at one house can bring the neighbors together in common interests such as safety. Baby-sitting co-ops can be very effective if well managed. Growing up together with other youngsters in a strong neighborhood builds lifelong friendships and good memories.

NEW YEAR'S EVE AND DAY.
Welcome the new year several times by celebrating with each time zone. Youngsters can go to bed after New York or any of the earlier celebrations and let parents celebrate right on to Hawaii. You can also make the event a progressive dinner in the neighborhood, walking from house to house for each course.
However, if New Year's Eve has been solely an adult event, make New Year's Day a family event. Celebrate with breakfast in pajamas while watching the parade on television. For an afternoon party, plan a three generation neighbors and friends open house and serve game foods such as hot dogs, chili, popcorn, and sodas. Give new year calendars as prizes for the best guessers as to the score and other elements of the football game on television. Let everyone make resolutions and seal them in an envelope for opening next January 1.

NIGHTMARES. *See also Dreams, Fears, Sleep.*
Nightmares are merely terrifying dreams from which the youngster can awaken in great fear. They usually occur in the early morning. Comfort is needed and a child usually falls back asleep easily. They seem to be

caused by emotional problems, rather than physical ones. Just as you can turn off or change the channel from a violent television show to a pleasant one, children amazingly have the ability, if told they can do it, to mentally turn off the nightmare. When they awaken during a nightmare, a parent can bring the dream to a conclusion. For example, tell the child that the water he thought was flowing out of the bathtub is no longer harmful and has become a beautiful waterfall where children can happily splash and play.

A night terror is quite different and occurs earlier in the sleep process, the youngster thrashing or screaming out and often not recognizing those who come to aid him. Since children don't remember the terror experience or the parent coming to help, it is of little use to question the child in the morning. Overly tired children or children with problems such as ear infections are more apt to have these terrors. Correcting the underlying trouble often means the end of the terrors, and most children outgrow them altogether by about age eight.

NOSTALGIA. *See Memories.*

NURTURING. *See Caring, Love.*

NUTRITION. *See also Fitness, Health.*

The seeds of good, balanced eating are planted in young children. Unfortunately, many don't want those seeds planted! Preschoolers can be very stubborn in their ideas of what they will or won't eat so be prepared to reward willingness to try new things.

Don't give in to "I won't eat that" attitudes. Encourage youngsters to have at least two tablespoons of any food. Call it a "royalty serving." Don't force feed, but rather cut back on snacks so youngsters come to the table hungry. Don't ask "Are you finished?" (most will quickly say "yes") but rather put a reasonable amount of food on a child's plate and expect it to be eaten.

Occasionally have a backward supper. A small dessert can be followed by the main dish, then soup or salad. Or, announce at breakfast that there will be a "WOW" food at dinner (that means something new or differently prepared).

Get to know the four basic food groups. Let picky eaters help you make a chart of the foods they already like to eat in each group. Then help the child find a new food in each category, letting him help to make nutritious menus and then shop with you for this food. If children balk at eating a food, reassure them that you do not serve poisonous food so it is safe to try it.

Breakfast is an important meal for preparing students to learn at school. Include fruit shakes, peanutty toast, cereal sundaes topped with yogurt, grilled cheese sandwiches, omelets, and waffles with toppings.

School lunches often go uneaten. With an insulated lunch box containing blue ice to keep things cold, a lunch can be more inviting than just a sandwich and chips. Consider cottage cheese with herbs, crackers and cheese wedges, a tuna-stuffed tomato, a half melon with cottage cheese, yogurt with fruit, meat balls, hot soup or chili in a thermos, or cold pizza. For dessert consider cookies and a container of frosting with spreader.

Snacks at home can be popsicles made of frozen juices, veggies with dip, muffins, even a small baked potato topped with cheese. Avoid soft drinks that have caffeine or are loaded with sugar—have a banana shake instead. Fruits make nutritious snacks, especially golden raisins, pineapple slices, and grapes.

For dinner, vary fish, fowl, and cheese dishes with red meats. Serve salads made attractive with olives, raisins, nuts, or corn topping. Potatoes are a good source of vitamin C and not high in calories if you control the toppings and use fat-free sour cream. And for desserts, consider gelatins, tapioca, puddings, and fruit. Before going to dinner at a fast-food restaurant, talk about and then order the more nutritious offerings.

Evening snacks can include popcorn, but go light on the salt and butter, using flavorings instead. Dried fruits are easier to digest than nuts and more healthful than candy. Younger children sleep better if they have a small bedtime snack (before teeth brushing) since it is a long time until breakfast.

OBEDIENCE. *See also Discipline, One-Chance Parent, Punishment, Rules.*

Parents don't know everything, but on most subjects they are wiser than their children. That is why they are the prime caregivers for children and why children should listen to and obey parents. That does not mean that youngsters should never disagree or express alternate ways of doing something. But it does mean that they should not arbitrarily and frivolously disregard parental ideas and orders.

With kid input, create rules and consequences and explain to them that these are means of protecting them from harm, foolish behavior, or unlawful activity, and are actually symbols of love.

OBESITY. *See also Anorexia, Bulimia, Eating, Nutrition, Teasing.*

Excessive weight is usually caused by a youngster consuming more calories than she burns. This may be triggered by long-established family eating habits, a hereditary problem, or depression. Eating habits form early so protect a child from later problems by insisting on healthy eating from the start. It is easiest to encourage good eating habits with a very young child, and much more difficult as years pass.

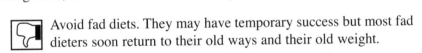 Avoid fad diets. They may have temporary success but most fad dieters soon return to their old ways and their old weight.

Take this problem seriously. Set up a plan to serve good, nutritious foods in all the food groups. Let the overweight child help plan the menus. Provide a container of snacks for the day so that a child can choose when to eat them, but understand that when the container is empty, there is no more for that day. This is an important lesson in self-control. Work together quietly and confidentially but get professional help if you are not meeting with success.

OBSESSIVE-COMPULSIVE DISORDER. *See also Perfection.*

Some children repeatedly perform rituals: acts such as washing hands, counting, sorting, checking things to the point that these actions interfere with their ability to perform normal everyday tasks and activities. Also, the child can have repetitive thoughts and impulses that occur time and again throughout the day, making it difficult for him to focus on other things. This disorder should be addressed when first noticed. A professional can suggest nonmedical and medical/behavior modification to alleviate the problem.

OMBUDSMAN. *See also Disagreements, Peacemaker, Problem Solving.*

To help settle arguments within the family or during play with others, appoint one child as ombudsman. They'll like the word, which means an official appointed to investigate complaints and maladministration. Have youngsters take turns holding the job. The ombudsman's decision is final, but he takes into consideration that bad decisions may kick back on him when others have the post. Give compliments to this judge when play goes well.

ONE-CHANCE PARENT. *See also Consequences, Parenting Skills, Punishment, Rules.*

Save your time and teach your children responsibility by being a one-chance parent. This means that you will tell a youngster what is expected one time only, and then give one warning (the one chance). After that, the child will be disciplined. It is important that you mean what you say since this is for the child's own progress toward maturity.

For example, your daughter knows the family rule not to yank toys away from others. But you see her doing this and give her the one chance to stop. If she does it again, it's time-out or other suitable punishment.

ONE-ON-ONE.

Honor the individuality of each child by having one-on-one times together each day. These can be with a snack after school or before bed. Also plan one-on-one activities that bring a parent and a child together for good times—things like bowling, a mall trip, visiting a museum, going out for breakfast, or going to a sports event. Don't do everything as a family group.

ONLY CHILDREN. *See also Loneliness.*

The number of families with a single child is increasing—by choice or because of a late start, divorce, or economics. The choice to have a second child shouldn't be to provide a playmate for the first child but because it is the parents' desire to have a larger family. Being an only child has benefits, but later in life, when parents are aged, it could also be a burden that can't easily be shared. Most child development specialists recommend that if parents have a choice, they should have at least two children.

Formerly it was thought that only children were more lonely, spoiled, and selfish. But, research shows that in most cases this is not true. Only children usually do spend more time alone and this enhances independence, creativity, and the ability to be comfortable with oneself.

However, raising an only child presents a few challenges. For example, there are no built-in playmates. Only children usually don't have as many opportunities to share their possessions, they don't easily learn how to care for a younger child, they are less apt to enjoy family games and other group activities. Of course, parents of an only child can certainly provide opportunities to mitigate these challenges.

Only children are often more adult oriented since they spend more time with parents and their adult friends than with peers. They are slightly more achievement oriented because their parents have zeroed in on their abilities more closely. But comparisons with children from larger families show that the differences are so slight that they don't really make much difference.

Research does show that only children tend *not* to have only children, and a child born into a very large family of siblings is more apt to have fewer children, even one. So, what it comes down to is that each child wants respect and attention and this can be provided in both large and small families.

OPENNESS. *See also Communication.*

A home environment that respects diversity, encourages good communication, and is not cruelly critical gives youngsters a great sense of belonging. The casual, almost airy feeling of this home life is called openness.

Tell youngsters often that you love them no matter what. Listen and appreciate as much or more than you talk. Avoid lectures. Keep everyone connected through daily updates on activities. Be willing to talk about almost anything. Put important things in writing. Do things spontaneously.

Avoid these openness killers: "Shut up." "What a dumb idea." "Not now, I'm busy." These comments close down relationships, rather than open them.

Consider these lines: "Let's find time to talk." "How can we accomplish this?" "That sounds like a good idea!" These show interest and open lines of communication.

In an open family, no topic is taboo, mistakes are not world ending, grudges last only a moment, and mutual affection is evident daily.

OPTIMISM. *See also Determination.*

A healthy point of view makes family life happier. Parents should watch the emphasis they place on problems, being careful not to go ballistic over small things. When mistakes bring shouting, followed by tears or guilt, a child develops a pessimistic and cautious attitude. Patience and a lighthearted approach help reduce discouragement. Make rejections and failures stepping stones to successes.

Avoid saying "This is hopeless." "I don't think you'll ever get it right." "Everything is a mess." Pessimism is depressing to both parent and child.

Consider these lines: "That's not so bad." "I know you'll get it eventually." "Let's see if we can solve it together." Optimism creates the feeling that "all things are possible"—or at least worth trying.

To be able to look on the bright side is an endearing quality in youngsters and one that will bring them through many hard times.

ORDER. *See also Choices, Environment, Messiness, Organizational Skills, Priorities, Responsibility, Self-Government.*

Prioritizing—knowing what's urgent and what isn't—helps a child to get through the routine activities of the day so that there is time for unstructured activity, creative play, and spontaneous fun. Time management and orderliness are lifetime skills you must teach. These help him through the mass of "must do" things each day and give him a sense of mental order. He needs to be taught how to think through what must be done first, what might be done next, what can wait for tomorrow, and what never needs to be done.

For a toddler, the first lesson in orderliness is showing him how to put away certain toys, games, and outdoor equipment at the end of the day—although toys in his own room can be left out until the room is to be cleaned. The next steps in teaching orderliness are how to tidy his room and bathroom and how to help clean up after a snack or meal.

When he enters school, he needs to learn an orderly way to accomplish homework. Don't think that this just comes naturally—it is an important skill for a parent to teach. He should have a desk with supplies and files for report cards, savings account passbook, letters received and to answer, pet information, and so forth. A bulletin board is helpful if it has a calendar showing the due date for assignments, times of after-school lessons, and club and social events. He also needs a shelf for displaying special awards, framed photos, and other memorabilia. All this gives order to a child's own space.

Once a month give each family member a bag and turn him loose in the house to collect things that aren't where they belong. It's fun to count up the number of items in each bag. Dump all the items on a table and sort them by room, letting each child deliver items to one or two rooms and put them where they belong, restoring orderliness. To promote order, make this a family motto: Don't put it down, put it away!

ORGANIZATIONAL SKILLS. *See also Calendar, Chores, Home Headquarters, Homemaking, Orderliness, Priorities.*

A happy and harmonious family is usually the result of good organization that efficiently handles the routine duties so there is time for more interesting activities. Here are some skills to cultivate:

• Keep a wall-sized family calendar of events in a conspicuous place.
• Assign chores and establish a method of seeing that they are completed.
• Give youngsters choices and even let them be "Parent for a Day" so they understand responsibilities.
• Write out family rules and the penalties for breaking them.
• Understand money management through an allowance and having respect for the family budget.
• Balance time for homework, chores, sports, and television.
• Learn to make lists and keep simple files.
• Take part in family meetings to consider activities and challenges.
• Set personal goals at least once a year.
• Care for possessions.
• Learn to communicate with respect.
• Practice home care skills such as cooking, laundry, mending/sewing, cleaning, simple repairs using tools, and basic gardening.
• Know how to respond to emergencies, deal with strangers, and act safely.

It seems as if it might take much time and energy to organize these areas, but if you bite the bullet and do it, you will find that this sense of order saves you a ton of time that you can use for noisy play or quiet reflection.

OUTDOOR PLAY. *See also Bicycling, Play Houses, Sports, Water Play.*

There's nothing like outdoor play, no matter what the weather. Looking for the first flower of spring while taking a walk, playing in a sprinkler, raking crackly leaves, or building a fort in the snow bring ingenuity and energy into play.

When looking for the family's first home, give as much priority to the backyard as to the interior of the house. While a park can provide hours of fun for a child, play in her own safe backyard is tops and you will feel much more comfortable about your child's activities than if she plays near the street.

Set aside a backyard area for active games, tetherball, digging holes, races, hopscotch and chalk play (on a patio), and catch. Provide a small wading pool that can be used when you're present and emptied at the end of play. If there's space, have swings and slides and a covered sandbox for young children. For older youngsters, have a lawn for croquet, slip 'n slide, badminton, and an obstacle course. Encourage active outdoor play with activities that include window painting on patio doors, making and flying inexpensive airplanes, sailing boomerangs, or games with spray bottles or balloons.

Make a private place to play outdoors using two card tables covered with sheets; or design a real tree house as a building project for parent and child.

As children get older and can safely play outdoors in the neighborhood, consider jump-rope play, sailing boats in puddles, drawing large chalk pictures or "traffic lanes" for bikes on sidewalks, bicycle riding, basketball, stilt walking, rocket launching, and flying kites.

Teach youngsters to play in all kinds of weather. Suitable clothing for rain or snow lets them have fun and get exercise at the same time.

OUTREACH. *See Service.*

PACIFIERS. *See also "Blankies," Thumb Sucking.*

With each passing decade, pacifiers go in or out of favor. Each parent must decide what works best for him. A fussy or crying baby may find comfort in a pacifier and the continued opportunity to suck, even though he has just been fed. As children grow older, the corner of a blanket or his thumb may become a pacifier.

If you decide to offer your baby a pacifier, buy one or two good ones of different designs and see if one is preferred. Some have a cord so that they don't end up on the floor; or you can attach one to a baby's chair with short nonfraying string that could not get around a child's neck and be a choking hazard. However, be sure to wash the pacifier regularly, using the same method you use for bottle nipples.

A pacifier usually becomes a habit and it is wise to find other ways of giving a child comfort as he grows older, such as hugging a beloved stuffed animal. However, never just take away the pacifier. Talk about it and see if it can be used less frequently, perhaps just at bedtime. Sometimes a toddler is satisfied by giving the pacifier to a younger sibling or tying it around the neck of a toy animal or doll. Dentists report that prolonged use by preschoolers can force the gums and teeth into a position that will require costly orthodontia later.

PARENTING SKILLS. *See also Calendar, Estrangement, Home Headquarters, Home Management, "I" Statements, One-Chance Parent, Organizational Skills, Single Parenting, Stepparenting.*

A successful parent plans time each day for:

- **Business work and/or home tasks.** Good parenting means using effective time management skills at both office and home.

- **Personal time.** A parent needs a feeling of self-worth, just as children do.

- **Interacting with children** so they don't feel left out or abandoned during the week.

- **Interacting with spouse** to keep the marriage alive.

- **Outreach to others** beyond the immediate family circle.

Create a family headquarters where you can have a desk, some files, and a bulletin board. Keep a very detailed calendar of family events so there is no confusion over who is where and when. This will let you see when family life is too crowded and activities need to be adjusted. Make the desk the family message center. Post on the bulletin board the family rules, information for sitters, the chores list, grocery list, and menus. To end the clutter and be able to find things, buy a monthly thirty-one day file to use for those things that occur on certain days of the month: days 15 and 30 for paying bills, invitations, meeting notices, theater tickets, and so forth.

It is absolutely essential for a parent to carve out some time for himself/herself. If parents fall apart, so will the family! Getting up fifteen minutes ahead of others, taking a long bath, reading before bed, going alone for a walk, taking a class are a few options.

Be alert to overparenting or not permitting youngsters to accomplish age-appropriate activities without parental input. Children need to be protected from real dangers but they also need to have some independence and adventure in their lives. Their mistakes will also teach good lessons. Underparenting adversely affects the development of children who need the stimulation of conversation and playtime with parents. Such interaction is not an option, it is an essential, not just in young babies, but also with teens. The time with children should not be the leftover time. Since few parents do things the exact same way, fathering is as equally important as mothering. It is beneficial for youngsters to observe that there is more than one right way to accomplish something. Learning to adapt to change is part of growing up. Research shows that fathers are no less effective than mothers in rearing children, providing they have similar goals for the children.

Be a good example of love and a happy marriage. Talk openly about the good things that happen when two people love each other. Show affection and use affectionate language to your spouse in front of your children. This adds a feeling of stability and comfort to youngsters—and to the spouse!

Outreach beyond the family and relatives shows youngsters the importance of caring for others. Working together at a care facility or doing good deeds in the neighborhood will set a good example for the youngster's adult life.

To fine tune your parenting skills, read *Six Weeks to Better Parenting* (Caryl Krueger, Belleridge Press, Escondido, Calif.).

PARENTS' DAY.

Traditionally the fourth Sunday in July, this day is unlike Mother's Day and Father's Day because no gifts are involved. The day commemorates the qualities that make a great parent as well as the qualities that make a happy child. Families often switch roles on this day, letting children take charge and show what they have learned about effective family life.

PARENT/TEACHER RELATIONSHIP. *See also School Grades, Teachers.*

Keep in touch with a child's progress by working closely with the teacher through school visits, meetings, interviews, phone calls, and notes. Some families even invite a teacher (and spouse) to a weekend lunch or dinner. These are things you need to know from a child's teacher:

- Is my child working up to the proper ability level?
- What are her strengths and weaknesses?
- What does the teacher take into account in grading?
- Is homework usually completed satisfactorily?
- Is the child self-disciplined, responsible, and cooperative?
- How does the child take suggestions and criticism?
- Are social skills and self-confidence developing?
- What simple things can a parent do to support the class or school?

Let youngsters know that you are vitally interested in their progress by daily talking about school and learning. Ask youngsters to assess their own progress and relationship with teachers.

PARTIES. *See also Christmas Parties, Entertaining; see also subsequent party entries.*

Memories are made from special celebrations. Parties don't need to be time consuming or expensive—but they do need to be fun for the celebrants. Prior to age three, the birthday party is mainly for adults. Make it a rule that there can be one friend invited for each year of age (thus a three-year-old invites three friends, a sixteen-year-old may have as many as sixteen).

A party should be two to four hours in length, shorter for young children, longer for teens. Make a time schedule for the party so that you can see there is adequate time for arrivals, games and crafts, opening packages, refreshments, and free play. Parties for younger children sometimes require help from other parents, but for teens your main assignment is to be a chaperone. Don't turn aside from this important job; it's your duty to be aware but not intrusive. For complete party details, see *The Family Party Book* (Caryl Krueger, Abingdon Press, Nashville, Tenn.).

PARTY DECORATIONS.

Go beyond balloons! For a younger child's party, consider hanging a sheet at the door on which you have illustrated the theme with marking pens: a clown's face, a birthday cake, a pirate ship. With a train theme, decorate the playroom with large cardboard boxes made to look like box cars, caboose, dining car, and engine. For older children, develop the theme by creating interesting places to sit: South Sea Islands made from pillows and fake palm trees made of PVC pipe, or cardboard boxes that are turned into space ships. For a wild west party, use bales of hay for seating. As soon as your child selects a theme, discuss what could be done to bring that fantasy to reality in the party room.

Just a change in light can make a room look different. For a dance, decorate with tiny Christmas lights strung around the room, giving just the right amount of light. Or, hang a mirrored ball with a spotlight aimed at it. Sometimes the decor can be as simple as a fire in the fireplace, streamers over the patio, or a variety of candles safely placed on various surfaces.

PARTY FOOD.

Until youngsters are preteens, party food is not too important. For younger children, serve it where it can be easily cleaned up. Younger children like pancakes with many toppings, dipping strawberries in chocolate or sprinkles, hot dogs wound in biscuit dough and baked, and individual cupcakes with relighting candles. Older kids like to get involved by making their own individual pizzas, subway sandwiches, or sundaes. Adults enjoy parties where everyone helps cook the meal. If the party location is outside, consider packing lunches in individual baskets or backpacks (cheaply purchased at an army surplus store).

Cakes are often the highlight and it can be fun to make big ones using various sized pans, a variety of cake mixes, lots of frosting, and lettering. Cakes can be made in the shape of boats, cars, rabbits, lambs, hearts, trains, and other simple objects to tie in with the party theme.

PARTY GAMES AND ICEBREAKERS.

Much of the party time will be taken up with games. Have an activity for the time while everyone is arriving: decorating the goody bags, face painting, or guessing how many candies are in a jar.

Here are some intriguing games for after everyone has arrived:

- **A Penny Hunt.** Scatter 100 pennies—some in the open, some slightly hidden—and give each child a sandwich bag for collecting and keeping.

- **Rembrandts.** Paint outside on glass sliding doors or with art paper attached on a fence.

- **The Tunnel.** Purchase a twelve-foot length of stretchy black tube material (an investment that will last for years) and let kids crawl through it individually, while being timed, or as a relay race with players coming from opposite ends and passing in the middle.

- **Tempting Tangles.** Make a string maze (strings laid out in one room from the doorway to across the room) with players picking up one end and not letting go until they find a little reward at the other end.

- **Weird Relays.** Players push eggplants with sticks to the finish line and back. (You will find that an eggplant has a mind of its own!)

- **Funny Faces.** Make big cookies and give youngsters icing tubes to draw faces on them. Give a prize for the funniest and then eat them.

- **Gone Fishing.** Give players sticks with strings ending with a large clothespin. Divide into two groups, half on either side of a sheet, each with a basket. Shuffle a deck of cards and give each side half. Each side sorts its cards on the floor to see what sets of four (four sevens, four jacks) it has and puts those in its basket. One side goes fishing by sending their strings over the top of the sheet. The other side attaches unwanted cards and then the first side checks to see if those complete any of their sets of four. Then it is the other side's chance to go fishing and the game continues until one side has matched all their cards into sets, or has the most sets of four.

PARTY PRIZES AND FAVORS.

Make prizes so plentiful that everyone wins and has something to take home at the end of a party. Some good prizes for younger kids are: rubber stamps and ink pads, stickers, masks, bubble stuff, books, sing-along tapes. For older youngsters: magazines, tapes, movie passes, jazzy pens, mod jewelry. For adults: coffee mugs, party napkins, paperback mysteries, fireplace logs, unusual candles.

191

PARTY THEMES.

Let the honoree choose the kind of party he wants, then work together to carry out the theme. It can be anything from a tea party with dolls to a sophisticated dance. Younger children like themes such as pirates, clowns, cowboys, and trains. Older kids enjoy themes such as safari, Olympics, Hawaii, video production, western, hobos, and space. Teen themes could be: karaoki, sweet sixteen, South Seas, pentathlon, pool or beach, progressive dinner, or a time capsule party.

You can also create a unique occasion for a party: the first day of spring, an April 15 tax party, a housewarming, kite-flying day, or a beach party with a castle-building contest.

PATIENCE.

One of the most difficult traits to learn is patience and it is best taught by example. Sometimes a bad example can be a memorable teaching tool.

 When a youngster begins to talk, and there are words you don't understand, patiently repeat the words you *do* understand and then ask the child to say the other words. Your patient kindness will encourage his willingness to communicate clearly. In teaching her to tie a bow or tell time, keep your cool as you go over the procedure step-by-step and time-after-time until she masters it.

With older children, you also need patience to teach and teach again, patience to put up with fads, patience to forgive mistakes, patience to let a youngster find his own way out of a mess. Being patient is not always easy, but impatience spreads the frustration without solving the problem.

Show patience with playmates and relatives, with the dog, with poor service, and point out to children how much more important it is to feel good about yourself than to fly off at someone else.

PATRIOTISM. *See also Politics.*

While it is an American "right" to complain about the American way of life, few people have found a better system. Talk about what is right in our country, what is wrong, and how the wrong might be changed. The object of our loyalty doesn't have to be perfect, just worthy of our allegiance.

Take time to observe patriotic holidays, not just Independence Day but also Memorial Day, Flag Day, and Veterans Day. Use an encyclopedia to share facts on our country, its founders, and its present day patriots.

 Put up a flag pole and let it be the duty of one youngster to raise and lower the flag each day. If you wish, you can focus a light on the flag so that it can be visible even in the dark. Teach youngsters the "Pledge of Allegiance" before they go to kindergarten.

True patriotism includes an inner sense of closeness to a country's land, its people, traditions, and a devotion to the welfare of the country. It starts with good citizenship within the family and then grows to good citizenship in the community. Talk about political issues that concern family and community life and what a patriotic person could do about these. After some investigation, pick one that is suitable for all the family and give time to work on it.

The core of patriotism is responsibility for one's own actions and love and caring for others. Discuss patriotic songs, use of the flag, heroes of the past and present, issues of nationwide interest, places to express patriotism, ways of settling disputes, legal and effective ways to "revolt," patriotism versus supremacy, and the importance of respect for the nationality, traditions, beliefs, and languages of other people.

PEACEMAKER. *See also Conflict, Fighting, Ombudsman, Problem Solving.*

Every home needs one person dedicated to bringing strife to a harmonious conclusion. Praise the child who usually prefers compromise to confrontation. Not everything is worth a fight. However, don't teach youngsters to knuckle under every time; solve the problem, don't give in to it.

PEDIATRICIAN.

When you choose a pediatrician or family doctor who specializes in children, carefully investigate in advance of your need. Your connection may be a long one so try to select the right one the first time. Consider recommendations from friends and check on each doctor's original training and subsequent training to keep his knowledge current. Interview the top two on your list and see how their philosophies and approaches vary, how comfortable you feel talking with them, how competent the entire facility and staff are. Decide if you prefer a male or a female. Determine the doctor's style. Does he listen and make suggestions? Does he prescribe medicine before he investigates? Does he enjoy children and have rapport with them?

Once you have chosen a pediatrician, keep in close touch and comply with the recommended visits. Don't try to second guess him by altering or ignoring his advice. Be thorough in your comments to him and keep good written records of each visit.

PEER PRESSURE. *See also Bullies, Sibling Rivalry.*

Even before a child knows the meaning of the words, she is using her skills to manipulate others. A preschooler shows a toddler how to throw food and laugh about it. A grade-school boy hands over his lunch money so he isn't pummeled by a bully. A teen takes an alcoholic drink so she looks grown-up like her friends. Peer pressure doesn't require deep thought; it is usually just following others to fit in. In advance of need, go over hypothetical instances where peer pressure might be used to force a youngster to make a bad choice. Talk about ways to avoid giving in to peer pressure.

PERFECTIONISTS. *See also Obsessive-Compulsive Disorder.*

Attention to every minute detail and the need to always excel can both frustrate and depress a youngster, especially those of above-average intelligence who think they should always be perfect. Such children often have highly capable parents and they perceive that the parent will be disappointed in anything less than perfection. Some, not willing to be anything less than absolutely perfect, suddenly decide not to try at all.

When a child is continually worried, and consequently suffering from eating and sleeping disorders or other unusual behavior, parents must step in with valid reassurance. Spend time with the child, assure her that you care deeply for her as a precious daughter—much more than for her triumphs. Show her that some things are not worth the time to do in a completely perfect way. Also indicate where you as a parent can cut corners to simplify or speed up a task. Introduce small joys, rewards, and casual fun into family life so life is more than a succession of things to achieve.

PERSEVERANCE, PERSISTENCE. *See Determination.*

PESTS, PESTERING. *See also Nagging, One-Chance Parent, Questions, Reminding, Whining.*

Pests are usually created by parents who permit children to ask repeated questions. It is usually the child's subtle way of asking for attention, to be heard, to be talked to. Often when parents fail to respond the first time, or give an unsatisfactory answer (in the child's estimation), the same question is asked again. It would be simpler to sit down face-to-face and answer the question the first time, ending the conversation with the question: "Is that what you wanted to know?" If you can't take the time to talk at the very moment the question is asked, make a definite appointment for later: "We'll talk right after dinner; you don't need to ask again."

Some pests are asking for a privilege. Having been given an answer the first time, an answer they didn't like, they think they may get a more favorable answer the second time. Unless you made a mistake, don't give in and change your answer. If you do, you're setting yourself up for more pestering.

 At the end of dinner, have a nightly question-and-answer time, letting kids ask anything they wish and getting a concise answer from a parent. Some of these sessions can be very illuminating.

PETS. *See also Responsibility.*

The care of an animal can be one of the best learning experiences for a young child. To select the right pet, choose one that a youngster can care for with minimum parental help. Before getting the pet, talk about how it would feel if neglected: not fed, talked to, or played with. Consider the cost to buy and care for a pet. Also, total up the amount of time required each day for the upkeep of the pet and decide who will be responsible for the tasks. Be sure it will not primarily be the parent.

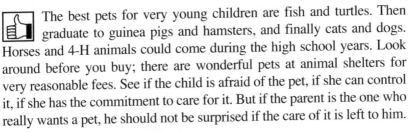 The best pets for very young children are fish and turtles. Then graduate to guinea pigs and hamsters, and finally cats and dogs. Horses and 4-H animals could come during the high school years. Look around before you buy; there are wonderful pets at animal shelters for very reasonable fees. See if the child is afraid of the pet, if she can control it, if she has the commitment to care for it. But if the parent is the one who really wants a pet, he should not be surprised if the care of it is left to him.

Have a yearly pet day when the family celebrates the pet's birthday with a new collar or fish bowl. At a yard picnic including birthday cake, talk about how the pet joined the family, and what the pet has learned and contributed to family life.

When a pet dies, take the passing seriously and consider a family memorial service. Talk about how much the family loved the pet and how much love the pet expressed. For young children, say "Sometimes a pet gets sick and cannot stay here with us anymore." Avoid morbid details.

 Don't immediately replace the pet. In the coming weeks, talk about what kind of pet to have next and who will care for it.

PHOTOGRAPHS. *See also Memorabilia.*

Photos are an important part of family history: monthly shots of the new baby, the yearly birthday picture, plus special pictures of graduations,

195

weddings, sports events, parties, and reunions. But don't forget to take candid pictures of the everyday life of your family. Make good use of the photos you've taken; send some off to distant relatives, put others in the family photo album and be sure to date them and identify the people and places in the photos.

PHOTOGRAPHY.

A simple camera is a good gift for a youngster at about age seven. Suggest she start with pictures of pets and pals and when the photos are developed, show (uncritically) how the pictures could be improved by framing or centering a subject, being sure the light comes from in front, or moving in closer. When a youngster gets proficient, let her graduate to more intricate cameras and video cameras and even become the family's photojournalist.

PLAY. *See also Activities, Games, Outdoor Play.*

Play fosters a child's positive self-worth and brings freedom from many rules and routines. It provides a sense of achievement and satisfaction, and most important, it brings happiness. Play promotes a youngster's language development and his ability to solve problems, often on his own.

Playtime is the chief joy of childhood. Freedom to play with toys gets lost when too much structure enters a child's life. Be sure there is time for making a city from blocks, doing puzzles, drawing and pasting. Rotate toys (put some away for a few months) so that there are regularly fresh ones with which to play.

Create play places (at least one that doesn't need to be cleaned up daily) in a child's room, a family room, a basement playroom, and in the backyard.

Bring organization to toys by providing plastic covered bins or cardboard boxes for storing blocks, trucks, small musical instruments, dress-up clothes, stuffed animals, art supplies, and so forth.

Let kids settle their own playtime disagreements as much as possible. After play with friends, talk with your child about what was good (or not good) about the play.

Never discipline your child in front of others, instead take him to another room for a corrective chat. Greet and feed playmates, but don't intrude on the play. Be prepared with ideas should boredom set in.

PLAY HOUSES. *See also Outdoor Play.*

Whether indoors or out, a special place of their own is a wonderful plaything for a child. A card table covered with an old sheet can be a clubhouse, a space ship, or a fine location for book reading or a nap.

Outdoor playhouses can come in all sizes depending on the age of the children. Start with a simple wood platform about one foot off the ground and placed under a tree. Sand it to avoid splinters. Use a bed sheet or tarp for a roof and attach it to the tree. Little ones can have fun jumping off of it, putting large cardboard boxes on it as rooms, and eating lunch on it.

The next step is to make a split-level house using this platform and adding another a few feet higher up the tree trunk, but not directly above the low platform. Securely fasten the higher platform to the tree or a nearby fence or support posts. Attach a sturdy rope ladder to get to the second level. Games or make-believe activities go well with this house.

Eventually youngsters will want a house way up in the tree, as high as safety permits. This requires more lumber and secure building. Attach sturdy netting around the top level so that inhabitants are safe. This three-level structure can be a quiet retreat for thinking or a noisy place for parties and sleep-outs.

Of course you can embellish these houses with walls and windows and a weatherproof roof, but part of the fun is first letting kids enjoy it in simple form. Later you can work together to make it a real mansion complete with a bell to announce visitors, a light fixture, simple furniture, and a waterproof box to hold supplies. Don't be surprised if teens and adults also want to spend time in the tree house, too.

PLAYPEN.

Considering the size of a baby in proportion to a playpen, it's like a small child in a cozy, safe room. A playpen used for fifteen to thirty minutes twice a day teaches a child to be independent and play alone. It is the safest place your child can be as you work on a project or answer the door or phone.

To intrigue baby, affix a shoe bag to the wall of the playpen and fill it with toys. Start to use a playpen when the baby is a few months old and can only lie there and look around. Soon she'll move toward the shoe bag and reach for items in the lower pockets. And eventually she'll be able to sit up and reach all the special toys there

A playpen lets a youngster learn how to entertain herself, it increases a youngster's attention span, it teaches choices (play with the toys or toss them out of the playpen), and it provides a padded place to learn to roll over and later stand up. Best of all, the playpen is a safe place from electric outlets and sharp corners. It increases a child's feeling of self-government and independence, and that's what growing up is all about.

POETRY. *See also Reading.*

Rhymes can be fun and soothing, that's why many books for young children are in rhyme. As children get older, continue reading poetry at mealtimes, bathtime, bedtime. Poetry expresses three essentials: the beauty of language, a sense of rhythm, and the understanding of people and places through word pictures.

POISE. *See also Conversation, Leadership, Manners, Shyness.*

Give a youngster opportunities that challenge him to think on his feet, to speak and act spontaneously. Encourage talk at home: to present new ideas, to make social conversation, to disagree pleasantly, and to ask intelligent questions. Practice oral reports at home.

Give youngsters opportunities to learn new things worth sharing. At dinner each night, let youngsters share something interesting that happened that day.

A poised child has been instructed at home in how to be a good leader, how to be a good follower, and also in table manners, conversation, introductions, safety, giving and receiving compliments. Older youngsters gain poise when they know how to ask for a date and make conversation during a date, how to dance and what to do when a dance is over, how to act in a public place when others are misbehaving, how to refuse alcohol politely, how to dress appropriately for special occasions, how to courteously open doors, offer an arm or a hand, and talk with adults.

Before a child goes to a party or is taken on an excursion, go over in advance how to greet her friends, how to be a good sport, and how and when to say "thank you." Suggest to children that when going to a social event they think in advance of five things they can talk about. If the trip is to a cultural event, read about the event in the newspaper or in an encyclopedia, and talk about how to act during a performance: what to read before it begins, when to applaud, and not to make conversation during the actual performance.

POLITENESS. *See Manners.*

POLITICS. *See also Business and Government, Patriotism.*

Your youngster may grow up to have different political beliefs than you. That's fine if you teach children at an early age about democracy, why it is important, and how it works. When a child is about five, talk about voting and even take her with you to the polling place. At election times, discuss the issues and how they will affect family and community life. Encourage youngsters to write letters to candidates on issues that affect them. Let each youngster follow one candidate and share with the family the positions that candidate takes. Stay up late on election night and see the success of your issues and candidates.

POPULARITY. *See also Friends.*

Being liked by others can be highly important to children. "I hate you and never want to play with you again" can be devastating words. You can help a child to be popular in *positive* ways, not in ways such as being faddish, showing off by spending money, or exemplifying bad habits such as promiscuity or using drugs.

 An unpopular child is argumentative, bossy, and often manipulative in order to get his own way.

 A popular child is willing to compromise, cares about the happiness of others, is optimistic and creative.

POSSESSIONS AND POSSESSIVENESS. *See also Play, Sharing.*

Possessions should merely be tools for increasing intelligence, happiness, and abilities. It is natural for children to want to have certain things and sometimes they feel it is a right to take those things from others. Pride of ownership is good when it teaches children to take care of their possessions. But there are even greater lessons learned through sharing those same possessions.

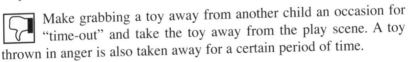 Make grabbing a toy away from another child an occasion for "time-out" and take the toy away from the play scene. A toy thrown in anger is also taken away for a certain period of time.

If one toy is very popular, use a timer to give each youngster an opportunity to play with it; or, find several other toys that can be played *with* the favorite toy.

Unfortunately, most children nowadays have too many possessions and too little time to play with them. Get rid of unused toys and rotate the ones that are left, letting some rest for a few months in a packing box on a high shelf.

Give youngsters places to keep their possessions. Make them responsible for the many little parts of some toys. A set of large stacking plastic see-through bins or cardboard boxes can help bring order to toys.

When a child receives her first piece of jewelry or watch, establish a box in her room where jewelry is kept. Teach this rule: There are only two places for your jewelry—on you or in your box. Jewelry left in bathrooms and other places should be confiscated by the parent and returned after a discussion of the rule.

POSTURE.

So important to good appearance in childhood and good health in adulthood is the care of the spine. Without being a nag, encourage good posture in youngsters so that standing straight and tall becomes second nature.

Be alert to problems caused by a heavy backpack or by carrying heavy objects on one hip. Better-designed and lighter packs are now available and many students are resorting to a cart with small wheels to tote heavy school books.

Rather than permitting lying down to do homework, provide a good chair at a desk or table so that the youngster sits comfortably but straight while working.

POT. *See Substance Abuse.*

POWER PLAYS. *See also Tantrums.*

Testing the resolve of a parent is called a power play. A child does something that makes him feel in charge of parental responses. This can take the form of tantrums, excessive anger, and repeated unacceptable behavior such as soiling underpants. Often the child is not bothered by being punished. The aim is usually to get attention. In some cases, it helps if the parent merely refuses to give the demanded attention.

When a child tries a power play, give him a choice: "Stop kicking your little brother or there will be immediate punishment." Stay calm and in control when the child is neither calm nor controlled. Don't be taken in when a child acts out, but at a later time discuss the wrong behavior with the child. Determine what triggered it and how to correct it. State clearly your disapproval and what the punishment will be if he tries a power play another time.

PRAISE. *See also Appreciation, Criticism, Put-Downs and Put-Ups, Self-Worth, Success.*

Praise can be the oil that helps a home run without friction. Praise has a more lasting effect when it is specific rather than general. This "pointed praise" can be more than "Thank you for helping in the kitchen" but instead, "Thanks for emptying the dishwasher and even finding where the pie pans go."

Use words of pointed praise similar to these: "You're wonderful to help your brother with his spelling." "I knew you could climb to the top." "That improved grade is incredible." "I admire what you did when no one else would help." "I'm proud of your Scout award." "Your drawing is well done, especially the colors!" "What a smart idea to hang your caps on the wall."

PRAYERS. *See also Faith, Grace, Religion.*

Prayer is merely talking to God and then listening. It does not need to include big words or long pleadings. Say prayers for babies and teach them to toddlers. Then suggest prayers for grade-school and teenage children.

Make prayer a natural response to challenges. Athletes, actors, politicians, business people, and medical doctors have witnessed the power of prayer. In fact, one doctor stated that in a decade from now it will be considered malpractice for a doctor to fail to mention prayer in connection with conquering health problems.

Here is a prayer for a baby.

Little one, I hold you near—
With God you're safe from every fear.
My kisses send you on your way—
So let sweet sleep now end your day.

This is a typical prayer for a young child to learn.

The day is over, the world's at rest.
Keep me safe, keep me blessed.
Tomorrow help me learn and play
Sharing love along the way.

201

Thank you for my family, too.
Make them pleased with what I do.
When in trouble, hear my prayer.
Now to sleep, safe in Your care.

Here is a prayer for a teen.

Dear loving Parent of us all,
Guide me through the coming day.
Give me strength to just say no
When temptations come my way.
Help me love when I see hate,
Let me know adventure, too!
Teach me what I need to know
But keep me safe in what I do.
With You I know I'm not alone
So help me make an honest choice
Free from fear and angry words.
Yes, I'm listening for Your voice.

Here is a prayer for parents.

As this day closes and I look back on its joys and challenges
Let me be grateful for raising a child in a free country
    for the loving support of family, friends, teachers
    for the progress made in giant leaps or faltering steps
    for the realization that my most important gifts to my child aren't
    things, but thoughts.
And for the day soon unfolding, give me
    a comprehension of my child's precious uniqueness
    the patience to show right from wrong
    the humility to lead and loose my child
    the enthusiasm to live adventurously as a family.
Thank you for the privilege of guiding one of Your children....
Let me do it with joy, with hope, and most of all, with love.

PREGNANCY, TEENAGE. *See also Abortion, Adoption, Sex.*

Children having children is usually the result of faulty education of teens and preteens who think "It couldn't happen to me." Many youngsters believe in three myths: they are invulnerable, it's normal to have a hard time planning ahead, and sexual activity is most enjoyable when it's impulsive. Despite the increased availability of contraceptive devices, youngsters let emotions take over. And parents hesitate to talk about pre-marital sex and pregnancy because they think that bringing up the topic gives it validity.

Start early and be very explicit about how babies are made. Your library will have books with good illustrations. The embarrassment of dis-cussing pregnancy is a lot less than handling it after the fact. Talk about how a life changes with a baby, the emotional toll of abortion, and the adoption option.

Should a teen become pregnant, seek professional help to help sort out the many ramifications. Research shows that babies born to immature youngsters are more apt to repeat the cycle. Opt for early education and break the cycle.

PREJUDICE. *See Cultural Differences.*

PRESCHOOL. *See also Child Care Facilities, Day Care.*
A preschool should be designed for play and for learning social skills. Avoid the school that is pushing a child out of the playtime years by encouraging age-inappropriate learning that could eventually bring on academic burnout. You want an atmosphere that is based on excitement combined with some routine. Be alert to these points:

• Two or more children the same age as yours.
• A curriculum of activities that support eye-hand coordination, motor skills, following directions, learning to dress self, using the bathroom, working with others, and increasing attention span.
• Teaching basic educational skills such as colors, some numbers and let-ters, writing one's name, knowing one's name and address, safety rules, using scissors, paste, and crayons.
• An outside play area with grass, sand, or wood chips for safety.
• A visually attractive room with smoke detectors, locked storage for harmful substances, and a nearby telephone for emergencies.
• A program of learning where the child has some options about what to do.
• An adult/child ratio of one to eight.
• Teachers and assistants with specific training in early education.
• A teaching philosophy that is pressure free.
• Teaching at a child's eye level, instead of "from above."

- A large library of quality books.
- A happy atmosphere.

PRESIDENTS' DAY.

Honor our heritage with a dinner that celebrates Washington and Lincoln but also talks about other presidents. If possible, invite a foreign exchange student to share dinner with you. Talk about patriotism and democracy and the contributions of these and other U.S. presidents.

PRETENDING. *See Make-Believe.*

PRIORITIES. *See also Order, Organizational Skills, Telephoning.*

Learning how to do first things first is a difficult subject for children. Show youngsters how there can be time after necessary tasks to kick back and have fun. Talk about the important things in life as opposed to trivial or transient events. Occasionally cancel your own plans so you can do something your child feels is important. Show him that his well-being is a priority for you. Use the word "priority" often: "What is our priority before bed?" "What's your top priority at school?" "What's our family's priority this weekend?" When a child has many things to do, help her to make a list and then number them, putting the most important first.

PRIVACY. *See also Modesty.*

Respect for the space of others should be taught early. Instruct youngsters to knock on closed doors, keep out of other's possessions, and not read mail addressed to others. Provide a locked drawer or box so a youngster can have a place to keep precious things. A youngster's room is his private domain and parents must have trust and not snoop in the room. The only exceptions are if you suspect that drugs or stolen property may be stashed in there.

Private times are essential, too. Respect a child who wants to bathe alone, read or play alone, or do homework alone.

PRIVILEGES. *See also Choices, Maturity, Rules.*

With each succeeding year, a youngster should be given more privileges and more choices to make on her own. Privileges differ from choices in that they are not automatic rights but are earned by showing responsibility. Privileges are granted by a parent or society, while a choice is a decision made by the child.

Privileges include: crossing a street, going to a movie alone, driving a car, owning a phone, and so forth. Youngsters need to show good sense before being granted these options. Review privileges with youngsters each autumn before school begins and, if possible, grant some new ones in keeping with the youngster's maturity.

PROBLEM SOLVING. *See also Arguing, Fighting, Ombudsman.*

Learning how to resolve problems is a vital skill. Encourage family members to keep a list of things that need to be resolved; just making the list takes away the stress. When the entire family has time to share ideas, then consider these listed challenges one by one, following these five steps:

1. Gather facts, not opinions.
2. State the problem concisely to the agreement of all.
3. List every possible solution, no matter how outlandish. This lets some be ruled out more quickly as everyone focuses on the workable ones.
4. Consider each alternative fully, showing how it will affect each family member and how it could solve the problem.
5. Choose the most likely solution for now and agree to try it for a specified length of time. If this solution does not work, try another.

Don't try to solve a problem when angry. If any participant feels he is losing his temper, adjourn the meeting to another time. There should be no winners or losers, just solutions.

A major consideration in problem solving is feelings: hurt feelings, anxious feelings, jealous feelings. As important as finding the facts is uncovering the feelings behind the problem and how one can respond to them with an equitable solution.

PROFANITY. *See also Communication, Language, Put-Downs and Put-Ups, Rudeness, Words, Yelling.*

Once reserved for exceptional situations, profanity has now sadly crept into everyday language, causing a deterioration in conversational skills.

The use of swear words starts when young children hear them from their parents or peers. Take immediate action to stop the use of these inaccurate, inflammatory, and unnecessary words. Do not giggle or freak out. In some cases, giving the true definition of the word will curb further use. Unacceptable words fall in three categories and are called "P words": profane words including the term God as in "Oh my God," potty words (the favorites of toddlers), and put-downs, which include name-calling. Youngsters can be given more acceptable words to use for emphasis. For response to a disappointing event, try "Thunderation!" and for a good result say "Hallelujah!"

Put a large glass jar with a slit in the sealed-on lid on the kitchen counter. The use of a word in one of the three "P" categories costs the adult or child a fine—under age six: ten cents, grade-schoolers: twenty-five cents, teens: fifty cents, and adults: one dollar. Use the money for a special all-family purpose.

It is encouraging that many schools are adopting a cuss-control policy, encouraging students to stop swearing and start searching for more meaningful words of expression. Such programs have been successful and have had the side effect of cutting down on hostility that formerly resulted in fights. The entire atmosphere of the school has become more pleasant. This can happen at home, too. Learning how to articulate without vulgarity when in an argument hastens the solution and improves civility.

Today, profanity and other objectionable topics are considered acceptable in movies, on television, and in websites. Parents have a right to prohibit the viewing of shows that are basically a string of profane words. There are products available to screen out objectionable material on the Internet.

PROMISES.

A person's word is of great value. Don't promise a reward you can't give or a punishment you aren't willing to follow through on. Use the word "promise" as an indicator of your love and care: "I promise to play a game with you when I return from work." "I promise to telephone as soon as I arrive."

Don't force youngsters to make promises concerning unlikely achievements, such as "I want you to promise to practice the piano one hour every day this year." Rather, express your hope they will do so and work out a plan to achieve this. To emphasize the importance of dedication, encourage the use of the phrase "I promise" when you feel a youngster is sincere and has the ability to achieve success.

PUBERTY. *See also Sex.*

The change from child to adolescent is called puberty and can be very emotional and confusing for the entire family. But it is not a given that the physical changes must lead to dramatic changes in family relationships.

Maturing is not a one-step process, it is evident in many steps: physical changes, sexual urges, selection of higher education or career, becoming old enough to drive, drink, or vote—these are just some of the passages that youngsters go through with ease or difficulty.

Some rebellion, some moodiness, some seizure of control is not unusual, and most parents can, with patience, good education, and communication, live through these. The sheer volume of changes in a youngster's life can be emotionally stressful if each step is not explained and parameters given for any new privileges. This is the time when parents must gradually find more and more areas where a youngster has control, to balance those areas where it is not yet wise to give up control. If parents permit harmless rebellions and don't go ballistic, the desired shock value of these is often lost.

Menarche, a girl's first menstrual period, usually comes between ages eleven and fifteen. If earlier, girls feel out of place with peers and may need special help from an understanding adult. Boys have similar problems with the changes in their bodies. Although their bodies are developing before age fourteen, most youngsters are not socially sophisticated before then; hence they are at a loss to handle changes. The issues of puberty are serious to youngsters and are not occasions for teasing but rather opportunities for healthy private discussions.

PUNISHMENT. *See also Criticism, Deprivation, Discipline, Obedience, One-Chance Parent, Rules, Spanking.*

Overlook minor wrongs but when you punish, be clear about the point you are making: that certain conduct is unacceptable. Mean what you say! Don't announce a punishment that you cannot carry out. If you don't follow through with punishments, kids will think you don't care and continue with bad behavior.

As much as possible, carry out punishments at home and fairly soon after the mistake. Because it is difficult to punish in public, tell children in advance what you expect and what will happen afterward if they act out. Then see that you carry out an effective punishment at home.

Parents should divide the correctional duties so one parent isn't the ogre, the other the sweetie pie. And, the punishment should, if possible, have some relation to the mistake.

Humiliation is no part of punishment. It erodes the self-esteem you've worked so hard to build. It is a not-so-subtle form of child abuse.

Behavior training starts with babies when you use a pleasant voice and smiling face (when the baby eats his food) or a somber face (when he throws all his toys out of the playpen).

Do not let youngsters appeal to the other parent for an easier punishment; stand united. When punishment is over, teach children to say "I'm sorry."

Don't be a nag. State what you expect one time. Let the punishment be known. Give one warning and then be quiet and let the child choose.

Consider these nonspanking ways of correcting unacceptable behavior:

Time-out (also called the Thinking Bench). Remove a youngster to a quiet place to think over what he's done. Let the place be without distractions, not his own room, but perhaps the laundry room. Have him sit on a little bench or chair and state clearly what he did that was wrong. If he seems not to know the mistake, explain it to him. Set a timer for three to five minutes. Before he's permitted to leave, ask him what he would do differently the next time. This is a good punishment for children under about eight. Even though it takes some time to put it into action, it will eventually save you time since the youngster will begin to think more about his actions in advance.

Deprivation. Take away certain beloved privileges or toys. This is very effective for most children and teens. It succeeds when you know a child well enough to know what the deprivation should involve: a very special toy, play at a friend's, phone privileges, car use, a night out, and so forth. Be alert not to let the deprivation affect other members of the family: don't say "We won't go to the circus if you keep hitting." Deprivation teaches a child that the loss of self-control and the resulting wrong behavior means the loss of privileges, as it does in the world outside his family.

Verbal correction. For some children, a lecture can be very impressive. A serious one-on-one talk is most effective when the parent explains the ramifications of the wrong action. It is best used when a child has done something dangerous or thoughtless such as playing with matches or running into the street. Repeat the message several times in different ways so that it is clearly understood. And, have the youngster write out the rule she has broken.

Written correction. Express disappointment by writing a note that the youngster can look at again and again. This is meaningful as it also says "My parent thinks this is important enough to write about it." (Be sure that along with disciplinary letters you also write notes of appreciation.)

Undoing the damage. Teach children how to remedy a wrong such as cleaning up a spill or mending or paying for what was carelessly broken. The parent may be able to undo the damage more quickly, but letting the child do it teaches an important lesson about cause and effect: that thoughtless action takes up his time.

Working it off. Assign extra work to a youngster who has thoughtlessly taken a parent's time. When a child cannot undo what he has done wrong, the parent must fix it, such as mending a hole in his shirt, cut while playing with scissors. This takes the parent's time, and in return, the child pays back by doing special work such as dusting or weeding. It should be quiet work so the youngster can think about the mistake.

A Special Project. This unique punishment is for those occasions when the mistake is of great magnitude. Reserve this for times when a child has done something to endanger life: drag racing, playing with guns, staying out all night. It worked well for a family when a youngster broke a rule about having no friends in the fenced pool area when an adult is not home. The offender had to do research and write an essay on the subject of responsibility that required interviews with neighbors and library time. In addition, the offender had to take an after-school CPR class that took away free time for a week. It was an effective deterrent to all the other children in the family and was also known in the neighborhood.

When any form of punishment is over, reassure the child that it was not he but his behavior that you did not like, and that your affection for him is the very reason he was punished. Use the line "I love you too much to let you act that way."

PUT-DOWNS AND PUT-UPS. *See also Criticism, Praise, Self-Worth, Words.*

While parents should learn to correct children without putting them down, many youngsters relish putting down their siblings and peers. Put-ups are the opposite of put-downs and accomplish far more than their negative counterpart.

A put-down is an attempt to make another feel lowly, unworthy, useless or unintelligent. Yet, unwittingly, these lines are used in everyday conversation. Parents say: "You never do anything right." Kids say "Hi, four-eyes!" A day of put-downs can send a child to bed feeling unloved, and if she hears a sufficient number of them, she may accept them as fact.

A put-up is a statement that gives a boost, that acknowledges a success, no matter how small. It must be a true statement, said with sincerity. "You were a great help cleaning the garage. I couldn't have done it as well without you." "You look nice in red." "You made my favorite dessert." While put-ups are usually compliments or happy comments, it's important to avoid superlatives that can be seen as puffery: "No one in the world had a better book report than yours." However, superlatives can be useful if the child understands them: "You were as strong as a tiger in separating your fighting friends."

Through an understanding of put-ups and put-downs, we can teach children the joy of recognizing good in others and in themselves.

QUALITY TIME. *See also Time Management.*

This popular concept has given comfort to busy parents who think they can make up for hours of separation by a few intense moments together with their child. Not true. Nothing can totally make up for the separation. And when that parent chooses to spend the quality time with the child, she may be involved in some other project, or too sleepy. So, along with quality time, there must be quantity time. That way a parent can be on hand to give input when a child wants to share something important or is troubled. Absent parents must be aware that they cannot just choose the times when their child will need their help.

Time spent with youngsters can take place in a variety of places: in the car, while folding laundry, cooking together, playing a game on the patio, or talking in the dark before bed. Of course quality time is important, but so is quantity time.

QUESTIONS AND REPEATED REQUESTS. *See also Pests, Reminding.*

Some youngsters don't take "no" for an answer and continuously ask the same questions over and over again, to the great frustration of a parent. This problem is not the child's but the parent's, a parent who does not mean what she says. For example, the child who has already had two cookies begs for another, is told "no," begs again and is told "no" again, begs again and this time the parent gives in. This exercise in repeated requests has taught the child:

• How to get his way.
• Repetition pays off.
• Being a pest gets rewards.
• Pleading has benefits.

- When mother or dad is tired, you can get them to agree to most anything.
- Parents don't usually mean what they say.

Whether it is "no," "yes," "maybe," "now," or "later," one answer should be sufficient. If not, kids will learn to use this repeated questioning device on matters far more important than cookies: bedtimes, doing chores, seeing a television show, curfews, or borrowing the car. And more repeated requests will follow in the years ahead. Thus it's important that parents mean what they say: *the first time*.

Good responses to repeated questions are: "I've already answered that," and "Didn't you understand what I said?"

QUIET TIME. *See also Homework, "Me Time."*

After school and play, children benefit from about thirty minutes of quiet time before dinner. This can be a time for reading, drawing, writing a letter, or doing homework. Research shows that grade-schoolers do the best homework in the time before dinner, utilizing a quiet, studious atmosphere. Teens are wise to at least get started on their homework during this period.

READING. *See also Books, Dyslexia, Library, Magazines, Poetry.*

If a child can read, he can do anything! Read to children for at least fifteen minutes each day, starting with babies. When a child learns to read, let him read on his own, but also read more advanced books with you. If a child has difficulty learning to read, get help immediately. Subscribe to age-appropriate magazines for children. Encourage youngsters to bring something they have read to share at the dinner table.

Let children see you reading. Establish a time to all read together. Let younger children choose a book each morning for reading during the day. Ask questions about the story as you read together. Make up new endings for familiar stories. Stop in the middle of a sentence and let the child fill in the next words. Introduce a children's dictionary. When the alphabet is being learned, let a child point out letters in books, along the roads, or in the grocery store.

For readers, put messages in lunch boxes. Let new readers "perform" by reading aloud to siblings. Start a book club at home, in the neighborhood, or through the school. Reward good reading habits with little gifts such as bookmarks or book plates.

Make a deal that for every hour of television watched, there will be thirty minutes of reading. And reward children with a fifteen minute later bedtime if they will read in bed.

Read in various places. Select a book for reading at dinner each night — for just ten or fifteen minutes at a time. Encourage reading in the bathtub, while listening to music, while riding in the car, while resting during a hike, at the beach, around the fireplace, and in a tree.

REBELLION. *See also Puberty, Running Away, Tantrums, Teen Years.*

Revolts are part of growing up. Show a child how to rebel in a responsible and respectful way. Youngsters as well as parents can change home life and community life for the better by presenting ideas in an organized and reasonable way.

Don't demand compliance when a youngster starts a revolt. Be calm and understanding, ask for facts and give facts, ask questions, see if a good compromise can be reached. Respect the youngster by giving him an active part in decision making when possible.

Give children many choices so they feel they are totally in charge of some things. Make it clear some decisions currently made by parents will eventually be made by the youngster. Pick the occasions when you must stand firm against rebellion, and give in when it is not a major issue. Let kids make a "presentation" to you about what they want, listen carefully, and be convinced when the reasons are valid.

When a child shouts "No I won't," keep very calm, ask why not, and see what you can agree on. Build on that agreement to come to a good conclusion. Starting young to handle rebellion will alleviate the problem in the teen years.

RECIPES FOR CRAFT PROJECTS. *See also Arts and Crafts Projects.*

Here are some handy money-saving formulas:

• **Dough.** Measure into a saucepan 1 cup flour, 1/2 cup salt, 1 cup water, 2 teaspoons cream of tartar, 1 tablespoon vegetable oil, and a few drops of food coloring. Mix all ingredients together in a pan over medium heat, stirring constantly until a ball begins to form. Remove from heat, cool, then store in an airtight container in the refrigerator until modeling time.

• **Paste.** Mix 1/3 cup nonself-rising wheat flour and 2 tablespoons of sugar in a saucepan. Over medium heat gradually add 1 cup of water and 1/4 teaspoon oil of peppermint or oil of wintergreen and stir well. Cool before using. This paste works well for making a collage.

• **Bubbles.** In a large container, mix 2 cups dishwashing liquid with 6 cups of water and 3/4 cup of light corn syrup. Pour 1 cup in a large shallow bowl and store the remainder, tightly covered. To make giant bubbles, cut off both ends of a large coffee or juice can and hammer the edges until they are smooth. Dip in solution and wave.

• **Space rocks.** Place some pieces of coal, porous brick, tile or cement in a bowl. Mix together 2 tablespoons of salt, 2 tablespoons of water, and 2 tablespoons of bluing (available at the grocery store). Pour it over the formation. The next day add 2 more tablespoons of salt to the solution in the dish. The following day add 2 more tablespoons each of salt, water, and bluing. Add a few drops of vegetable coloring or ink to each piece of rock. Keep the formation in an open dry area and watch the crystals develop. Some will look like rosebuds or coral. To keep it growing, just add more of the original solution from time to time.

• **Papier-mâché.** This French modeling clay is easy to make by cutting regular newspapers into one-inch size strips. Put the paper in a pail and cover with water overnight. The next day divide into balls and knead the soaked mass, squeezing out the excess water in a strainer. Mix in ordinary paste and you have the material to mold into small objects. When dried, they can be painted.

REJECTION. *See also Self-worth, Teasing.*

Being excluded by friends is a major hurt. Parents need to determine the cause of the continuous rejection of a child, which could be the result of overactive pride, aggression, lack of social skills, or unpleasant appearance. Soon a child gets a general reputation for being undesirable and the rejection increases. This is where parents must step in with home training on cleanliness, sharing, settling disputes calmly, kindness, and empathy. But before that, the parent should reassure the child of his great value. When some changes in the child's character have been made, it may be helpful to have her invite a classmate over, then gradually form a circle of friends who are accepting.

RELIGION. *See also Ethics, Faith, Morality, Prayers, Spirituality.*

Research shows that the strongest families and the most capable youngsters have a religious base to their lives, especially when religion is not just a Sabbath day event, but lived each day of the week. Belief in a Supreme Being adds stability to family life and provides comfort during challenges.

Find a religious community where you and your spouse are both comfortable and where your children are eager to join in the activities. Don't fall into the trap of letting the difference between parents' religions be an excuse to avoid all religious training. Weekly religious observances should be a given part of family life starting when children are babies and continuing for all the years they are under your roof.

⌦ Do not permit kids to drop out. One dad says "As long as you eat at our table, we want you to enjoy the feast God has prepared for you." Also, discourage activities that interfere with the times of service. Make sure the starting time for sports events can accommodate religious services. Don't degrade other religions, learn about them. Help your children to understand various Christian and Jewish holidays, Buddha Day, the Swedish Saint Lucia's Day, and so forth. When traveling, visit another church or religious site, and talk about the differences and similarities with your own church.

👍 Make religion part of daily life: grace at meals, evening prayers, and considering how to act using the question "What would Jesus do?" Learn one Bible verse each week, simply by repeating it at mealtime. Help youngsters understand the Ten Commandments by translating the commands into modern language for present-day situations. Do provide youngsters with their own Bibles or other religious books. For young children, Bible stories make excellent bedtime stories. As children are older, Bible charades can be fun.

Learning about religion from an historic or literary point of view may be the first step toward a belief in God and the acceptance of religious teachings that give youngsters strong ethical and spiritual perspectives. As your own faith grows, tell kids that you pray for them each day. Also help them to put their needs into words of prayer.

REMINDING. *See also Pests, Questions.*

Parents who don't mean what they say the first time will end up spending a tremendous amount of time reminding their children. These kids rely on parents to remind them, knowing that the parents will remember for them. Why should a child have to remember when a grown-up will tell him what to do until it gets done. Learning to remember is an important lesson for a youngster in his progress toward responsible maturity.

Encourage a good memory: tell a child one thing you want him to remember. Then when he masters that fairly well, give him two things, and then see if he can remember even more. Encourage him to write down some of your requests that don't need to be accomplished immediately.

RESOLUTIONS. *See also Goals.*

Once a year have a family get-together to make resolutions. Many choose New Year's Day as the time. Resolutions could be: to daily share some good news (not just problems), to do something outdoors each weekend, to communicate with relatives regularly, or to read thirty minutes each day. Write these down, keep them in a safe place and bring them out in about six months to check how you're doing. At the same time of year, you may want to set some goals as suggested under "Goals" in this book.

RESPECT.

Admiration for the good qualities in others, along with politeness and consideration, is the basis of respect. While a youngster may not always like you, he should respect you for the stand you take for integrity and love within the family. Being a parent with honor will eventually bring respect.

In turn, parents should respect children's rights and not demean them in any way. Both parent and child should act in such a way to respect themselves, their bodies, their thoughts, and their actions.

 At dinnertime, exchange names and allow time for thinking about respect. Then share ideas about what you respect most about the person whose name you drew. It could be a sense of humor, loyalty, honesty, companionship, or any qualities worthy of respect.

RESPONSIBILITY. *See also Choices, Copping Out, Leadership, Marriage, Order, Organizational Skills, Self-Government.*

Teaching responsibility is actually teaching a child to be free. Let a youngster know what you expect her to do and what happens if she doesn't do it. When you teach the right and ethical things to do, you can loose her more confidently to go out on her own.

Stimulate independence by giving opportunities to be self-governing at home. These opportunities are granted gradually: a toddler is taught to pick up his clothes, later to choose what to wear, then to launder clothing, do simple mending, purchase clothes within a clothing budget. The same gradual increase in responsibility can be given a youngster regarding activities away from home, doing school work, or spending free time. This increased feeling of being in control is important and also develops leadership.

A child constantly prodded doesn't learn to act responsibly on her own. Be willing to let a child suffer the consequences of being irresponsible, as long as it is not physically harmful. Only by experiencing both failure and success will he learn to choose the better way.

Don't save youngsters from mistakes thinking this is a sign of your love. While you would protect her from dangerous mis-

217

takes, you must let her try her wings in most areas. Don't make a child feel stupid when she's done something irresponsible. Calmly discuss how she could have had more success.

Compliment successes, no matter how small. Encourage persistence. Give youngsters an increasing number of choices as they get older. With your children, go over these steps that youngsters can take to show greater responsibility and thus gain greater privileges:

- Get up in the morning without being reminded.
- Have a system for accomplishing the seven morning tasks: go to the bathroom, wash, dress nicely, make the bed, tidy room, brush teeth after eating a good breakfast, and do one helpful thing.
- Read for pleasure at least fifteen minutes each day.
- Use after-school time for play, sports, crafts, homework, chores, rather than television and computer games.
- Choose wisely and spend no more than one hour on television during week days, two hours on weekend days. This will give extra time for active fun.
- Don't be a complainer. Say "OK," "Yes," "I will," "How can I help?" and "Thanks" more times than whining "No."
- Be committed to worthwhile activities such as teams, lessons, Scouts.
- Do your part at home. Keep your own possessions in order and establish a place for a messy project that can be cleaned up occasionally. Do assigned chores without being reminded and do something extra as a surprise.
- Be proud of your homework and get help when confused. Plan ahead for big projects. Don't cheat. Don't complain. Just do the work.
- Grow each day by learning something new. Start a collection, have a hobby, train a pet, read a book or newspaper. Get smarter each day.
- Eat nutritious meals and arrange your activities so you can eat with the family. Take part in conversation and remember basic good table manners.
- Remember what you're supposed to remember. Quit saying "I forgot." Put important things in safe places such as drawers, boxes, shelves, file folders. Train your brain but also make a list of the things you're to do.
- Show and tell love. Do it by the way you act, but also use the words "I love you."
- Communicate with parents, siblings, and other relatives with the same enthusiasm that you use when talking with friends. Write thank-you letters for gifts. Share the use of the phone.

- When you go to bed, stay in bed, and don't pester your folks. Get enough sleep so that you can function well in the morning.
- Have fun. Being a kid is a great time of life. Be adventuresome, but be safe. Show that you are a bright, unique, and awesome individual.

Consider giving each of your youngsters a copy of these aims.

RESTAURANT EATING. *See Eating Out, Manners.*

REUNIONS. *See also Heritage.*

Organized family reunions are great occasions for sharing love and history, and they provide youngsters with both roots and wings. Let kids participate in preparations, starting at least six months ahead. Here are some steps to take:

- Choose a date and lodgings.
- Select others to help you with communications, finances, food, activities, kid activities, travel, and housing.
- Set a theme such as a major anniversary, holiday, or plan it for every ten years.
- Make a complete list of those to invite. Later make a list of attendees with addresses, phone numbers, and e-mails.
- Promote the event with an initial mailing that gives all the particulars and probable costs. Then continue to promote it monthly.
- Depending on the location, vary the food. Consider a potluck for the first night, a picnic for a day full of activities, a box lunch during a tour of a local attraction, and a more formal final dinner.
- Select and order souvenirs and remembrances such as: T-shirts, caps, mugs, totes, family calendars, memory book, and family cookbook.
- Arrange for a qualified family member or professional photographer to take a group photo and also make a video of the highlights.
- Plan a place and decoration for a table for name tags, photo and family tree displays.
- Select an emcee, guest(s) of honor, and those who will receive special recognition: oldest, youngest, most children, recent graduates, newlyweds, those who came the farthest, and so forth.
- Organize activities such as excursions, hikes, talent show, sports, games, relays, dance competition, square dancing, family quiz show, storytelling night, and worship service.

For step-by-step details on planning a reunion, large or small, see *The Family Party Book* (Caryl Krueger, Abingdon Press, Nashville, Tenn.).

REVENGE. *See also Getting Even.*

There is an old saying "Living well is the best revenge," but a better statement would be "Doing right is the best revenge." Do not permit vengeful activities by children. Revenge should be punished with the same force as the original offense. Vengeful children are not happy children and hate is not healthy. As difficult as it may seem at the time, promote forgiveness instead of revenge.

ROLE MODELS. *See also Coaches, Grandparents, Teachers.*

Most of what children learn, they learn from parents, their everyday role models. That's why it is important for parents to be honest with children, to let them see/hear some disagreements and the respectful way to handle them, to observe how parents treat each other in loving ways, and to see how they relate with caring concern to others beyond the family circle. Grandparents, teachers, coaches, religious leaders, and group leaders are also role models and a wise parent needs to be sure that these adults uphold those ethics that are important to the family.

ROLLER BLADES, ROLLER SKATES. *See Bicycles.*

ROOM ARRANGEMENT. *See Environment.*

ROUTINE. *See Morning Routine, Order, Organizational Skills.*

RUDENESS. *See also Profanity.*

A child who speaks in an unkindly way is often seeking attention. Start by outlawing (fining, punishing for) rude and profane words. Show youngsters the acceptable way to get attention by making eye contact and talking and listening. Some children can be cured by ignoring the rudeness, but most require a firm, corrective response.

RULES, FAMILY. *See also Consequences, Family Meeting, Obedience, Safety.*

Parents are usually wiser than their children and should be the final authority, but they should also admit their own mistakes. Corrective conversation should be *with* children, not *at* them, so they learn to manage challenges.

Start with toddlers to create a picture book illustrating family rules. This first book should cover, for example, coming when called, where to eat food, and rules concerning hitting, biting, crossing streets, or playing with matches.

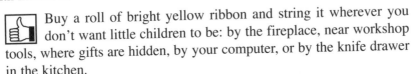 Buy a roll of bright yellow ribbon and string it wherever you don't want little children to be: by the fireplace, near workshop tools, where gifts are hidden, by your computer, or by the knife drawer in the kitchen.

When a child can read, write out rules concerning computer use, television viewing, homework, lesson practice, and so forth. Teens and preteens need rules that cover such things as phone use, curfews, drugs, tobacco, and alcohol. Include what will happen when these safety rules are broken. Post these family rules on a bulletin board where all can see them.

Make a "When Can I?" list, showing the age when a child can cross the street alone, go to a movie with friends, have ears pierced, go on a group date, wear makeup, go on a double date, and go on a regular date.

For younger children, print out these silly rhymes, one per page, illustrate them with pictures cut from magazines, and read these at least once a week. You can omit the subject of the rule that is given before the rhyme.

Coming when called the first time: When Mom or Dad calls my name, I come as fast as a speedy jet plane.

Being excused after a meal: We eat together for family fun, and ask to be excused when we're all done.

Coming in from play: I wipe my feet when I come in the door. That helps me keep mud off the floor.

Manners: "Please" and "thank you" are easy to say. How many times have you said them today?

Helping: "Can I help?" are words I can say. When work is done there's time to play.

Responsibility for a pet: I pat my doggie in a gentle way and remember to feed him every day.

Car riding: In the car there's one way to be: seated and belted means safety for me.

Crossing streets: When crossing a street, a hand I hold. That's the rule till I'm five years old.

Talking with strangers: I do not talk with strangers I see. This rule for safety is important to me.

Fighting over toys: If I argue about toys and don't act right, the toy is put away, out of my sight.

Snacks: When I get hungry and want a treat, I ask permission before I eat.

Not interrupting: Taking turns is the way to talk. Speak one at a time and please don't squawk!

Bathroom etiquette: After using the toilet, the thing to do is wash my hands and dry them, too.

Hitting: Hitting hurts and makes me sad. I remember what's right so I won't be bad.

Television viewing: Once in a while I see TV, but only if the program is good for me.

Picking up toys: When finished playing at the end of the day, I quickly put my toys away.

Clothing: My clothes never get thrown on the floor, just in the wash or in my drawer.

When it's bedtime: When I am told it's time for bed, I don't argue or shake my head.

Getting ready for bed: Before I go to bed each night, there are four things that I do right: go to the bathroom without a fight, wash my hands with all my might, brush my teeth so they'll be bright, give a hug and say "good night!"

Staying in bed: When I'm tucked into my bed, I say my prayers and rest my head. I don't get out of bed and play, I think about the fun today.

RUNNING AWAY. *See also Anger, Rebellion.*

Far more children think about, talk about, or threaten to run away than actually do it. But before the situation becomes that severe, meet with the youngster and an impartial mediator (a relative, friend, counselor) to uncover the cause of the unhappiness and to see how it can be cured. Runaway kids think they can care for themselves but end up on the street in truly dangerous circumstances. Should a youngster actually leave home without informing you of her whereabouts, take the necessary immediate action to find her. When you locate her, first enfold her in your arms and express your worry and loneliness, not your anger. Then when everyone is calm, talk about how to avoid a repeat performance. This may take many sessions and outside intervention, but it is vital to the family's well-being.

SAFETY. *See also Car Seats, First Aid, Guns, Molestation, Playpen, Strangers.*

Because a parent can't always be with a child, teach safe practices starting when kids are very young. You may even want to make an illustrated book of safety rules. Topics to include are: guns, knives, matches, poisons, and medicines. Also create role-playing examples for: answering the phone, calling 911, opening or not opening the door, talking with strangers, what to do when followed, and what to do when lost. Be sure to practice how to leave the house in case of fire and locating and using a fire extinguisher. Teach simple first aid for home emergencies and be sure everyone in the family knows where the first-aid kit is kept. Make using seatbelts a given and teach youngsters to get in their seats and buckle up quickly without reminding.

Take a good close-up photo of a child every six months. One way of finding lost or kidnapped children is through a current photo. Young children should be taught their full name, address, and phone number.

At an appropriate time, talk with teens about what to do if lost in the wilderness, how to handle road rage, what to do in a riot, what to do when the car breaks down late at night, or when there is a boating accident. For bicycling insist on a well-fitting helmet and for roller-blading and skate-boarding, the use of a helmet and pads for elbows, wrists, and knees should be mandatory. For some workshop projects, goggles are a necessity and they can also be a protection when mowing the lawn.

Teach safety without fear. Tell youngsters you want them to know these things, not to frighten them but because you love them and want them to be safe. Work with neighbors to create a Neighborhood Watch or other mutual surveillance system. Teach youngsters to be alert to their surroundings in malls, parks, parking lots, and other public places. Alert youngsters to leave any scene that becomes violent.

Sometimes family members need to get the attention of others in the family or find one another in a grocery store. Devise a distinctive family whistle and practice it around the house so that everyone can be confident of doing it in public.

Countering youth violence is a parenting responsibility. They must block out inappropriate television and movie viewing, ban playing violent video games, and prohibit viewing trash on the Internet. Decades of research back up the fact that violence "taken in" can become violence "given out."

Gun control starts at home. Games and sports that use guns should be outlawed; there are plenty of alternatives. Guns at home should be locked up and ammunition should be stored elsewhere.

SANTA CLAUS. *See also Christmas.*

Parents should decide early what to tell youngsters about Santa. While the myth has charm, there is also sadness when the truth is revealed and some youngsters feel fooled or betrayed. Many families find it preferable to tell youngsters that Santa is the spirit of love at Christmas and that they will see many Santa figures sharing love. Often it is the parent who wants to perpetuate the Santa myth and the child is happy to go along, suspecting that he will get fewer gifts if he no longer believes. Most youngsters will admit that they knew the truth long before others told them.

SARCASM. *See also Rudeness.*

Younger children's thinking modes do not run to sarcasm; it is more of an adult way of responding. Teens pick it up from peers and parents. While it may at times be funny, in school and career it is not acceptable. Do not use sarcasm as a way of dealing with youngsters. Set a better example by responding kindly.

SAVING. *See Money.*

SCHOOL. *See also Attention Span, Child Care, Education, Homework, Preschool, Teachers. See also subsequent listings.*

The school is your child's other home. Actually, many youngsters spend a greater number of awake hours at school than they do at home. For this reason alone, a parent should be vitally involved in what goes on at school, and what does *not* go on. For some students, parental involvement can make the difference between a great school experience and just a waste of time. Of course, home is still a center of learning and maturing, so parents must not abdicate their own part of the teaching role.

School is far more than what is learned in the classroom—it includes what happens on the playground, in the library and gym, in the hallways, and in extracurricular activities. School gives the opportunity for a youngster to be an individual, to have a distinct identity, and to function successfully without parental input.

A child can benefit greatly from school even when the facility is not state-of-the-art. One-room schoolhouses still turn out bright graduates. The quality of the teachers and administration is what makes the difference.

SCHOOL FEARS. *See also Bullies, Teasing.*

The fears of youngsters in school are endless. There are the fears of leaving home and parent, meeting new children, maybe having a wetting accident, being teased, or finding the classroom. Then come fears of making a book report, remembering to bring a paper from home, and having to compete on the playground. These are small compared with fears of undressing for gym, of not being datable, of not getting good grades, or being accepted in college.

Get to the bottom of each fear and assuage it. If he reports that the school bus trip makes him nauseous, or that students on the bus are threatening him, talk about his fears of throwing up or being beaten. Let him talk with an interested adult friend or even the bus driver who is not as emotionally involved. The bus driver could assure the child he will be protected while on the bus or suggest the best place to sit to avoid motion sickness. These conversations could result in the fear being overcome. If the child continues to be afraid to take the bus, you may have to drive him for awhile.

Home preparation and support can allay many of these fears, and talking with a school counselor can also help if the student feels confident in doing so. Schools always provide opportunities to succeed, to get attention, to take pride in good work—things that should balance fears.

SCHOOL: FIRST DAY. *See also Kindergarten.*

The first day of school, whether it is kindergarten or later, should be a special day for youngsters, preceded by plenty of sleep the night before. Start this important day with the child's favorite breakfast and let her sit at the head of the table. Also let her choose a favorite outfit to wear. Be sure to arrive on time. If possible, arrange for two children in the family, or one child and a friend, to go together.

Emphasize how proud you are of her and the importance of a good education. Prior to the first day, change the bedtimes to a later time than the previous year and extend some privileges as signs of growing responsibility. To avert first-day gripes at dinner, ask each family member to share the best thing that happened during the day. Then ask what might be changed to make tomorrow even better.

For kindergartners, parting from a parent can be very difficult. Ease the transition by visiting the school in advance and even checking out the playground. Give a child a secret pocket reminder of your love. It could be a shiny penny, a new colored pencil, or a tiny angel pin. Without anyone else knowing, she can slip her hand in her pocket and remember that you're thinking about her and loving her.

SCHOOL GRADES. *See also Homework.*

While grades are not the only indicator of learning, they usually give a parent some idea of how well a youngster has grasped the material taught and how well he can convey it to the teacher through reports and tests. (In some cases grades show how much a youngster can mimic a textbook or please a teacher.) Grades rarely show the true depth of understanding a topic. All this aside, the traditional report card is what most parents and students have to contend with and it is usually an adequate measure until something better is invented.

Your conversations about grades will be important if you ask questions such as "What did you learn that you can use later?" "How can this information learned in arithmetic be used to help you in your science class?" "Do you enjoy this subject even though it is difficult for you?" "Does this class serve as a foundation for another class you hope to take?"

Should children be paid for good grades? School is a child's work, so pay can be an acceptable reward, but other rewards can be just as effective, depending on the youngster. A much-wanted gift, a trip, or extended privileges can be equally important as money. If you do pay, give a bonus for a grade raised or for good character traits noted, and deduct for a grade that goes down. Do this for each middle-of-term and end-of-term grading period for a year and then discuss the system with your child to see if it has encouraged better grades. For some youngsters, pay is an incentive to improve. However some children hesitate to improve because parents will then expect even higher standards of excellence.

Some youngsters sabotage their success out of fear of failure. Rather than risk the effort of success, it is easier to do nothing, especially when they start to fall behind and get poorer grades. A youngster with very smart parents and siblings finds that by hiding her intelligence she won't have to enter into competition with them. Her great fear is that she will be tested and found less worthy. Some youngsters take up using drugs so they can blame failure on the use, not on themselves.

Don't permit grades to define your child to the exclusion of all other factors. If a child feels she's only valued for her grades, this form of parental control can cause her to rebel against the control by doing poor school work. Many parents have found that if they don't mention grades for a semester, the youngster accepts the responsibility as her own, and the grades improve since the arena for arguments has been removed.

Social promotion has been popular in the past to the point that many young people are promoted right out of high school without the necessary skills for workplace survival. In the early classes, repeating a grade can overcome frustration and bring success to a student who learns a bit more slowly. However, the emotional strain that being held back could put on a child can be great and it may be better to search out alternatives such as tutoring, remedial help, or summer school in order to keep a student with her same-age peers.

Alternatives for young children include: delayed entry into kindergarten, obtaining special instruction during the summer before first grade, entering an after-school learning program, or dedicated learning at home specializing in reading, drawing, and logical thinking.

Don't wait for a report card to know how your child is progressing. Attend conferences, make phone calls, and ask questions.

SCHOOL HOMEWORK. *See Homework.*

SCHOOL LUNCH. *See Lunch.*

SCHOOL PREPARATION.

Make preparing for the start of school an important event for your child. Choose a quiet time to discuss his educational progress, and especially how content he is with his life. Set a later bedtime (even if just ten minutes), increase his allowance, make a list of clothes needed, and talk about possible extracurricular activities. Encourage hopes and offer your help to make them realities. Make shopping for clothes and school supplies into a special day or early evening, perhaps arranging to do this as a twosome and then have supper out together.

SCHOOL SELECTION.

As a taxpayer or a tuition payer, you should know if you are getting your money's worth. Visit the proposed school with your youngster and assess the following:

- **Class size:** twenty-five or less is ideal but teacher's aides can make a difference.

- **Atmosphere:** should be upbeat and orderly whether the facility is old or new.

- **Safety:** established rules concerning violence and other safety issues.

- **Staff:** experienced and dedicated, of both sexes, and varied ages.

- **Grading:** a system that does not ordinarily permit social promotion.

- **Fundamentally sound:** Solid education in the basics with early teaching of second language, art, and music as part of the curriculum.

- **Equipment:** quality computers, scientific supplies, an extensive library, a rigorous program of physical education, and extracurricular opportunities.

- **Trained professionals:** counselors who are alert to and understand the moods and needs of youngsters.

Don't hesitate to ask questions. And if you visit when other children are present, observe them to see if they appear to be enjoying school.

SCHOOL TESTS. *See also School Grades.*

Tests usually reveal how effective the school teaching is and identifies the strengths and weaknesses of the students. While it is true that some students don't test well, this is often an excuse (given by students, teachers, or administrators) for low test scores. Schools should be encouraged to teach students the needed skills for taking tests.

Ask your youngster to inform you of upcoming major tests. The day before should be free of chores and tiring activities. Serve a pleasant dinner, encourage bathtime and a sensible bedtime followed in the morning with a favorite and hearty breakfast.

228

Be alert to areas of study where the student's scores are low and get help to raise the scores. This is important since several different tests are used by colleges and universities as one basis for admission and scholarships.

SCIENCE. *See also Recipes for Craft Projects.*

The sciences teach exploration of the past, analysis of the present, and discoveries for the future. Scientific activities are important to a child's development and should begin in the early years and continue; don't wait until he's old enough for a chemistry set! Don't put down childish inquisitiveness. Even preschool children can begin to take part in scientific experiments in the home.

Because microscopes, binoculars, telescopes, and chemistry sets are expensive, you can satisfy youthful inquisitiveness with some simple home experiments:

- Give youngsters small jars in which to mix food coloring, making different colors. In season, let them pick flowers to put into the jars, or handfuls of snow.
- Make bread together and learn how yeast makes the dough rise.
- Show how gelatin makes a liquid solidify.
- Make salt crystals by adding salt to a very small quantity of boiling water, then set the pan aside until the water has evaporated and you can see the square crystals through a magnifying glass.
- Plant seeds and watch them germinate.
- Take a magnifying glass and observe bugs in the grass or creatures in tide pools.

Older kids can make a pulley with string and empty thread spools, identify leaves, learn about the stars, discover the wonders of snorkeling, or make an inclined plane by elevating one end of a piece of plywood. With this they can roll cars down the wood to see how the steepness affects the speed.

Show youngsters how and why things work and let older ones learn to use a compass, take apart unusable small appliances, connect a battery to a buzzer, or make a radio crystal set.

Don't ignore those "how" or "why" questions. If you don't know the answers, find them.

SCOUTS. *See Clubs.*

SCRAPBOOKS. *See also Memorabilia.*

Encourage youngsters to keep a simple scrapbook of important things: the baseball or ballet program, a good school paper, an award, a special postcard, or ribbon. When old enough to write, let him write a few words about the item pasted in the book. This idea helps a youngster get rid of clutter and organize many of the things that might otherwise be tossed out. Some families also keep a yearly scrapbook of events, or a scrapbook for each family trip.

SCREAMING. *See Crying, Profanity, Yelling.*

SECRETS.

Explain that things told in confidence with peers or parents are not to be shared (unless it is something illegal). Practice telling secrets by telling a child something "only between you and me." Show children the fun of keeping a secret, such as a surprise party and gifts for Father's Day.

SECURITY, SUCCESS, SATISFACTION. *See also Maturity.*

SECURITY + SUCCESS = SATISFACTION. These three qualities are essential to the maturity of a child. Security is the confidence of being loved and needed and comes first. Add to this opportunities for a child to accomplish something, no matter how small, giving her the feeling of success. The result of the first two is satisfaction, the inner joy of knowing she has done well, whether it is acknowledged by others or not. The three are closely tied together. An insecure child can be hesitant about trying to achieve something and thus miss out on the feeling of satisfaction, which is closely tied to self-worth.

SELF-DISCIPLINE. *See Choices, Discipline, Self-Government.*

SELF-ESTEEM. *See Self-Worth.*

SELFISHNESS. *See also Sharing.*

Fear is usually the basis of selfish actions. A child insists on his way, holding onto his toys, or saying and doing anything he pleases because he fears that he will otherwise lose control of his world. The selfish child needs to know that there is enough good (both good things and good activities) to go around, and that sharing gives just as much satisfaction as fiercely hanging on to one's possessions.

Selfishness often stems from a family where the child is the focal point of everything, but of course, the family should be the focal point, not one person. As much as parents love their children, they should not permit them to become tyrants, demanding everything to their own satisfaction. A selfish child is not well liked so help him learn otherwise by giving him opportunities to share toys, to help others, and to put other's desires before his own.

SELF-GOVERNMENT. *See also Choices, Discipline, Independence, Morning Routine, Priorities, Responsibility.*
   How to know the right thing to do without being told is self-government and is a great skill for children to learn. Of course you can get youngsters to do the right thing by constantly reminding, but this is time consuming, irritating to both of you, and doesn't really teach. Therefore, giving choices and extending responsibilities enable a child to be self-governing.
   These are the basic skills that should be mastered in the early years:

- Get up when the alarm goes off or suffer the consequences of over-sleeping.
- Accomplish the seven essentials of the morning routine before play.
- Be punctual in accomplishing tasks, returning favors, and coming home.
- Complete quality homework assignments on time.
- Remember to take along needed items for school, sports, and activities.
- Make a list of things that must be done when there is more time.
- Keep clothes in order: clean, mended, and where they belong.
- Tidy the bedroom at least once a week.
- Determine priorities: things that must be done first and what can wait.
- Keep important things in a special place: a box for jewelry, a bank or wallet for money, file folders for guarantees, awards, and other important papers.
- Recycle what is environmentally useful and get rid of what is junk.
- Return phone calls and write down phone messages for others, putting them in the designated place.
- Respond to invitations and thank for invitations and for gifts, the latter in written form.
- Rarely borrow things and always return borrowed items promptly and in good condition.
- Be aware of family activities, especially when scheduling own events.
- Accomplish tasks with a minimum of reminding.

How great life would be if we all practiced these sixteen self-government skills! An important aim of parenting is to teach a youngster to do the right thing without reminding, rigid routine, or written-down rules. Self-discipline means that a youngster has learned to control his actions at first in just one area, eventually in many areas.

SELF-WILL. *See Willfulness.*

SELF-WORTH. *See also Choices, Depression, Encouragement, Put-Downs and Put-Ups, Rejection, Responsibility, Self-government, Suicide.*

Distinguish between attempts to build self-worth based on mere "feel good talk" as opposed to important "feel good opportunities." Many schools are currently going overboard in teaching youngsters to chant "I am a good person" without giving them the experiences to back it up.

The feeling of being essential or worthy isn't something "given" to a child through words that puff her up. Self-esteem is the result of a youngster's positive experiences each day. So, what a parent can give are opportunities to gain self-worth. These include making decisions and occasionally suffering the consequences, taking responsibility for her actions, finishing tasks and homework in a timely manner, and volunteering help and caring for others. Such activities lead to self-respect, but this self-worth should never lead to a feeling of being better than others; instead it is founded on humility.

All important is a home and school climate that respects individuality, differences, and genuine emotions. The aim is to produce youngsters who are responsible citizens of home and community, who are happy, well-adjusted, caring, and are effective as leaders and team players. This leads to resilience, or the ability to bounce back from a defeat.

From a child's first attempts to speak, walk, or play with a certain toy, make a firm distinction between *doing* something that is good or bad and *being* someone who is good or bad. A bad experience needn't damage self-worth. A youngster can accept some failures when she can also recall successes. So, it's up to the parent to notice achievements and comment favorably on them.

Be alert to put-down statements. Couple merited criticism with helpful suggestions. Make sure you say something positive to a child each day. However, don't protect her from simple mistakes. Let her learn how to cope in the real world.

Build self-esteem by helping a youngster keep a list of good things she accomplishes. Encourage her to add to the list, keep it in her night table or on her bulletin board, and look at it often. Teach the value of life, that each person has work that only she will do and that each person's contribution is needed. This will negate tendencies to regard life as meaningless, which can lead to suicide.

Research shows that children with self-worth come from parents who believe that a child is basically good and has value. Winning or being the best should not be the prime emphasis. Doing a good job, working up to one's capacity, doing better than before, finishing the task or trying hard are all acceptable results.

Praise of good work is an essential because young children can later recognize a repeated good work and feel good about it even without the parental approval. Thus it is important to be specific in your praise, describing what the child has done by saying "What a great tower you built!" as opposed to the more general words "What a good girl!" In the same vein, specific criticism helps a child to know what to improve, while just saying "You're a bad girl" is not at all helpful.

Be alert to the number of good messages you send in proportion to the "bad girl" messages. What a child hears of himself is often what he believes is true about himself. For more difficult-to-praise children, phrases such as "that's a good start!" and "You're getting it!" can encourage.

A child's self-image is sometimes a mirror of what he believes a parent is thinking about her. Some children try to conceal their low-esteem feelings out of fear that the parent will support the conclusion. When a child states "My face is ugly!" the child's feelings should be accepted, not denied with a statement such as "that's silly." Instead determine why a child feels this way; was it something said by a peer or relative? Is she comparing herself with models in magazines? Often a mere discussion, assuring the child of your interest and that she is worthy of your concern, can dissipate the problem.

A parent's best tool for developing self-worth is giving a child a life of opportunities, a life beyond school and television, a life punctuated with praise.

SEPARATION ANXIETY. *See also Fears, Fears at Bedtime, Homesickness, Kindergarten, Moving.*

Whether it is the first day of preschool or of college, parting from parents is one of the largest emotional challenges to the entire family. Even the most self-reliant youngster can fold under the stress. The clues to successful separations start with short separations early in childhood and include very complete verbal preparation.

The more the youngster knows of the new experience—be it a new neighborhood, new school, a week at Grandma's or camp, or a morning at a play group—the easier will be the separation. Seeing the location in advance can help. Also, meeting the person who will be in charge or getting to know someone from the group or neighborhood will ease the tension. The daily routine (play, stories, exercise) can be talked about and even followed to some extent at home.

Talk about homesickness in advance. Although it may be hard to describe, explain that it is a normal reaction. Be sure you are not sending subtle messages about your own concerns. Talk eagerly about the fun ahead and the new things that will be learned. For a camper, reassure the child that you will keep in touch and that things will be fine at home.

Don't ignore cries for help. If a child away from home continues to be upset, contact the school, camp director, or relative and see if there is a deeper problem. Tell a child that it is okay to miss family and that you are not disappointed if the time away really needs to be cut short. Perhaps he will feel more comfortable another time.

Acute cases of separation anxiety often stem from a youngster who has been severely deprived of dedicated care during early childhood. Then, when someone begins to care for him, he remains so fearful that he doesn't wish to be separated for even a moment. This results in wanting to have the parent or caregiver always in sight and preferably within touch; the child wants to be held, rocked, soothed, and slept with. While this is distressing and time consuming to the parent, the child usually grows out of it.

SERVICE. *See also Caring, Christmas Outreach, Empathy, Giving Versus Getting.*

Teach youngsters how giving to others enriches oneself. Make it a family practice to give service to others and make youngsters an integral part of the giving. You can work through organized groups to make dried flower arrangements for seniors, place mats for hospitals, toy boxes for ill children, scrapbooks of pictures and puzzles for shut-ins. But beyond this is spending time in contact with others: leading an exercise or singing group at a care facility, teaching musical games to children at a park, working in a charitable thrift shop, or being a mentor. Many preteens and teens find these activities enriching.

There may be people within your own neighborhood who need help with running errands, raking leaves, shopping, helping with children, learning computer skills and so forth. Many of these tasks are ones that grade-schoolers can accomplish and at the same time find the joys of service.

During the holidays, your family can "adopt" another family and supply food, gifts, clothing, and holiday decorations. A social service agency can connect you.

SEWING.

Boys and girls need sewing skills, so don't raise a helpless child. Show them how to sew on a button, mend a simple tear, and change a hem. For each child, prepare a small lidded box to use as a sewing kit with thread, needles, pins and pin cushion, thimble, and small scissors. Encourage him to keep it in a bedroom drawer for ready use, and to take it along when going to camp, on a trip, or off to college.

SEX, SEXUALITY, SEX EDUCATION. *See also Abuse, AIDS, Homosexuality, Living Together, Masturbation, Molestation, Pregnancy, Puberty.*

Society gives youngsters far too many "don'ts" in relation to sexuality and far too few "dos." Youngsters need to hear the words: "Feel good about your body, feel good you are a girl (or boy), feel good that your body works as it was made to function." There is nothing better or nothing worse about the different ways that male and female bodies work. Be calm in handling occasions when preschool children comment on or show their body parts to other children. This is a natural curiosity. Explain that our bodies are nothing to be ashamed of, but that they are our own special property.

From infancy onward, boys and girls are often treated differently: boys get more verbal bolstering, more physical play, and more freedom; girls get more advice, more occasions for quiet learning, and more rules. Parents need to be alert to sexual stereotyping in activities, in the selecting of friends, and especially in choosing classes to take. There is no reason, other than old-fashioned tradition, to reserve certain fields of study for boys and others for girls. Computer science, astrophysics, wood shop, or home-management classes should be considered as suitable subjects irrespective of sex. Be alert to your own gender bias when assigning tasks around the house.

When young children begin to ask questions of a sexual nature, emphasize that a good relationship is based on how much we love and care for another person; add discussions on the privileges and benefits of marriage. You may want to start by telling of your first date and first love. In discussing sex with even the youngest child, don't make up cute names, use the actual terms for body parts. Teach children early that others should not be permitted to touch any part of their body that a bathing suit would cover. Tell children that they should always report to the parent any instance of inappropriate touching, no matter how minor it might seem.

A child's first questions are usually of a curious nature about the mechanics of sex. Give a simple response to the question asked and don't elaborate. Sometimes a good answer is "that's the way our body is made to work." Only later do matters of unwanted pregnancy, abuse, rape, and sexually transmitted diseases become issues. Television, movies, and music lyrics can be springboards for helpful discussions. Older children need a thorough education, best given by a well-informed and caring parent. Prepare yourself with a visit to the library. Don't count on school sex-education classes, which can be biased, to do the job for you. Ask to see a curriculum summary for the class and discuss points of divergence with your youngster.

"Prior to need" should be a parent's motto when it comes to questions of sex. Don't wait until a youngster is going on a first date! Start early. Don't fall into the trap of thinking that kids will ask about sex when they need to know about it. That's often too late, thanks to the free, and often faulty, education that television and movies provide. While you can't totally control a child's sexual behavior, you can be a great influence if your conversations are not one-time specials but rather continuing serials. Don't pretend to have all the answers (but know where to get them) and don't be afraid to admit that this is an involved and sensitive topic.

Let youngsters clearly understand your family values. Give moral and religious reasons for your values. Above all, tell youngsters that you will always love them, even if they should make mistakes.

To have or not have premarital sex deserves factual information, and abstinence should be discussed as a viable alternative to contraception or pregnancy. Explain that there is nothing wrong with sex but that there is a right time. Use the analogy of flying an airplane. As much as a little child might want to fly an airplane, you wouldn't want him as pilot because there are many things to be learned before the piloting experience can be safely and successfully enjoyed. The same is true of sex; there are many steps that lead to a satisfying and safe experience.

Keep the lines of communication open. Sometimes youngsters feel it will be more comfortable, and believable, to talk with another authoritative person: a counselor, doctor, minister, or aunt or uncle. You can encourage this if you're sure that person will convey the same values that you have.

Don't permit youngsters to see television and movies that give immoral ideas about sex. If they do see inappropriate material, talk about it, don't just assume it went over their heads.

Talk about babies and where they come from. Let youngsters understand the birth process but, in most cases, exclude them from the actual birth. However, they should be encouraged to see the baby and hold him as soon as possible. In the case of adoption, tell a child that the baby grew "in my heart rather than under my heart."

Sexuality is not some hush-hush topic. Keep the discussion a natural part of your ongoing complete education process for your child.

SEXUALLY TRANSMITTED DISEASES. *See AIDS.*

SHAME. *See also Humiliation, Sorrow.*
Although "shame on you" is a popular parenting phrase, shame is a much less desirable emotion than sincere sorrow. Shame is a painful mental feeling of having done something wrong, dishonorable, or ridiculous, and can have a lasting effect if the child who has done wrong is not shown more acceptable behavior. Shame is an abusive form of punishment, as when a child who has soiled himself is made to remain in that state as a corrective measure.

Most youthful mistakes are not shameful but rather are opportunities to recognize more proper behavior, to feel and express sorrow for any inconvenience caused, and to be forgiven and go on to do better the next time.

Never shame a child. Feeling guilty focuses on the problem at a time when you want to focus on a solution.

SHARING. *See also Conflict, Play, Possessions, Service, Taking Turns, Toys.*
Make opportunities to share—it's a lifelong skill. Let a child cut one cupcake in half, knowing that you will get to choose your half first. Show

how to use a timer so that others get to play equally with a favorite toy. Since you can't have two of every toy, show how two different toys can be played with together. Compliment children who willingly share.

Don't force a child to share a favorite possession if she doesn't wish to. Just put the toy on a high shelf during her play with others. If there is fighting over a toy, immediately remove the toy from play.

Keep precious or breakable toys out of reach or in a child's own room. Some toys should be kept on high shelves as decorations to look at and brought down only when a child is willing to handle them carefully. Toys that all can play with should be in the play area or family room.

Encourage children to hand down toys to younger siblings when they are no longer their own favorites. Sorting out toys can be an enjoyable once-a-year occasion at the end of summer. Donate them to child care facilities or a holiday toy drive.

SHOPPING. *See also Errands, Excursions.*

Errands and shopping are a part of family life and they need not be stressful. Never go shopping when you or your child is tired or hungry. Shopping with younger children can be made easier with the Walk/Talk/Gawk Rule:

- Walk—no running or pushing permitted
- Talk—no crying or shouting allowed
- Gawk—look but don't pester for things

On a grocery trip little children can name pictures, letters, and colors on items, or choose things to be eaten in the car as a "rolling lunch" on the way home. The parent should name items he sees so that the trip builds vocabulary. Older youngsters can shop as a team for specific items, comparison shop, be in charge of coupon buys, or estimate the total cost.

When shopping at a mall, take along a sack of toys to amuse little ones when you're in the dressing room. Although clothes shopping is best done alone, preteens and teens sometimes enjoy being advisors about what to buy. Before going shopping for youngster's clothes, make a budget that can cover the needs but not extravagantly. Reward good behavior with an ice-cream store stop afterward. Give children choices: "We can have the treat if you choose to behave, or we can go directly home if you whine."

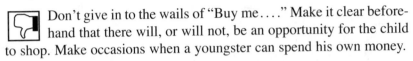 Don't give in to the wails of "Buy me...." Make it clear before-hand that there will, or will not, be an opportunity for the child to shop. Make occasions when a youngster can spend his own money.

When shopping for toys and gifts for others, ask children to tell what they might like themselves and write these down so you have ideas for up-coming gift occasions.

SHOW-AND-TELL. *See also Communication.*
You don't need a kindergarten classroom for show-and-tell. The object of show and tell is to get children to verbalize. You can have show-and-tell at home by taking a toy (bear, truck, book) and letting a child tell you about it. This can be done at playtime or during mealtime. When taking something to school for show-and-tell, see that it is labeled with the child's name, is in good condition, and is carried in a bag for easy storage at school.

SHOWING OFF. *See also Attention, Need for.*
A child who constantly shows off is seeking attention. A show-off should not be catered to, but in age-appropriate terms should be told that his actions do not please you or others, and are not an acceptable way to gain attention. Look for many occasions to give him your full attention so that he doesn't need to offend by being a braggart.

There is also a good side of showing off. This occurs when a youngster is expected to speak to others (aunties, teachers, peers) and is able to act in a comfortable outgoing way. This is heartening for parents just as it is disheartening when a parent says "tell Grandma about your doggie" and the child hangs his head and says nothing. A shy child may be greatly helped by being given occasions to talk within the family and even rehearse things he could say to others.

SHYNESS. *See also Poise, Visiting.*
Almost every child has shy moments. These are often caused by her inability to handle a social situation such as what to say or do when called on in school or when visiting with others. Prepare a child for new occasions and remind the child of past successes. You can help erase tension by suggesting the first line of something she can share. For example say,

"Aunt Carol loves dogs and would like to hear what Cringle learned at obedience school." And when she wants to play with other children, you can teach her the words that can let her join others, such as "Can I help build?" or "My dolly would like some tea, too."

Avoid situations that force a child to show off in front of others; encourage, but let her choose when to participate. And remember that youngsters develop poise at different rates, so don't be quick to compare or label. Find successes and build on them.

SIBLINGS, SIBLING RIVALRY. *See also Birth Order, Competition, Favoritism, Tattletales.*

Growing up with a brother or sister can be one of the joys of childhood—someone to play with, confide in, and share ideas with. It can also be a miserable time if sibling rivalry tries to creep in.

Celebrate the uniqueness of each family member, emphasizing special skills and attributes. Rivalry is increased when the age difference is smaller because the older child has not had sufficient experience to show he knows his precious place in the family.

This rivalry often begins when a new baby joins the family. As soon as the mother begins to show the pregnancy, bring the child into the loop by explaining in age-appropriate terms what will happen in the next months. A visit to the hospital will allay the fears of the child, especially if he can safely see the maternity section (some hospitals will not allow this). See that the older sibling has the same amount of physical contact and conversation with a parent, especially the mother, after a baby is born as before the birth.

Along with purchases and gifts for the new baby, see that the older child has a gift. Some parents present a gift at the hospital as being a gift from the new baby.

When the baby is brought home and is getting care for her needs, be sure to give the sibling extra love afterward so he knows that he, too, is greatly valued. Refer to the baby as "our baby." Help older siblings to letter on one of their shirts "I'm the BIG brother" (or sister). Give the older child special privileges. Comment on things he can do that the baby cannot.

Arrange opportunities for him to play with you when the baby is asleep so that his world does not totally revolve around the baby. Each day, let the older child perform some simple form of care, such as gently stroking the baby's hand. When visitors come to see the new baby, see that the older child gets to participate by leading the way to the nursery or opening a package for the new baby.

> Don't let older siblings play in a baby's crib or carry the baby. Sitting and holding the baby, playing with him in a safe place on the floor, helping to feed him, are safe means of interaction.

As children grow into early childhood, the rivalry takes on new aspects: arguments over toys, hatred when the sibling is perceived to be more loved, constant academic and athletic comparisons and competition. All this can be tiring and frustrating for a parent. Assigning blame doesn't really help since it makes one child a winner and the other a loser. What fighting siblings are trying to do is to establish in their relationship who is dominant and who is subservient, so a parent can recognize this and point out that each child has areas of supremacy. Help older youngsters to develop acceptable social behaviors, not just for use with siblings, but also with friends. Show them how to control situations that could lead to sibling rivalry.

When siblings play together and arguing interferes with happy playtime, immediately step in and remove the toy or toys being played with. This is preferable to criticizing/correcting one or both children, unless you know all the facts. Ask older kids to settle disputes themselves, but say that you will settle the problem if they cannot.

To reduce sibling fighting, quickly separate the two fighters into separate rooms, without making any judgment. They'll soon figure out that playing in harmony beats being alone. Offer a simple reward to both siblings, such as a rented video, for a week without complaints.

Sibling rivalry sometimes carries over into early adulthood and even beyond. However, the parent's emphasis on the importance and distinctiveness of each child at an early age can defeat adult sibling rivalry.

SICKNESS. *See Diseases, Health.*

SIDS. *See Sudden Infant Death Syndrome.*

SINGING. *See also Lullabies, Music.*

Sing songs to babies, teach songs to toddlers, sing together as a family. Use times in the car, around the fire, and at holidays with relatives as singing times. Let youngsters teach you songs and, in return, teach them songs: folk songs, patriotic songs, hymns. If you do this, youngsters will not be self-conscious about their singing voices. Vocal music classes are often one of the first cuts in a school budget so parents need to reinforce the fun of singing at home. Inquire what would be needed to form a school chorus, or a children's choir.

SINGLE PARENTING. *See also Divorce, Parenting Skills.*

Going it alone is a lot of work, but it can be done. Don't make the mistake of thinking that many two-parent families are similar to single-parent families because one spouse is too disinterested or busy to participate. There is a huge difference since the single parent *never* has a spouse to help, consult with, or call on when totally tired or in an emergency.

The main challenges of single parents are overwork, anger, frustration, loneliness, guilt, and lack of funds and lack of time. Whether a single parent by choice or circumstances, you are going against the odds, but with organization and inspiration you can triumph and raise wonderful children.

These are the most important tips taken from the book *Single with Children* by Caryl Krueger, and available at the library. These tips are based on hundreds of interviews with effective single parents:

• Build a strong support group of relatives, friends, and neighbors that you can call on when times are tough. Be a good support to them in return.
• Find role models that fill in for the missing parent.
• Settle nagging questions such as custody, why a parent left, death of a parent, an unknown parent, abandonment, adoption. When questioned by the child, be prepared with brief, honest, nonjudgmental answers.
• Learn as much as possible about saving money and living economically. Make it a game with children. Create a budget that provides the necessities and an occasional reward, and stick to it. Vow to keep out of debt.
• Work diligently at your career and see if you can arrange to work through lunch and then leave early to have late afternoon time with your children.
• Learn parenting skills to help you become a great parent. Be alert to problem areas, such as substance abuse, and get help immediately.
• Don't treat a child as a substitute spouse by involving her in age-inappropriate decisions that are best made by you.
• Find adult companionship for fun and relaxation.
• Continue to grow as a person. Practice forgiveness, optimism, and a positive attitude. Take a little time for yourself. Read, take a class, be active in a social or religious group. This lowers your stress level and prepares you for life after your family is grown.

• Above all, love your children and yourself. Say it and show it often. There are many support groups for single parents that supply both information and social activities.

SITTERS. *See Caregivers.*

SLEEP. *See also Bedtime Routine, Crying, Naps, Nightmares.*
While a child's sleeptime may give parents a sense of relief, it can be an anxious time for some children. They fight it or are frightened by it, resulting in sleep disorders that are detrimental to parents who are sleep-deprived because of the child's unsettling difficulty.

The problem begins when parents slip a sleeping child into the crib after feeding time. Thus the child doesn't understand how sleep comes and can be frightened and demanding of attention when he suddenly awakes on his own and alone. Your aim is to let a child fall asleep *on his own*. You can accomplish this by putting the baby to bed when drowsy, though not asleep. The crib mobile, the music box or other simple diversion will be seen as comforting alternates to the parent.

Try not to let a child fall asleep while having a bottle, or in your bed, in a carriage you are rocking, in front of television, or in a place other than his own bed. When a child wakes, having fallen asleep in such places, he is upset because the bottle, the closeness of a person, or the feeling of movement is not there. So to sum it up, your job is to put the child to bed when it's time to sleep.

Of course, illness and changes in the family routine can cause stress that leads to sleep disturbances. Parents give extra attention under such circumstances and soon the child is dependent on a parent's presence in order to sleep. If a parent is completely sure that there is nothing physically wrong with the child, one answer is to ignore the cries, unless they are persistent and continuous without quiet interludes.

A bedtime routine with pleasant rituals aids sleep and is discussed in this book under the topic "Bedtime Routine." The activities should lead to sleep, becoming slower and quieter as the evening progresses. Activities that overstimulate can increase wakefulness and the need to be held.

For a baby who finds going to sleep difficult, you may want to consider swaddling, offering a pacifier, or placing a wrapped, warm (not hot) water bottle next to him.

Not all children require the same number of hours of sleep but an attentive parent will see the signs of too little sleep: fussiness, meanness, inattention, drowsiness. Cutting down on naps will improve nighttime sleep. The average for two- and three-year-olds is twelve hours, and four- and five-year-olds need about ten hours. It is normal for children to have different sleep patterns at night as they move from drowsiness to the dream state, to deep sleep, during which they may awaken briefly. Until a child learns to return to sleep on his own, a parent may have to stand by reassuringly.

Older children often fail to get adequate sleep, causing learning difficulties in school, disruptive behavior, and the need to sleep in over the weekend. Some of the time that teens use for television viewing and computer game play could be used to better advantage by sleeping. If you see signs of teen sleep deprivation, do everything in your power to encourage adequate sleep.

SLOW LEARNING. *See also Failure to Thrive, Hurried Child, Tardiness, Tutors.*

Some parents panic if their young child is not keeping pace with the neighbor's same-aged child. It is comforting to remember that preschool children learn at varied paces but most equal out at about age eight. However, when a child enters school and is having difficulty grasping skills, it is best to get help as soon as possible since new material is usually based on what has already been mastered. Consultation with a teacher should help.

Unfortunately, some students just learn more slowly all through their school lives. They deserve extra loving encouragement from parents and teachers to complete a basic education. This is vital to their feeling of self-worth so they can find a useful place in the after-school world. Often they will discover one particular talent that they enjoy that can be useful in selecting a career. Never give up on a slow learner or he may give up on himself. There are community agencies that will support your work.

SNACKS. *See also Mealtime, Nutrition.*

Minimeals, at midmorning and midafternoon, are fine providing they are nutritious. Healthy snacks include fresh fruits, dried fruits, cereal, low-calorie popcorn, low-salt crackers, simple cookies, veggies with dip, and yogurt.

Chips, candy, and ice cream have a place but are not ideal as snacks. Limit their use by having a small quantity in the house and saving them for special occasions.

Spanking

Rather than eating directly from packages, prepare a snack by setting out the amount that it is wise to eat. Then sit down together and use the opportunity to talk. Eating alone usually results in overeating. Parents should keep on hand reasonable portions of healthy snack foods for youngsters to choose: a jar of peeled carrots kept in fresh water, cubed cheese in a plastic bag, raisin boxes, granola bars, or other favorites. Make a cut-off time (two hours before mealtime is reasonable) after which there should be no snacking.

SOCIAL PROMOTION. *See School Grades.*

SOCIAL VISITS. *See Visiting.*

SOCIALIZATION.
This is the term used to describe a child's ability to cope effectively in a normal environment at home and beyond. A child who is socialized is not afraid of others, is able to speak when spoken to, can put into words her needs, can be left with a competent caregiver, and will act in a thoughtful rather than impulsive way. A child who is not socialized is fearful, silent, uncooperative, and often prefers being alone. Good parenting automatically socializes a child.

SORROW. *See Death, Grief.*

SPANKING. *See also Deprivation, Discipline, Punishment, Rules.*
Spanking, slapping, and other forms of physical correction have been popular in the past because they have an immediate effect and help a parent work off frustration. But, research shows that spanking is not as effective as other forms of correction (described in this encyclopedia) that will take more time and thought at first but have the benefit of correcting wrong behavior on a long-term basis. Since a change of behavior is the object of correction, it is wiser to use the methods that bring the better results. A parent's aim is not to show he is powerful or mean, but rather to be an example on how to act and react to wrongs.

Physical punishment such as spanking shows a child that an appropriate and adult method for solving a problem is hitting/slapping/spanking. While some child psychologists think spanking is effective on some occasions, the majority feel that using reason is better since it is less damaging to the parent-child relationship and cuts down on resentment. Spanking

245

doesn't permit the child to respond to any reason being voiced since he is busy focusing on the discomfort and humiliation of being spanked, rather than the wrong action.

Discipline is defined as "training that produces self-control." Proper parental discipline leads to a child's self-discipline that contributes to his self-worth. Thus parents should use a form of discipline that encourages a child to exercise self-control, to make good choices, and to have time to think about bad choices. Because you cannot watch a child every minute of the day for eighteen years, you want to raise a youngster who understands the correct way to act when you aren't on hand to remind or discipline.

SPEECH. *See also Communication, Grammar, Language, Profanity, Stuttering, Words.*

Good speech is an asset to most everyone except a hermit. While childish mispronunciations, even lisps, are sometimes viewed as cute, in the big picture, proper speech is preferred. Good speech is learned mostly by ear, so be careful what you say!

If a youngster has difficulty with a certain word, say it correctly, and have her repeat it. Do this several times in rhythm to establish the correct pronunciation. Reading to a child lets her hear the correct way words are pronounced. When you're finished reading a story, let a child tell it to you in her own words, and you will note that she picks up both vocabulary and inflection from your reading. Listening to well-read children's books, available on audio cassettes at most libraries, is another way to boost a child's good speech practices.

SPIRITUALITY. *See also Religion.*

The spiritual side of each child is her permanent essence—pure and perfect. While spirituality was formerly discussed mainly in religious terms, today it has a broader meaning, relating to the enduring aspects of each person. This animating principle is distinct from the body and is tied to a child's highest nature. It is expressed in joy, love, courage, forgiveness, peace, and confidence in something greater than the material person.

Children have moments of great spirituality when the human spirit is lifted to new heights that amaze even the most materialistic parent. Do not make fun of a child's spirituality but instead carefully nurture it.

SPOILING. *See also Parenting Skills.*

Spoiling a child, giving in to every whim (right or wrong), is a great disservice to both the youngster and to society. Children raised as the center of attention can be prideful, demanding, and obnoxious. Good parenting skills enable concerned mothers and fathers to create a balance between parental parameters and childhood demands.

It is unlikely that a baby under six months of age can be spoiled. However, sometime later in the first year infants begin to polish the skill of getting their own way. Patience and persistence on the part of the parent will help make a youngster who grows to be caring and appreciative and who also understands more acceptable ways of achieving aims than screaming or whining. A spoiled child has not been properly socialized or disciplined and sometimes a parent has to go back to basics to bring a youngster out of this unbecoming attitude. It's never too late to help a spoiled child.

SPONTANEITY.

With so many activities and duties that must be accomplished on schedule "or else," we need to work on our sense of adventure and the fun of surprises. The home offers many opportunities for teaching flexibility. Consider changing a boring routine, asking kid help in rearranging a room, eating different foods in different places, going somewhere together on short notice. When a spontaneous suggestion is made, think "Why not?" rather than "No." Get rid of the phrase "We've always done it this way." You'll be surprised at all the new things you learn and the more exciting things you do.

SPORTS. *See also Fitness, Games, Health, Outdoor Play, Sportsmanship, Team Sports.*

Sports are a healthy alternative to school work and computer and television viewing. Even if you aren't sporty, see that your youngsters are exposed to various athletic activities like catch, tag, obstacle races, relays, skating, badminton, swimming, dodge ball, and so forth. Then move on to sports such as volleyball, basketball, soccer, golf, baseball, skiing, scuba diving, or football. One of the best all-family sports is bicycling. Don't overlook inside sports and exercise: Ping-Pong, shuffleboard in the garage or basement, and a chinning bar. And don't restrict certain sports to boys, others to girls. At least thirty minutes of a sports activity each day is ideal.

For older youngsters, consider extracurricular school teams, joining a sports club or the Y. Equipment and uniforms can be expensive so start simply and see what sports appeal to the child. Parents and children playing a sport together, such as tennis, has added benefits, and certainly parental attendance at games and meets is important. College scholarships are available for young men and women who excel at sports and are willing to spend time and energy playing them.

Before a child is old enough to join in, start building interest in sports through attendance at neighborhood and high school games. Show him what to observe in the play. Expose him to the sports section of the paper and sports magazines. Choose a professional or college team to follow for a season.

SPORTSMANSHIP.

Winning is not as important as we often make it seem. Show your child that you're proud of her—and love her—whether her team is the champ or not. Celebrate the sport and good sportsmanship with an after-game event at the ice-cream parlor or back home. Talk about the things the team did well: good plays, scores, and the effort and exercise involved. Talk about respect for other players and how to improve skills without engaging in trash talk. Make it a point that it is truly *how* you played the game that counts.

STABILITY. *See also Divorce, Love, Parenting Skills.*

A stable home with stable parents (whether there are two parents or just one) provides children with the needed stability to function without fear. That they are loved, respected, and cared for gives them the freedom to work outward from the home base and be more confident in school and play. A sense of permanence is invaluable when the going gets rough.

Never threaten to leave a child or get rid of him. The attachment between parent and child, even when not always strong, is the life link which provides steadiness in everyday life.

If there are parental arguments, reassure the child that he is not the cause of the trouble. And if there is divorce, good relationships between the former spouses can still provide the needed stability for their offspring.

Stable homes are sanctuaries that do more than provide beds and meals. They are the centers of a full life and the source of affection.

STDS. *See AIDS.*

STEPPARENTING. *See also Divorce, Parenting Skills, Sibling Rivalry.*

Parenting a spouse's children is most effective when there is complete agreement between the parents, both the presently married ones and the ex's. When a new family is created, new roles must be defined—between all parents and children and between children and children.

The bad reputation of stepparents usually comes when items of major importance have been brushed aside by the euphoria of the dating period and the new marriage. The parent and stepparent need to settle their expectations regarding work/career, authority over home and children, managing money, and the place of the divorced parent.

Of course "getting to know you" sessions prior to the marriage will help the blended family work together for common goals. But it is also necessary to have regular family meetings after the marriage to iron out areas of conflict. Topics will vary with the ages of the children but matters that need defining usually include:

Discipline. Who is in charge and when. Discipline methods. The role of each parent as it relates to the children of the other parent.

Rules. Actually write them down so that there can be no confusion. A blending of rules of each family works best.

Traditions. The best of each family should be explained and retained. Family stories and photos can help each to appreciate the traditions of the other.

Territory. It will be natural at first for children to be possessive of their own toys and space, whether it is an entire bedroom or a portion of one. If possible, choose a new house or at least give each youngster her own private space. Screens and folding doors can help accomplish this.

One-on-one time. Respect is needed between birth parent and child and the new parent needs to see that this connection is maintained without criticism or hurt feelings.

Favoritism. While it can be natural for a parent to feel closer to her own child than her stepchild, both parents must bend over backward to see that there is equality in dealing with all the children. Parents may feel protective of their own children but expansive love can include them all. Rivalry among stepsiblings is common but can be lessened by both parents uniting with rules that pertain equally to all. Birth order may change with the remarriage and the baby of the family may lose his precious place and the big girl may find she has a bigger sister.

Stepparenting is most successful when youngsters learn early that the parent and stepparent are united in their aims, and that it is lasting relationship. Problems arise when a child tries to play one parent against the other and such machinations should be dealt with swiftly and firmly.

Effective stepparenting requires the parents to teach children how to respect the new parent. While you can't legislate love, you can require respect. And the new parent should move slowly and with loving consideration to correct unacceptable behaviors of stepchildren. Good lines are: "Yes, I know I'm not your mother, but I am your parent. As your parent I have certain obligations to fulfill in seeing you grow up correctly. And I have certain rights that you must respect, just as I respect your rights."

Don't rush to make many changes in a blended family. Take your time and let love do some of the work for you. It may not always be easy, but strive to be a real family, rather than just get through the stepparenting years.

STORYTELLING.

A child's creative thinking is encouraged through storytelling. For bedtime stories, a parent can elaborate on an episode from his own life. Or, a parent can start at the end of a favorite story and create what happens after the prince finds Snow White or after Heidi grows up.

Storytelling can be done with just two or with a group. Choose interesting places for storytelling: in lounge chairs on the patio, around a fire, by candlelight, in the car, or in a dark room. If everyone is to take part in the story, the first storyteller often sets the mood for the others by starting with a spooky story, a silly story, or a futuristic story.

Sometimes it's fun to let everyone tell part of a made-up story. One person begins with a few sentences and then each person adds to the story, giving it interesting twists and turns. This is called "round-robin" storytelling and it can also be used when a parent has finished telling a story to children and then asks them to tell it back to him.

Some stories can be true stories from the family's past or about historical characters. Children don't have to know the story is true until the end.

Subjects to take off and run with include: the best day in my life, a trip I liked, my first job, how I'd change the world, my first love, an animal I've met, my scariest night. The more these stories are embellished, the more fun they are.

Create storytelling props with cards or paper in two different colors. These cards are going to get good use, so write legibly. One stack is called the "Word Stack." With kid help, write out about twenty-five cards with one word or phrase on each card: some nouns, some verbs, adjectives and adverbs. These could be: baseball bat, puppy, jump, frugal, grandfather clock, cookie, snore, computer, moon, hug, spaceship, moose, Eskimo, looney, menacingly, balloon, creepy, full moon, toothpaste, diamond ring, monster, creaking, dinosaur. It doesn't hurt to have a few new words that must be looked up in a dictionary as using them will increase vocabulary.

The second stack is called "Happenings Stack." In it are things that will take place in the story. These lines could be: suddenly the candle dies, the cereal bowl is filled with cookies, a coyote howls in the distance, the store gives free toys, Fido speaks, the water turns purple, a pilot asks who would like to fly the plane, the teacher does somersaults, the car turns into a hot air balloon. Kids are great at suggesting these.

Turn over the two stacks on the table and let each storyteller draw one from each stack, but she should not show the cards to the others. Then, one person begins spinning the tale, just a few sentences, and then the next person picks up the story, each person trying to use the words and happenings from his cards. Both cards must eventually be used as the story goes 'round and 'round. Depending on the size of the group, set a timer and see if all the selected words can be used in that length of time.

The story might go like this with each person giving just a sentence: "A coyote howled in the distance and I hid my head under the covers and put my arms around my puppy." "The puppy needed to brush his teeth, but our family was too frugal to buy doggie toothpaste. However, the puppy did wear a diamond ring on one paw." "It was a full moon so I decided to go outside to find the coyote, my puppy pulling on the lead as we headed down the hill." "Suddenly, I felt someone following me. It was my teacher doing somersaults." So the story goes, no winners, no losers, no prizes, just fun.

STRANGERS. *See also Safety.*

Explain to children that a stranger is someone that we don't yet know. Without creating fear, tell that many adults like to talk to children, but that we must be polite and careful. Even if a stranger looks nice, offers candy, a ride, or says they know you or your family, they are still a stranger until a parent or other responsible adult has introduced them.

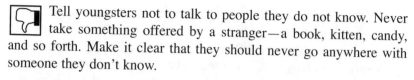

Tell youngsters not to talk to people they do not know. Never take something offered by a stranger—a book, kitten, candy, and so forth. Make it clear that they should never go anywhere with someone they don't know.

Do create a code word and tell it to young children. The word is to be used by another person who has been authorized by the parent to pick up a child from school or another location.

Tell children to stand a certain distance from someone who asks him a question when out on the street. The distance should be described as the length of two bicycles or two squares on a sidewalk. If he doesn't know the person, he should quickly leave.

Compliment children on safe practices with strangers. So you know what the child might do, give a series of "what would you do" questions and see the responses. "What would you do if I didn't pick you up after school?" "What would you do if someone said they had been sent by me to get you?" "What would you do if someone offered you a five dollar bill?" "What would you do if a stranger asked you to look at a map?"

It is necessary to reaffirm your teaching about strangers on a regular basis, even with older youngsters.

STRESS. *See also Parenting Skills, Time Management.*

While stress is a current buzzword, the results of overwork and over-stimulation have long been a problem. See that youngsters have daily periods of free time, and the structured time for homework and chores. Don't fill every free moment with activities, clubs, and lessons. Let there be time for casual conversation, board games, a long bath, or a back rub. Life is long and getting longer so everything doesn't have to be crammed into the first eighteen years of life!

What used to be termed anxiety is now generally classified as stress. In today's faster-paced living, overworked parents and overscheduled children suffer meltdowns that can interfere with their normal activity. Cause of stress can be fear of going to school or work, lack of achievement, little free time due to too many duties or activities, appearance, low self-esteem, or guilt over past mistakes. Before the stressed-out level is reached, take time to assess all the activities of the day. Weed out for the present those that are not essential. Keep a list of things to do at a later time. Sometimes just writing down things to do eases the mind and says that they will be dealt with in the future.

Set goals: easy-to-fulfill ones for the present, bigger challenges for later. Take steps to change what can be changed. Agree with yourself not to spend time fussing over what cannot be changed. Establish a time each day for quiet reflection, meditating, reading inspirational or other upbeat material, enjoying a simple sport or game.

STUBBORNNESS. *See also Willfulness.*

A stubborn child can be sending many messages: he can be using this as a means of getting attention, or he can be very sure he is right, or he may be afraid of doing something different. Usually stubborn preschool children become mellow by school age. Balky young children can be quite wise, so reasoned conversation can often talk them out of their set ways.

Stubbornness in older children is usually based upon fear of trying new things and contentment with the past. Encourage new activities that can be accomplished without judgment by parents, peers, or others. For the child who is adamant about her way always being the best way, challenge her to suggest an equally good way of doing the same thing. Your own bullheaded actions can also be encouraging children to emulate you, so be careful not to stubbornly get bogged down into ruts.

STUDY HABITS. *See Homework, School.*

STUTTERING. *See also Disabilities, Speech.*

Stuttering is a complicated problem that has long baffled scientists looking for a cause. Putting aside the cause, the focus is currently on the cure and thankfully success rates are high. It seems to afflict boys five times as often as girls. Young children may stutter when they search for an unfamiliar word. Children who are naturally lefthanded but are forced to be righthanded are more apt to stutter and this is linked to the control centers of the brain.

Don't say "Slow down," "Relax," or "Just take a breath." This only further flusters the speaker. Whatever you do, don't finish the sentence of a person who stutters. This can be confusing, demeaning, and increase nervousness.

Do try these suggestions for alleviating this exasperating problem. Maintain normal eye contact. Patiently wait until the child finishes speaking. Don't act embarrassed. If you don't understand what he's saying, say "I'm sorry, tell me again." Set a relaxed pace of speaking yourself and indicate that you are really listening to what is being said, rather than how it is being said.

If stuttering persists, professional consultation can greatly help.

SUBSTANCE ABUSE.

Alcohol and drugs cannot become addictive if a person doesn't even start their use. The home environment is the biggest influence in keeping kids free of these life busters. It is in late grade school that youngsters usually experiment with their first smoke, toke, drink, upper or downer. They see this as symbols of growing up. Frank discussions with parents and even former users are extremely important for deterring use.

Recent research shows that most teenagers find it easier to talk about drugs with their mothers than with their fathers, and those who don't have a good relationship with their fathers are at far greater risk for experimentation and extended use. Teens in two-parent families who have poor relationships with their fathers are 68 percent more likely to be users than those in average households. Mothers seem to be more inclined to partake in confidential give-and-take conversations and to give nurturing advice than fathers. And, the research also shows that youngsters who never have dinner with their parents have a 70 percent greater risk of substance abuse! Parents can get much helpful information by calling the National Clearing House for Alcohol and Drug Information at 1-800-729-6686.

Here are some things you should know:

Marijuana. Don't believe the myth that marijuana is harmless. Today's grass is ten times stronger than a generation ago and can result in impaired judgment, reduced attention span, vision and hearing problems, reduced learning ability/brain cell impairment, loss of coordination, increased heart rate, anxiety, panic attacks, and loss of motivation. The drug stays in the system for an indefinite time, decreasing resistance to infections and damaging lungs even more than cigarettes. Research also indicates that the use of marijuana by a mother during the first month of breastfeeding can impair the infant's motor development. Explain to a youngster that the use of marijuana will make him a poor student and athlete, an unsafe driver, and eventually a hacking, wheezing adult.

Cocaine, PCP, LSD, and heroin are drugs that can end life quickly. Cocaine (coke) is a powerful stimulant of the heart and brain that can last for days, then cause intense depression or paranoia, resulting in a craving

254

for a new high. Cocaine-related deaths are often the result of cardiac arrest or seizures, followed by respiratory arrest.

Angel dust or PCP is cheap and deadly, causing hallucinations, mood disorders, hostility, and brain damage, with symptoms sometimes recurring years after use. It can also interfere with normal growth and development and with the learning process. Many who have used it once will not knowingly use it again since it causes feelings that are violent and suicidal.

Lysergic Acid Diethylamide or LSD is an unpredictable drug that can cause severe psychotic symptoms, bad "trips," and permanent mental damage. The physical effects include dilated pupils, higher body temperature, increased heart and blood pressure, sweating, loss of appetite, sleeplessness, dry mouth, and tremors. Most frightening are the acute adverse reactions of a trip, including flashbacks for a year or more after use.

Heroin is an expensive hard-to-kick drug that requires a fix several times a day. Apart from fatal overdoses, it causes hallucinations, spontaneous abortion, collapsed veins, liver disease, other infectious diseases, and is associated with HIV/AIDS and hepatitis. Withdrawal from its use causes chills and nausea, muscle and bone pain, insomnia, diarrhea and vomiting. Because addicts often share needles, it is a primary cause of the spread of AIDS.

These expensive drug habits cause many users to turn to stealing and other criminal habits in order to support the need. And the bottom line is mental and physical exhaustion, sexual dysfunction, and frequently an early death.

Inhalants. Fumes from nail polish remover, glue, cooking spray, furniture polish, paint thinners or solvents, gasolines, and other aerosols can cause a temporary mild euphoria. But they can also damage the nerves that control breathing, and can cause damage to hearing, bone marrow, liver, and kidneys. Frequent use can lead to heart failure, coma, and death. Even firsttime users can suddenly die from sniffing Freon, butane, and propane. The problem with inhalants is that they are readily accessible within the home and youngsters feel it is fun to experiment with them.

Tobacco. Cigarettes and cigars, and chewing tobacco, are highly addictive and can cause heart disease and cancer. As lungs deteriorate, the victim is in extreme pain prior to death. Tobacco use can result in depression and fatigue, and also ruins the speaking and singing voice. Withdrawal can result in anger, aggression, the loss of social cooperation, and the impairment of motor and cognitive functions. Secondhand smoke usually causes illness and sometimes kills innocent nonsmokers who must breathe the polluted air.

Ecstasy. Also known as MDMA, ecstasy is a designer drug made popular in dance establishments. It can be swallowed, inhaled, or injected and increases emotions, energy, and sensuality. It greatly raises the heart rate and blood pressure, causes confusion and severe depression, and can result in death from dehydration and exhaustion. Even low doses destroy brain cells and the damage may not be immediately apparent. Parkinson symptoms (lack of coordination and possible paralysis) eventually emerge.

Liquid Ecstasy (also called GHB) is odorless, tasteless, colorless. The alcohol-like stupor caused by just a few drops can be followed by a tremendous ill feeling. If accompanied by alcohol or in an overdose, bodily rigidity, seizures, cardiac arrest, coma, and death can occur. It has been used on occasion as the drug for date rape.

Amphetamines, methamphetamines. Called speed or uppers, these stimulants are often available by prescription. While there are some medically legitimate uses, they are sometimes misused as a treatment for obesity. Energy, alertness, and increased athletic ability are sought-after results, but increased heart rate, violent mood swings, elevated blood pressure resulting in strokes are a few of the side effects from misuse. Unfortunately kids think that these prescription drugs are harmless since they are somewhat related to ingredients in cold remedies, appetite control pills, and no-sleep pills. Even small amounts seriously damage the central nervous system, causing irritability, insomnia, confusion, convulsions, paranoia, and even death.

Steroids. While these may increase muscle mass, strength, and the ability to train longer and harder, people who inject these run the risk of contracting HIV or hepatitis. Side effects include liver tumors, jaundice, high blood pressure, severe acne, and trembling. For males, they can cause infertility, baldness, and shrinking testicles. For females, they can bring on maleness features such as facial hair, deepened voice, and change or cessation of the menstrual cycle.

Alcohol. Alcoholism is a subtle addiction that starts early and leads to the leading cause of teen auto accidents and death. Alcohol use can result in cancer, brain damage, malnutrition and liver problems. In addition, alcohol abuse leads to the failure of careers and marriage. Babies born to parents who are heavy drinkers often have mental and physical defects. Alcohol is used as a crutch for those who think it relaxes them and helps them forget their troubles, but it is actually a depressant and requires more frequent and stronger drinks to get a lift. Thus it becomes more difficult to control, ruining the lives of the abusers and many others.

Educate yourself by getting authoritative information. Set an example by being a responsible adult. Make your house a drug-free, alcohol-free, nicotine-free zone. When your children give a party, be alert and don't permit the use of any controlled substance. Prohibit gatecrashers, or guests coming and going, which is often a sign of drug use. There is much free literature available for parents and children. Don't rely on the schools to do your job.

Don't hide behind your ignorance. It is your right to ask and know what is going on. If you find drugs or alcohol, or suspect their use, confront your youngster. The warning signs that every parent should be alert to include: a sudden drop in grades, a new set of friends, loss of interest in activities, altered eating and sleeping habits, weight loss, and a change in behavior from a happy youngster to one who is wary, withdrawn, depressed, rebellious, or aggressive. Often your best solution is to get professional help before the problem goes too far.

Get to know the parents of your youngster's friends. Work together to be vigilant and say and mean these words: "If you see my child breaking the rules, tell me, because I need to know." Find the causes for substance abuse and work to solve them, whether it is low self-esteem, peer pressure, depression, boredom, or revenge. Take action sooner rather than later.

SUCCESS. *See also Achievement, Appreciation, Determination, Failure, Praise, Self-Worth.*

Provide opportunities for a youngster to be successful. Don't underestimate what she can do, but occasionally repeat an activity that you are sure she can do. This success brings a wonderful sense of self-worth and security to a child who may be struggling with feelings of inferiority.

Verbal praise from others is important, so parents and grandparents should acknowledge good school work, good craft work, and good sportsmanship. Once in a while, write a brief letter of appreciation to your child, telling your pleasure at something she has done. Feeling essential and loved is important, especially when a child needs to be corrected and could consequently feel less worthy. So, be sure to note her successes that can counter her failures.

When school is over, plan a special dinner out, honoring a successful year for the students in your family. Let them share what they think were their successes. If report cards are worthy of compliments, even of the smallest variety, do mention these, too.

SUDDEN INFANT DEATH SYNDROME (SIDS).

The sudden death of an apparently healthy baby is a tragedy that at present has an unknown cause. Known as SIDS, it seems to mostly affect babies under six months of age. It more commonly afflicts high-risk babies, those born prematurely, or those whose parents use alcohol, tobacco, or illegal drugs. While it was formerly recommended that babies sleep on their stomachs, there are some indications of a connection to SIDS. Thus, it is now considered preferable to have young babies sleep on their backs.

SUICIDE. *See also Depression, Self-Worth, Substance Abuse.*

The choice to end human life is not ever a solution to problems, actually adding to them by creating havoc and guilt to those left behind. Give youngsters a good sense of the value of life and their unique opportunities to contribute something good to the world. If you have a religious background, you can point out that life goes on and suicide is not an advantage.

Never make light of a child's threats to commit suicide. Even if he is not sincere in that desire, he is saying that he feels his life isn't worth living. Get professional help at once. Children with low self-esteem and those who are easily depressed are candidates for suicide. Drug abuse may cause suicidal tendencies. A change in friends or a sudden lack of friends, lower grades, lack of interest in appearance, giving away belongings are all symptoms of a disturbed mind. Don't ignore any of the warning signals that are cries for help to be noticed, to be appreciated, and to be loved.

Suicide statistics cross all socioeconomic barriers. In fact, suicide is on the rise among intelligent kids with affluent parents whose misplaced priorities—devotion to career and social status—may have replaced tangible or visible love for family. These children feel a lack of intimacy and the pressures of competition with their parents' other time-consuming activities.

Suicidal tendencies don't come on suddenly. Parents who keep close to their children can sense the symptoms and take action before tragedy strikes.

SUPPORT SYSTEM. *See also Parenting Skills, Single Parenting.*

Parents can't know everything so a support system is essential. Before the first baby arrives, find dependable help in a variety of areas.

PEP. A PEP (parental enrichment partner) is an experienced friend who is a backup when unexpected things happen.

Trading Partner. You will also want to find another parent to be your trading partner, enabling children to play together at the partner's home and yours.

Baby-sitter. When a child is young, you will want a knowledgeable baby-sitter so you can have free time at least once a week. Interview sitters and ask for references. Be sure your baby-sitters enjoy children, are instructed in home care and safe practices, and knowledgeable about your rules concerning television, snacks, and bedtimes. Consider hiring a reliable and well-taught teen who lives nearby and whose family you know.

Professional help. You will need professional help, which should include a pediatrician or other health-care practitioner.

Community resources. Social service agencies are sources of good parenting information, as are parent support groups in your area or at schools. Religious advisors and professional child-development lecturers and writers can also add to your knowledge.

Teachers and leaders. One of your most important supporters are the teachers of your children. Get to know them and keep them informed of your child's special interests and needs. Also, leaders of your child's group activities and sports teams can give valuable input.

SWEETS. *See also Nutrition.*

Limit the amount of candy and other sweets given to children and don't use candy as a reward. Desserts, both the sweet variety and the fruity variety, should be part of the daily menu. Cookies made with grains and nuts and a minimum amount of sugar make good snacks. Once a child develops a taste for sweets, it is difficult to curb it, so start early to control that sweet tooth.

TAKING TURNS. *See also Sharing.*

Sharing isn't a problem with the firstborn since she usually plays alone, but it can cause battles when there is more than one playing together. To teach an only child how to take turns, a parent can join in the play, acting as a playmate. These are aids to learning how to take turns:

• The minute there is a tug-and-pull, remove the toy from play for that day.
• Divide popular toys into two stacks and let youngsters trade.
• Provide a simple timer and let the second child have the toy after three minutes.
• Give the child who wants the toy, but doesn't have it, a toy that goes with it and suggest a line of play. For example, if two children are arguing over the train engine, give the other child the gates so she is in charge of traffic at the crossing.
• If a child refuses to give up a toy and you don't want her to make a scene, engage the other child in playing with something special. Soon the first child will want to join in that play.

Learning to take turns is part of teaching youngsters to be caring and unselfish, and this basic training with toys will carry over into other activities as kids get older. An example of this is when teams are chosen and youngsters who appear less talented are usually chosen last. If the activity is set up so that kids take turns being the chooser, there are less hurt feelings. Better yet, the team captains should meet in advance, make up balanced teams, and just announce them.

Help youngsters overcome the "me first" desire. This can be helpful when waiting in lines, when choosing an activity, when dividing chores, or when a teen driver comes to a four-way stop.

TALENT. *See also Lessons, Sports.*

Every child has talent. Some may excel at an instrument or sport while others may excel at math or the willingness to try new things or to make others laugh. Never compare talents between siblings; and never degrade a child's abilities.

And remember that many youngsters are multitalented. Don't let them get stuck in just one activity. Give youngsters many opportunities to try new things until they discover more of their talents. Don't push a talent, rather let a child enjoy it without excess pressure or parental manipulation.

TANTRUMS. *See also Anger, Attention, Destructiveness, Rebellion.*

Annoying for a parent and scary for a child, tantrums are not unusual during toddlerhood. The first things to do are: take a deep breath, be sure it is not a seizure or other physical problem, and see the child is in a safe place where he can kick or thrash. Sympathy is the next step, so casually say to the kicking child: "I know you're angry, but it will soon be better."

While some tantrums just fade away, others require parent action. During a tantrum a parent can feel helpless and want to do something. In some cases, holding the child and telling him that you love him and that everything will be okay is sufficient. Other times, a music box or cassette may distract and soothe. Try going out on the grass or onto soft carpet where both of you can kick and shout together; he may be surprised and stop to watch you! Putting a child's hands in cool running water may stop the screaming.

Most often the child is frustrated over something and is using this inappropriate way to seek attention. Don't give it, just turn your back and don't look; depriving him of attention may quiet him down.

When the tantrum is over, see if you can talk together about what caused it. The tendency to have tantrums stops when a child's verbal skills are improved.

Don't treat the child roughly, this only aggravates the problem. If the child wants something, don't give in to him. This only reinforces the use of tantrums by the child. Tell him why he can't have what he wants. Don't worry about what any bystanders are thinking since most of them have been through this stage with their own kids.

Remove the child from the scene of the tantrum even if you only go a few yards away, this indicates that you are in charge. If a child is difficult to pick up, roll his body in a sheet, with his face uncovered, lift him into your arms, and rock him gently.

If tantrums become violent or persist, professional help is needed.

TARDINESS. *See also Morning Routine, Slow Learning, Time Management.*

Children can manifest two kinds of tardiness: the child who is late for everything (often due to loafing or distraction) and the child who learns things a bit later (the ten o'clock scholar). Both need help with easier-to-attain goals and a bit more attention to routine.

Work out a morning schedule with a school child who is often tardy, showing what must be done and how long it takes, hence when he must wake up. Figure in a ten minute cushion for playtime after the routine things are finished. Then make a time schedule for after-school activities and duties and talk about it often until he masters it. Let him do assigned tasks and homework somewhere near a parent. Vary the tasks and punctuate the hard work with periods of relaxation. To reinforce his successes, give praise daily for keeping on each part of the schedule, possibly in front of someone else so that his worth is recognized. Your aim is to let the child eventually schedule his own time without your supervision.

Require less than you feel he's capable of doing at first, but establish "the must dos" and stick to them. You may have to include some punishment for tardiness that affects others as in carpools or the entire family when going on an excursion. Don't make tardiness an easy habit by ignoring it.

Remind him that it is his decision to accomplish things on time and feel satisfied, or ignore things and reap the punishment. Acting responsibly at home gains more privileges. Turning in quality homework on time results in better grades.

Don't give up on a child who is slower to learn. Just like physical growth that comes in spurts, mental growth can seem stagnant and then leap ahead. With help from the teacher, prioritize, selecting just one or two of the things most important for him to master. When these are learned, build on these successes.

TATTLETALES. *See also Sibling Rivalry.*

Getting others in trouble can be a tantalizing game for some children. They become very excited to tell what another child is doing, especially when it's something bad. Of course a parent needs to know about serious infractions of family and school rules or community laws, but most parents are already aware of the bad habits of their children and probably don't need to be told.

If a child is a constant talebearer, you can say "Tell me if it is very very important." Or, "Why not tell her (the other child) what you wanted to tell me?" Or, "I will listen to your complaint if you first tell me something nice about her." Or, "I think you should help me come up with a solution so you don't have to take your time to tell me these things."

By not overreacting to tales, you take some of the fun out of it, and you'll find that the tattletale may start using his dramatic talents in more productive ways.

TAXES.

Parents are entitled to certain tax savings. Be sure you take all the child-care credits and exemptions due to you. See your tax advisor for details on dependency exemptions, child credit, child and dependent-care credit, college tuition credits, higher-education interest and deductions, earned income credit, adoption credit, college-savings bonds and many other new and helpful exclusions.

TEACHERS. *See also Education, Parent-Teacher Relationships.*

A school teacher is one of the two greatest influences on a child. (The other is the parent, of course.) Get to know the school teacher, attend parent functions and conferences, and offer your help. Be ready to hear both praise and criticism about your child, and make it clear that you will do all you can to support improved schoolwork.

Ask the teacher (and spouse) for dinner at your home. Most will welcome a free home-cooked meal after a busy day. While some youngsters are apprehensive about this, once they've experienced it, they are eager to do it again. Kids will find that teachers are regular human beings, have a sense of humor, and have interests beyond the schoolroom.

Be supportive of the teacher's aims, but complain if the homework load is so huge it does not allow time for other activities. When there is a student/teacher problem, hear both sides before judging. If you ever think that a teacher is doing something inappropriate (anything from swearing to molesting), report it to the administration. When the problem is resolved, but if the child continues to feel uncomfortable, it is sometimes best for the student to be transferred to another class of the same grade.

See that teachers are respected and well paid for their invaluable work. This is not something out of your domain; your phone calls and letters to boards of education and influential government officials can lift the teaching profession to a higher status in our society and also bring people of superior talents into the field of education.

TEAM SPORTS. *See also Fitness, Sports, Teamwork.*

Carefully supervise your youngster's participation in team sports. Don't just sign her up and forget it. There can be great pressure from parents, peers, and some team managers for youngsters to participate in sports that are not age-appropriate or safe. Despite the safety rules, carefully consider the physical risks in certain sports and perhaps suggest alternatives to your child. Attend practices and games to see that the coaches are fair, not overly competitive, give opportunities for play to all participants, and do not berate young players. Talk to your youngster about her feelings and be vocal to those in charge if you feel that she is always sitting on the bench and not learning anything but patience.

Don't force a youngster into a team sport. But, if there is to be a commitment, tell the youngster that it has to be for a certain amount of time in order to give it a fair try. Remember that a parent also has a commitment to be supportive.

Team sports can take up a great proportion of a youngster's time. Keep it in balance with other activities and be sure not to let academics end up in second place.

TEAMWORK. *See also Sportsmanship, Team Sports.*

Group activities have many benefits beyond athleticism. They also provide opportunities for academic, social, physical, and emotional experiences. They teach ingenuity, honesty, leadership, followership, and poise. Most important is learning how to work and play effectively with others. When considering extracurricular activities with youngsters, suggest at least one that includes opportunities for teamwork, such as a debate team, drama group, or climbing club. Group activity can be a useful microcosm of society since teamwork is vital to home life, careers, and community projects.

TEASING. *See also Cultural Differences, Name-Calling, Profanity, Rejection.*

Making fun of one another can be miserable or it can be fun. With young children, it is usually a test of power to see which child is in charge.

With school-aged children, it is often just silliness and they may not yet realize that certain words are hurtful. And, as children mature, teasing can become downright vicious as those who are "different" are picked on. By adulthood, teasing has become a form of camaraderie.

When teasing is a child's main method of communication, a parent should step in with not-too-subtle lessons in social skills. Taunting others, goading them to do certain things, saying words that degrade, and making fun of everything, can be an indicator of a child's feelings of inadequacy. He feels that attacking in this way will take the focus off his own short-comings. Therefore, emphasize activities that develop self-worth.

Don't ignore cruel teasing or tell the victims to just ignore it. Rather empathize with the hurt child and reassure him that you are supportive. If a parent doesn't give attention to the teaser (and instead gives attention to the teased), the teaser will not find as much satisfaction in doing it.

Ask the teaser if he knows what the words mean. Sometimes inappropriate teasing is really a language misunderstanding. Practice gentle teasing between parent and child and be ready to laugh at outrageous remarks.

TEEN PREGNANCY. *See Pregnancy, Teenage.*

TEEN YEARS. *See also Appearance, Dating, Fads, Haircuts, High School Concepts, Rebellion, Rules, Sex.*

When youngsters accept more responsibility and wish for less parental input, it is still important for parents to continue instilling good values and adherence to family rules and standards. In a few years teens will be on their own, and these teen years are the last years for a parent to give guidance on how to live a fulfilling life. Just because a child is a teen and thinks he is endowed with all wisdom, do not abdicate your job as parent, but complete your job with vigor.

TEETH. *See Dental Care.*

TELEPHONING. *See also Privileges.*

With each year of age, the use of the telephone increases to the point that it can become the main means of recreation for some youngsters. Conversations are rarely based on new information, but rather a rehash of something that has happened in school or at a party. The phone provides emotional support during the adolescent years from someone of their own age and similar experience. A telephone is presumed to be a private tool where one can share innermost thoughts.

Teach cooperation so all family members can have equal use of the phone. Consider voice mail and call-waiting services. The buzz of call waiting should be an immediate indication for the one talking to politely take the second call and say that they will be called back within a short time. Then, the first call should be terminated in a reasonable amount of time or called back later if necessary. While some people feel that call waiting is rude, if handled properly it is a good tool for keeping peace in the family and also letting the second caller know that someone is home. In some cases, a pager or e-mail are good alternatives to the desire to keep in touch.

When a youngster asks for a phone extension in her own room or a cellular phone to carry, consider how trustworthy she is now and has been in the past. Have family rules and limits been adhered to consistently? How well do you know the values of the youngsters that your child will probably be talking with? Is personal safety a reason for the youngster to have a cell phone? Remember that when you give a youngster this connection with the world, it is a step of separation from the family and you lose some of the options for monitoring her relationships.

If you do decide to let a youngster have her own phone line, state clearly that a parent will have the ability of seeing the child's phone bill. Ask the phone company about teen rates. Discuss how the bill is to be paid. Teens might pay for their long-distance and toll charges, and a percentage of the rest of the bill.

Don't provide a child with a private line until after age twelve. If you have more than one youngster, let them share the line. When kids have their own line, they must not also tie up a parent's line except in an emergency. Prohibit using the phone to reach sex or pornography numbers and say that it will be immediately removed the first time it is misused.

Make telephone use contingent on acceptable grades and behavior. Don't hesitate to unplug the phone if homework and chores are being ignored. Set a time limit if the phone is overused and set hours of use.

TELEVISION. *See also Activities, Video Games, Videos.*

Don't let television take over the life of your child. Certainly there are some benefits of television: it can educate, relax, stimulate imagination, improve vocabulary, and entertain. But it can also introduce inappropriate themes, promote aggression, cause apathy and passive learning, and take time away from more important activities. Parents need to help youngsters find a balance. Wise parents know what their children watch, in fact many make a list of approved shows so even caregivers know what can be viewed.

Don't have the television on during dinner, for when the news-caster is talking the family isn't talking. Don't turn on the tele-vision without knowing what you plan to watch. Don't let youngsters do homework with the television on. Don't let Saturday morning be hours of cartoons; provide good videos or alternate activities when par-ents want to sleep late. Don't permit viewing shows with gratuitous sex, violence, or vulgar language, as research shows what is seen does influence the actions of children.

Take turns reading the television guide and recommending what the family or youngsters only should see for the week. Do per-mit a maximum of one hour of television on week nights and two hours on weekends, letting youngsters recommend what they believe is most important to view. Do preview new weekly programs and give your approval or disapproval. You may wish to view the same programs in midseason since some have a tendency to get raunchier as the weeks go on. Do allow kids to occasionally stay up beyond their usual bedtime in order to see an especially good program. View television *with* youngsters when possible and talk about it afterward.

Research shows that youngsters who overdose on television are more apathetic about life and violence prone than those who see a minimum amount. Obesity can result from fatty snack foods and minimal exercise. And excessive television viewing is related to poor schoolwork. If a grade falls to an unacceptable level such as a C-minus, terminate weekday view-ing until the grade improves.

There are many means of controlling television, so use what works best for the benefit of your children. The use of a video cassette recorder will let you tape shows to see when you want to see them, free from commer-cials if you fast forward through them. Don't let television become a pas-sive baby-sitter. Reason combined with intriguing alternative activities are the best ways of cutting back. If need be, get locks or try a month without any television at all.

THANK-YOU'S. *See Appreciation, Gratitude.*

THANKSGIVING.

Modern Thanksgiving celebrations can recreate the sharing atmosphere between the pilgrims and Native Americans with everyone bringing a portion of the meal as a symbol of the gratitude for bounty of the past year. As guests arrive, give them a strip of colored construction paper about eight inches long and two inches wide on which to write something for which they are grateful. Staple these into a "grateful chain" to hang over the eating table. Other activities could be a corn-on-the-cob eating contest, a contest for the best photo of the year, and a piñata—not exactly a pilgrim custom, but lots of fun!

Next to a large place card marking each place at the table, put a pen. Between the feast and dessert, each person passes his place card to the right and that person puts a word on it, something she's grateful for about that person (a sense of humor, caring, adventure, musical ability, and so forth). The cards continue to go around the table with more qualities put on them until they get back to the owner who now has a memento of the good things others see in him.

THEATER. *See Drama.*

THINKING BENCH. *See also Discipline, Punishment.*

Learning to think through a problem to a solution is a great skill to teach youngsters that can even be taught to toddlers. That is why the thinking bench or time-out is a common form of behavior adjustment. When a youngster misbehaves, such as hitting a friend, he is sent to the thinking bench, which is located in a quiet place such as the laundry room. A timer is set, and if he comes out before the time is up, the timer is reset for a slightly longer time. Until a child understands the system, a parent may have to remain quietly nearby, reading or working.

While sitting on the bench, the youngster is to come up with a better way of acting, which he will share with you when the timer goes off. His solution may not be adequate so that the parent will have to suggest ideas. Then the parent points out that he missed play because of what he did, and in order not to miss play again, he should try hard not to repeat the offense. This has the advantage of teaching the young child that there are consequences to inappropriate behavior and he can choose how to act. It also permits a time for the child to calm down without parental threats.

As soon as a child begins to recognize those actions that result in a trip to the thinking bench, the parent will save time and have less input, but the child still needs to acknowledge what he did and how he should have acted.

THUMB SUCKING. *See also "Blankies," Pacifiers.*

A child does this because it gives her comfort. Most children give up this habit by about age two. If it persists beyond toddler years, it could become a power play. Don't make it into a struggle; ignoring the thumb sucking may cause it to go away naturally. It may only occur in sleep, as it does in many adults. Carried to an extreme, thumb sucking can change the angle of teeth and gums and be a cause for orthodontia, so you may want to enlist the help of your dentist to persuade a child to stop.

Never punish or threaten a thumbsucker. See if you can show children other means of self-comfort such as curling up with a book, thinking of a good happening, cuddling with a favorite toy.

TIME MANAGEMENT. *See also Calendar, Chores, Fun, Home Management, "Me Time," Quality Time, Quiet Time, Tardiness.*

Finding time to be a good parent is a matter of priorities. Busy parents need to set their expectation level (what they hope to accomplish) high, but not too high. And they need to scale back less-worthy activities as soon as they feel frustration or guilt about not spending adequate time with their kids.

Most people have a tendency to do the smallest projects and the more pleasant tasks first. However, it is better to start with a hard job, then reward yourself with an easier, more pleasant one. Learning to "work in the cracks" is an important tactic. This means that while hanging on a phone line you make a list of "to do" items, or write a thank-you note. This means that when you leave one room, you look around it to see what needs to be carried to another. This means that you group errands or other trips, doing small things on the way to bigger things.

Good time managers learn to do two things at once. Many people save time by having a bathroom radio so they can catch the news while dressing or showering. When cooking a meal, many parents include youngsters as helpers and use the opportunity to talk together or go over a book report or a spelling test.

One time management skill is to know how long certain projects take: the drive to work or school, the time to get dressed (both children and parents need to know this), the time needed to prepare and eat breakfast. It also means that many household tasks are done as a team, and that some things can be left undone. And, when both parents work, the chores at home should be fairly divided. Imbalance (one parent doing far more than the other) is detrimental to the marriage relationship and also sets a bad example for youngsters.

There are six times each day that parents need to manage the time to connect with their children. I call them *touch-base times.*

1. **At breakfast.** This is for reminding about plans for the day and reaffirming love.

2. **After school.** A check-up for safety and activities. This can be done in person or by phone.

3. **The before-dinner reunion.** A reuniting time for winding down and sharing, even if only a few moments before starting dinner preparations.

4. **Dinnertime.** This all-family event includes conversation on the day's events, upcoming family activities, world events, even reading a chapter of a book.

5. **The evening hour.** This could be as little as fifteen minutes but is an important time for a game, walk, or one-on-one activity. Then youngsters go on with their evening tasks, homework, and going to bed.

6. **Bedtime.** This is a vital connection between parents and children of all ages, a time to reaffirm close family ties.

These touch-base times provide opportunities to communicate and counsel and overcome fears of separation and loneliness. Touching base at these six times also alleviates the guilt of not having enough parenting time.

Keeping a monthly calendar can also help plan events so there isn't too much activity one week and too little the next. And parents need to be aware of their own needs for quiet times and social times; a parent needs to be a "whole" person, which is an aid to being a good parent. Taking time to develop those interests that go beyond children will be important when the children are grown and the parent has more time for career and other activities.

TIME-OUT. *See Thinking Bench.*

TOASTS. *See also Appreciation.*

One of the most enjoyable ways of showing appreciation to young people is through toasts given at dinner the last night of the month. Think of a toast for every family member at the table—for good sportsmanship, for helping around the house, for an improved grade, for a delicious meal, for earning money, or for a special kindness to someone. Use juice or nonalcoholic sparkling drinks in classy glasses and let everyone raise their glasses and their voices in appreciation.

TOBACCO. *See Substance Abuse.*

TODDLER CONCEPTS. *See also Early Learning.*

The years prior to age five are great learning years, in fact the brain grows to 90 percent of its size during these years. Here are some concepts that should be mastered: name/address/phone number, bathroom training, simple table manners, use of please and thank you, how to dress oneself, taking turns, left and right, throwing and catching, various childhood games, and the love of books. These are especially important years to spend with your child. If at all possible, postpone a career until a child enters kindergarten, but if not possible, look very carefully for quality care.

TOGETHERNESS. *See also Family Life Essentials, Parenting Skills.*

What is the "Togetherness Rating" for your family? Count your "yes" answers to these easy questions:

1. Do you have at least ten minutes together in the morning for breakfast and going over the day's plans?
2. Do you use car time to listen to one another and initiate meaningful conversation?
3. Do you ask daily what youngsters are learning in school, in sports practice, or by reading at home?
4. When you return home in the evening, do you spend at least ten minutes with other family members before reading the mail or newspaper, before changing clothes, or before preparing dinner?
5. Does the family eat dinner together at a table with the television off, with conversation and interesting stories about the day and plans for the weekend?
6. Is there usually an after-dinner event, such as a walk, game, or craft that brings the family together for a short period of time?
7. Instead of being totally engrossed with your own evening projects, do you make yourself available for conversation, homework help, and problem solving?

Toilet Training

8. No matter what the age of your youngster, is bedtime an occasion for conversation and expressions of love and appreciation?
9. Do you take time to plan ahead for an enjoyable family event each weekend?
10. Do you work together (and thus talk together) each weekend, doing repairs, washing the car, gardening, or cleaning?
11. Does the family have a religious observance each weekend and an in-car conversation (on the way home) about the sermon subject, or about ethics and morals?
12. Do you take an active interest in your youngster's activities: sports, music lessons, scouting, and so forth?
13. Do you build memories by creating traditions around major (and minor) occasions, activities, and holidays?
14. Have you taken time to know your youngster: likes and dislikes, talents and problems, tastes in music, food, clothing, and hopes for the future?
15. Do you include your child in talking about your own challenges, hopes, and dreams?

Twelve to fifteen "yes" answers is a sign of a family that practices good togetherness. If less than that, discuss this list with your family and try to make some improvements.

TOILET TRAINING. *See also Bed-Wetting.*

Parents often make toilet training into a bigger deal than it merits. Just as learning to talk, read, and ride a bicycle can occur at different ages, so does toilet training. It should not be a matter of parental pride or guilt. Don't be intimidated by the father of a sixteen-month-old who tells you his daughter is trained, and don't be despondent over your four-year-old who hasn't mastered it yet. There are numerous books, tapes, fancy equipment, even "targets" to encourage success, yet far more important is your calm, consistent approach.

Although the time is somewhat the child's choice, don't hesitate to encourage that choice. After all, the parent has had much more experience in using a toilet. It takes a certain level of understanding and readiness on the part of the child, and some are ready sooner than others.

To some extent, the training is of the parent, not the child. Parents should calmly talk about the process and soon they may recognize signs indicating the child's need to go. Don't ask "Do you want to go to the bathroom?" Rather say, "Let's try to go, but it's okay if you don't." It will

272

happen (sometimes in just a day or two) and sometime between the ages of two and four. The more you try to manage it, the more it becomes your issue and not the child's.

Staying dry all night may take longer. At some point a child may recognize the need to go and awaken herself, but this is more difficult than daytime training. A good training time is the naptime when a child can go to the toilet beforehand and stay dry for the one- to two-hour stretch. Don't fall into the habit of over-using pull-up diapers. Pull-ups can be a detriment if a child doesn't register the displeasure of being wet. They have a short-term purpose and continued use can promote lazy bathroom habits.

Use the same words: real words, not cute words, but words you wouldn't be embarrassed to hear in public. We think that pee-pee and poo-poo are easy for a child to say, but "Toilet please" is just as easy and will sound better through the years. It is degrading for an adult to say "I have to pee."

Encourage a child to tell you when she needs to go, is going, or has already gone. This is a first step in the right direction. If a child has been dry for about two hours, put her on the toilet. Let a child see a parent, usually of the same sex, use the toilet. Buy a sturdy, simple junior potty and let it be seen in the bathroom before you suggest its use. Be simple in your appreciation when the potty or toilet has been used, and try to use the same positive words such as "You used your toilet!"

Don't start the training just because you're tired of diapering. Avoid using the words "good" or "bad" in relation to success or nonsuccess. Don't shame a child for a mistake. And don't be discouraged about periods of regression—they usually don't last long. When a new baby joins the family, the older child often begins to wet again, seeing the attention the baby gets. That's the time for praise such as "You can do so many things the baby can't do. Maybe you will teach him to be dry."

Toilet training teaches self-control so do not use shame, which only undermines the important feeling of self-esteem.

TOOTH FAIRY.

Losing a tooth can be frightening for some children. She sees that part of herself is actually falling apart and wonders what will be next! Be sure to share your own stories of tooth loss and how a new tooth always came in. By the time a child loses a tooth, she usually knows that fairies are part of fantasy, but it's still fine to play the game of hiding the tooth under the pillow for the fairy to find. When the parent takes the tooth away in the night, it can be replaced with money or a very small gift.

TOUCHING. *See also Failure to Thrive, Hugs.*

Research shows that lonely and depressed children long for loving touches, contact with another living, breathing being. Yet, they don't know how to ask for that important contact. Touching is very important to the development of every youngster, starting at birth. Research has shown that babies who are not touched when very young often have developmental difficulties later.

Certainly we don't like people who are overly touchy-feely, and we abhor those who use improper forms of touching. But loving touches can do much to bring comfort, stability, and warmth to family life. While babies get touched a lot, children after the age of two get decreasingly fewer touches in the years that follow because the parents don't feel that the child needs as much of this form of care. However in these early school years, touches are even more needed since the child needs support as he reaches for more independence.

Consider these ways both parents can casually and comfortably touch children during the course of the day:

Morning "high five." When you first meet in the hall on the way to the bathroom or kitchen, give a spirited "high five" to start the day with friendly vigor.

Breakfast squeeze. Even if it's a brief breakfast, let the family congregate around the table and hold hands, sending squeezes. Three squeezes can mean "I love you" and four stands for "Have a great day."

Farewell hug. No matter how rushed you are, it takes only four seconds to give a big hug as you say "I'm looking forward to being with you later." (Always link parting with meeting again.)

Welcome home hug. This is the same as the farewell hug, but it's important to take the time to tell family members how happy you are to be together again.

Suppertime grace. More than 65 percent of Americans have a quiet moment before dinner, and many hold hands during this simple expression of gratitude for the day.

After-dinner walk. Go hand-in-hand or link arms for a short walk. Or carry a young one piggyback.

Evening book reading. Let a young child sit in your lap with your arms enfolding her as you read. For older youngsters, sit shoulder to shoulder on the couch or stretch out on the floor close to one another as you read.

After-bath wrap. Use a large towel to envelop a child, then touch noses together. Let a child sit in your lap as you comb out her hair.

Off to bed. Take a young child by the hand and swing arms as you walk. Or carry her fireman's style. Or let each parent take one hand and swing the child between them. An older child may enjoy an affectionate slap on the back as he goes off to bed while others like to continue the hug and kiss.

Tucking in. With one child and two parents, have a triple hug, the parents standing and holding the child between them. Then make it a practice of carefully tucking the covers all around her body. Rub noses like Eskimos, kiss a child's hand or forehead, or make a game of kissing all toes, two elbows, and two knees.

Aloha sandwich. This is made when the family stands in a very tight circle, each placing a hand on top of another making a stack, then letting the bottom hand move up to the top. Do this faster and faster and hear the giggles!

Moonlight madness. Sit shoulder to shoulder in a circle on the ground, with arms linked. Then all lean back, look up at the moon and stars, and howl like wolves. Lean in and then do it again.

These simple ideas take practically no time at all but are vital to keeping a close physical connection within the family.

TOYS.

A few, creative toys are all a child needs. Children who have too many toys are often bewildered by them and seem confused about how to even start to play with them. Regularly work with youngsters to hand down toys they've outgrown.

When a youngster purposely throws or mishandles a toy, remove it quickly and keep it out of sight until you think she is ready to play with it carefully. Don't give youngsters toys that are beyond their capabilities; you want kids to stretch but you don't want toys to frustrate. Avoid fad toys that can be expensive.

Here are all-time favorites for various ages:

For younger children: big building blocks, play dishes and pantry items, puppets, sturdy rolling toys that can even be sat on, art easel, construction toys such as Lego or Lincoln Logs, musical instruments such as a xylophone, a plastic or pop-up playhouse, a doll family, a zoo or ark with many animals, very easy-to-play games.

For older youngsters: a doorway gym bar, camera, a tape recorder, a microscope, a variety of cars and trucks that can be played with together, sports equipment, a waterproof watch, computer accessories, games such as dominoes, Scrabble, Yahtzee, and Uno.

TRADITIONS. *See also Christmas Activities/Decorations/Traditions, Memorabilia, and Specific Holidays.*

Traditions are a key block in building good memories within the family. Doing pleasant things again and again creates anticipation and illustrates caring love. Try many activities that have appeal—keep some, toss out the ones that don't work. Talk about your own family traditions and the special things that "we" do.

Traditions can be part of each day. At breakfast there can be morning songs and prayers, the new word-of-the-day, farewells in foreign languages. Messages can be tucked in lunch boxes. Dinner can feature special seating arrangements, candlelight, "royalty servings" (just a tablespoon of a new food), toasts, and book reading. At bedtime there can be bedtime tag, a bath with boat races and refreshments served in the tub, and a fifteen-minute bedtime bonus for reading in bed.

Ordinary activities can become traditional: an evening walk, Sunday night popcorn and singing around the fireplace, taking turns being "parent for the day," a week of everyone playing box games, buying supper at the grocery store and eating it in the park, serving an all-family breakfast in one person's bedroom on Saturday morning.

When in the car, there can be the traditions of playing games, singing, or taking turns as navigator. To nurture a child's spirit, there can be traditional weekly religious education, setting personal goals, one-on-one sessions to solve nagging problems, and regular outreach to the community.

Special occasions call for traditions: a crown to wear and also the practice of doing a good deed on a birthday, a neighborhood cookie exchange, breakfast in bed for honorees on Mother's and Father's days, an ice-cream social on July 4, making of a "grateful chain" at Thanksgiving, special pillowcases for the month of December, making a unique Christmas candle, a Christmas family to help, cutting the Christmas tree in the woods, and New Year's goal setting.

For details on 289 traditions, see the book *Family Traditions* (Caryl Krueger, Abingdon Press, Nashville, Tenn.).

TRAITS. *See Character Building.*

TRAVEL. *See also Car Trips and Games, Grandparents, Vacations.*

Travel with youngsters is both educational and fun if you make it so. Plan ahead with car games, maps, songbooks, and some structure: time to read, nap, talk, and eat. Consider inexpensive trips by car, bus or train and save plane and ship travel for older youngsters.

Start building anticipation about the trip by visiting a travel agency for ideas and brochures. Write tourist bureaus, visit the auto club. Pouring over maps can be fascinating to youngsters. Provide means for recording the trip: show how to use a camera and encourage youngsters to keep a journal or scrapbook of each day's events. If during the school year, ask the teacher if there can be extra credit for a related project or presentation.

Before leaving, help youngsters to make a packing list and then see that they check it as they leave each stop. A copy of this list left at home can be invaluable if luggage is ever lost. Provide a carry-along case or backpack that has a sweater, book, snack, small toy, notebook and pencil, comb and other needed personal items, plus a plastic bag or two for collecting things.

Vary the seating arrangement in the car every few hours, letting youngsters serve as copilot and navigator, food chairman, toy and games chief, shopping coordinator. Car games can lighten boring stretches of road. Try these:

Magazine Madness. Using old magazines, let kids tear out pictures of outdoor things: houses, cars, animals, buildings, and so forth. Then "deal" them out picture side down, three for each player. When the driver says "Go," the children turn over their three pictures and start looking for the thing shown in each picture. The first one to find his three wins. When all the pictures are found, turn them over, mix them up and play again.

Pint-sized poets. A parent makes up the first line of a poem. A child completes the second line with a rhyming word at the end. They don't have to make a lot of sense, for example: "I want to stop—because there's a cop." "Sit on my knees—unless you sneeze."

Odometer ogling. One person indicates a distant point along the car's path: a hilltop, a building, an intersection. Each child quickly tells how many tenths of a mile away he thinks it is. Watching the odometer, see who is the best estimator.

Don't let car activities distract the driver, but do use car time for fun and learning.

👍 When older, responsible teens have time for a vacation, permit same-sex travel with firm rules about driving, safe accommodations, staying together, money, no drinking, no picking up hitchhikers, and so forth. A bus, train, or car trip of about three days is a good way to start. Parents should have an itinerary and a nightly phone call. It's a way of "letting go" and it can be a happy time if the travel rules are made very clear.

👍 Grandparents can be enjoyable travel partners. Some take a grandchild on an overnight trip when six years old. At twelve, there could be a week-long trip with the youngster helping make the choice of destination. There can be a special trip to commemorate a graduation.

Plan a "memory night" after the trip when pictures, mementoes, and ideas about future travel are shared.

TREATS. *See also Sweets.*

Rather than rewarding youngsters with candy, select treats that are healthy or helpful: a bookmark, a fifteen-minute bedtime extension, sugar-free gum, an extra-long story-and-snuggle time. Rewards don't have to be things; just as valuable are your sincere words of appreciation.

TRUTHFULNESS. *See Honesty.*

TUTORING. *See also Grades, School, School Tests, Tutoring.*

Don't permit students to slide behind in any subject. Your options begin with discussions with the teacher. Then, student mentors may be available to help. But it may be necessary to have the student professionally tutored so that he can keep up and pass the class. Tutors are usually paid by the hour. If the student has fallen behind because of his own negligence, he should pay a portion of the tutoring cost. Be sure to take action sooner than later as many courses of study build on what has been previously learned and if the basics are not understood, subsequent work is extremely difficult.

UNSELFISHNESS. *See also Affection, Caring, Selfishness, Service.*

What a joy to know a child who puts the welfare of others ahead of her own personal agenda! She usually learns this by living in a home where others give of themselves.

Unselfish activities for youngsters begin with learning to share when playing, by being a friend to a new student, by taking part in clubs where there is a service project for other children, for seniors, or for those in hospitals. Teens can have regular positions as volunteers at senior centers, hospitals, and playgrounds. Give special appreciation for unselfish acts, especially as youngsters get older and are more into their own agendas.

VACATION FROM SCHOOL. *See also Travel.*

Freedom from school days can be a beneficial change or a waste of time. For long vacations when the initial freedom begins to turn into boredom, provide some structure through special activities and classes. Make a list of possible vacation-time projects such as rebuilding a car engine, reading twenty-five books, learning to swim, building a treehouse or bookcase, or sewing a new wardrobe.

Set vacation goals: to learn to ride a bike or pass the driver's test. Make an educational goal to keep minds learning in preparation for resuming school. This could be daily book reading or computer learning.

VACATIONS. *See Travel.*

VALENTINE'S DAY.

Celebrate this holiday built on love. Let kids make and decorate a Valentine box for the center of the dining table. Encourage them to make handmade cards. Put these cards and some small, wrapped gifts inside the box. A parent can include a love letter to each child, telling him all the ways he's special. At supper on Valentine's Day, open the box and distribute the contents one at a time.

Serve a red-and-white meal: red gelatin, white chicken or red corned beef, red beets or tomatoes, white potatoes or cauliflower, white cake with red frosting. Look up Saint Valentine in the encyclopedia, read about his life, and discuss how the family can be more caring.

VALUES. *See also Character Building, Ethics.*

Each family has distinctive things that are special to just themselves — things they believe in and stand for. These can be traditions, character traits, or certain ethical standards. Take time to instill in your children the family values that you deem most important. Live them, talk about them, share them.

 Don't let what others do make you lower your standards. When kids try to use this as an excuse, stand firm.

 Make your values known to your children: words or actions that support love, honesty, loyalty, democracy, opportunity, fairness and so forth.

VIDEO CAMERA.

Recording a youngster's growing years is easily done with a simple-to-operate video camera. Some families make a yearly video about the entire family, others keep an historical record for each child by setting aside one videotape for that child. On it they record her special events for the year: making Valentines, bike riding, birthday party, helping to cook, teaching the dog a trick, opening Christmas gifts, and so forth. Then on New Year's Day, look at all the wonderful events of the previous 365 days. Older children like the creativity of making their own video production, and viewing these spontaneous videos can be great family entertainment. For a party, have a roving video reporter asking for questions and comments from the party guests about the people, food, and activities. Play it at the end of the evening.

VIDEO GAMES. *See also Guns, Killing.*

Whether played at home or in arcades, video games can be exciting, interesting, and good fun or they can be harmful, time consuming, and addictive. Psychologists also find that they promote stress, since players are always striving for higher scores, much like a chemically dependent person's obsession with "scoring" by using greater amounts of the addictive substance. In addition, violent games can trigger negative behaviors such as aggression, lying, tension, and sullenness.

Can it be considered play when a child loses and reacts with frustration and even anger? Worse yet is the amount of time taken up by these games that could be used for far more satisfying activities. Also consider the big expense of video arcades and the purchase of games for play at home.

Shop for quality video games. There are some truly unique ones out there that don't have scoring or killing as the main components, but involve reasoning and strategy.

VIDEO RENTALS.

One answer to better television viewing is to rent videos. By the time a movie comes out on video, you will have heard about its merits from family and friends so you are less apt to choose a loser. Make viewing an event in a darkened room with popcorn and sodas. Fast forward through the beginning promos. For an occasional weekend, rent several videos, letting each family member choose a favorite, but for all to watch. Then see whose selection was the most popular. Don't forget that conversation, sports, and games make excellent alternatives to overdosing on videos.

VIOLENCE. *See Aggression, Guns, Safety.*

VIRTUES. *See Faith, Honesty, Humility, Love, Openness, Optimism, Responsiility.*

VISITING. *See also Poise.*

The art of visiting is part of a child's maturing process—being able to make conversation with people of various ages and backgrounds, having good manners, asking proper questions. A little advance planning will help make visiting an event that is looked forward to.

Choose a time when a youngster is well rested and see that she has something to show and tell on the visit. A photo album, a few garden flowers, a new toy can be brought along. Sometimes it is nice to bring a small food gift like candy or baked goods.

Explain the purpose of the visit: to cheer someone, to welcome a new neighbor, to show Auntie Amy her rock collection, and so forth. Give a few conversational clues in advance and explain about food that might be served. Above all, keep the visit short.

VOCABULARY BUILDING. *See also Language.*

A young child's first vocabulary is dependent on the parents who indicate the one-word names for people and objects. Parents can increase a child's vocabulary by reading to him, by introducing a new word each day at breakfast and seeing who can use it at dinner, and by expanding their own vocabulary. For computer-friendly children, the computer thesaurus will broaden the vocabulary by showing synonyms for over-used common words.

A young child should be taught to use and understand the basic twenty-five words and phrases vocabulary: yes, no, maybe, please, thank you, now, later, today, tomorrow, come, stay, sit, stop, help, ask, tell, share, pick up, give, follow, quiet, up, down, hello, good-bye, I love you.

VOLUNTEER WORK. *See Service.*

WAGONS. *See Bicycling.*

WATER PLAY. *See also Outdoor Play.*

The beach is a highlight for most every youngster, but backyard water play can be equally fun. Here are some activities that are wet and wild:

Paper sailboats. Fold stiff paper or aluminum foil to form a boat, one for each player. Lay a string straight across one side of a wading pool to form the finish line. Line up boats in a row at the opposite side. Then, kids use lung power to blow their boats to the finish line.

Cool feet. Even adults will enjoy this game on a hot day. Participants sit on the ground around the wading pool with knees bent and feet in the pool. Place a bowl next to each one and start play by dumping a large quantity of ice cubes into the water. The object is to move the cubes from the water to the bowl, but only using the feet. It's cool fun.

Balloon bashing. Fill inexpensive balloons with water. Then, using a very fine needle, poke a small hole in each balloon so that there is a slow leak. Players fire the balloons at one another and keep tossing them until they run out of water. For neatness and safety, have the players pick up all the spent balloons and put them in the garbage when the game is over.

Spinning sprinkler. Take turns being a player or being the "Hose Master" in this game. All participants should be in swimsuits and you'll need a rotating lawn sprinkler attached to a hose. Set it in a grassy area where the Hose Master can see the area but be in charge of the faucet. Turn the sprinkler on full to note how far the water can spray and mark that circle with string. Players must stay within the circle. The Hose Master watches the players as he turns the faucet on and off. Players can jump over the spray or get drenched.

Sponge tag. All ages can play in a grassy area. One really big sponge and a pail of water is all that is needed. One player starts by soaking the sponge and then tagging a player by hitting him with the wet sponge. That player soaks the sponge and the game continues. Use several sponges for a larger group.

Wet relay. End the day with a relay race. Set up evenly divided teams and a relay course that has three elements that each team member must do: a wading pool (jump in, sit down, then stand up), a chair with a spray bottle (sit down, spray the top of the head), and a bowl of ice cubes (player must put five cubes inside his swimsuit), then complete his run tagging the next player on his team. This hilarious game is equally fun to watch.

WEEKENDS. *See also Quality Time.*

Weekends are the most important family times and an all-family activity should be a highlight of every weekend. Of course there will be errands and chores, team play, religious services, some homework and quiet play, and social events for children and also for parents. But a planned, and announced in advance, activity is both enjoyable and bonding. Activities can include excursions to the library, museum, park, zoo, dairy, ball game, concert, play, and so forth. Be sure to end the weekend on a high note — a simple supper by the fire, an all-family game after dinner, or ice-cream sundaes. Tell youngsters regularly how much you enjoy being together with them on weekends.

Don't let "must do" activities (sleep, errands, home maintenance, chores, sports practices) take time from the family activity. Planning in advance can provide time for both the "must do" and "want to do" activities.

An interesting and inexpensive Saturday morning event is going to a yard sale. Give each youngster fifty cents and see who can come up with the best buy.

WEIGHT. *See Obesity.*

WELLNESS. *See Health.*

WHINING. *See also Nagging, Pests, Repeated Questions.*

Whining usually begins before a child has the language to express the problem. So she repeats words or sounds in hopes that someone will glean the need. If parents don't understand, and if they don't respond in any way, the whining gets more intense and can turn into crying or a tantrum. The best response is to pick up the whining child, comfort her and say "Use your words" in hopes that you'll get some clue. If not, ask her to show you the problem.

In older children, the whining has usually become a habit, even though the child has the necessary words. Whining, muttering, complaining has often resulted in the child getting her way, thus she has found that whining wins. Parents can cure this type of whining by insisting on words and then settling the problem with patient logic.

WILLFULNESS. *See Determination.*

WINNING. *See Sportsmanship.*

WISH LISTS. *See also Gifts, Toys.*

Many gifts that children receive are played with just a little or not at all. One solution is to let a youngster keep a continuing wish list, telling what gifts he hopes to receive at some gift-giving occasion. Of course, the entire list may never be fulfilled, but it does provide ideas for relatives who may not know the specific interests. A wish list should be reviewed occasionally and kept on a child's bulletin board where others can surreptitiously see what he wants.

WORDS. *See also Communication, Criticism, Language, Praise, Profanity, Put-Downs and Put-Ups, Speech.*

What comes out of our mouths greatly influences our lives. Also our attitude and body language further depict our words. The same words shouted or said soothingly can have different results.

 Words parents don't like to hear include:
"How come I never get to?"
"I could never learn that."
"You don't understand."
"I don't know why you make me do all this stuff."
"It's not my turn."
"Not now, I'll do it later."
"I don't like that food."
"But everyone else does it."

 Words parents love to hear include:
"What can I do to help?"

"Thank you."
"You're right!"
"You look nice."
"I'll sure think about it."
"I understand what you're telling me."
"I'm willing to try."
"I know you love me."
"I'll be home on time."
"I appreciate your help."

 Words kids don't like to hear include:
"You never do anything right."
"Who do you think you are?"
"I'm too busy!"
"How stupid."
"I never change my mind."
"You think you're so smart, don't you!"
"How many times do I have to tell you?"
"Just see if I ever let you borrow it again."
"Why? Because I said so."

 Words kids love to hear include:
"That's okay, you tried."
"We give you our permission."
"I'm proud to be your dad."
"I couldn't wait to hear your voice."
"Let's fix it together."
"I miss you."
"But what do YOU want to do?"
"You can stay out thirty minutes later tonight."
"I trust you."

WORKING PARENTS. *See also Parenting Skills, Time Management.*

Separated from home and children, a working parent must have a dual-track mind to be effective on the job but also to be alert to the needs of his or her children.

If the company doesn't have a good family-oriented policy, encourage it to develop one. There should be comprehensive health care, maternity and paternity leave, time off for a child's health care, and opportunities to attend special school events with the ability to make up the work in other ways or at other times. Working parents must not abuse company time, but a midafternoon phone call to check on at-home children should be permitted and encouraged.

Parents of both sexes have proved that they can be very effective and professional at work, and at the same time still be caring parents. Sometimes a change in work hours can permit a parent to work less time, only during the hours kids are in school. You won't know if this is possible if you don't ask. A motivated employee is valuable and management may possibly honor this request. And, with computers, many parents are now enjoying work time at home. This is practical if the parent is sufficiently disciplined to accomplish high-quality work and give the employer his money's worth.

Help youngsters understand why parents work and just what they do. Take part in special days when parents are encouraged to bring kids to the workplace. When appropriate, let youngsters help with office work: keying in information, sealing mail, delivering memos, sorting mail, listing tasks, dialing phone calls.

When parents and youngsters come together at the end of the work and school day, it is important to take a few moments to reconnect. Don't immediately change clothes, read the mail, or start dinner. Instead, serve glasses of juice, show interest in your child and find out something that happened during the hours of separation that can then be more fully explored at the dinner table. This moment of relaxation makes everything that follows go more smoothly because the child is less likely to be pestering for attention.

Avoid the myth of quality time and give as much quantity time as possible, especially first thing in the morning, after dinner, and on weekends.

See that care providers are topnotch. A working parent needs to feel very comfortable about the facility where children will spend most of the day. And, when the child is in school, the parent needs to be equally concerned over the quality of teaching as well as after-school care.

For effectively combining career and parenting, read *Working Parent/Happy Child* (Caryl Krueger, Abingdon Press, distributed by Belleridge Press, Escondido, Calif.).

WORSHIP. *See Religion.*

WRITING.

Encourage writing by hand and by typewriter or computer. Writing helps organize thoughts and encourages good grammar. Support the school activity of teaching children to form each letter in both upper and lower case form. Clear printing can be a great asset, even when super-seded by cursive writing.

When a child is bored, work together to write a book—a true story, fantasy, or mystery. Use old magazines to illustrate the story and bind the pages with ribbon. Use cardboard for the cover, which should include the title and author's name.

Writing letters and keeping a journal or diary will keep a child's writing skills alive. A youngster with a talent for writing should be encouraged to write for the school newspaper and to enter writing competitions.

X-RATED WORLD. *See also Profanity.*

An important parental duty is to protect your children from the unsavory aspects of an X-rated world that includes movies, videos, television, magazines, books, Internet, and unsuitable friends. Of course you can achieve some of this through being a watchdog or employing electronic devices to inhibit certain activities. But you can't be with your child everywhere every moment.

The aim of good parenting is to show youngsters what is the right thing to do and how to do it on their own, by their own choice. Out of respect for parents and also for themselves, well-taught youngsters will not be attracted to X-rated information and will not bring it into the home. Research shows that young people who are not exposed to X-rated activities in the home and do not hear X-rated comments in the home, are far less apt to take part in these in their adult years. So, a parent's example is highly important.

YEARLY GROWTH CHART.

Once a year, let the family measure up: height and weight. For the height, use a pole (about 1" x 6" x 6 feet should do), which you can take along should you move. Using an indelible marking pen, write on it the name and height of each person and the date. If you wish, you can also show the weight, opposite the height. It's fun to see how kids grow.

YELLING. *See also Arguing, Disagreements, Fighting, Profanity.*

The ability to speak with tremendous volume is useful when cheering one's team or calling for help in an emergency, but in most cases yelling is not an acceptable form of communication. It is the words, not the volume, that carry the message, and when the volume is too loud, the message is actually lost. So, outlaw yelling in favor of expressive speech. It is much more effective to get your important message across with a calm, low tone of voice. And, you'll be pleased about your self-control if you don't yell. Set up a system of fines for yelling and use the money for an enjoyable family excursion.

Parents who yell at their children, rather than speaking firmly to them, are really defeating the purpose of teaching or correcting. The only thing yelling accomplishes is to blow off steam, and this looks out-of-control in the eyes of others.

ZEAL.

If your family doesn't know the meaning of zeal, it's time to learn and exercise this important quality for living together. It means enthusiasm, hearty and persistent effort, animation, and a zest for living. It may be at the bottom end of the alphabet, but zeal is at the top of the list of qualities that make for great parenting.